Women and Language

Women and Language

Essays on Gendered Communication Across Media

Edited by
MELISSA AMES *and*
SARAH HIMSEL BURCON

McFarland & Company, Inc., Publishers
Jefferson, North Carolina, and London

LIBRARY OF CONGRESS CATALOGUING-IN-PUBLICATION DATA

Women and language : essays on gendered communication across media / edited by Melissa Ames and Sarah Himsel Burcon.
p. cm.
Includes bibliographical references and index.

ISBN 978-0-7864-4944-6
softcover : 50# alkaline paper ♾

1. Women. 2. Women — Language. 3. Language and languages — Sex differences. 4. Mass media and women. 5. Technology and women. I. Ames, Melissa, 1978– II. Burcon, Sarah Himsel, 1965–
HQ1176.W66 2011
302.23082'09 — dc22 2011004692

BRITISH LIBRARY CATALOGUING DATA ARE AVAILABLE

Front cover design by Victoria Fenstermaker (www.showcasedsign.com)

Manufactured in the United States of America

McFarland & Company, Inc., Publishers
Box 611, Jefferson, North Carolina 28640
www.mcfarlandpub.com

To the women in our lives,
especially our mothers and sisters,
whose conversations have inspired this collection

Table of Contents

Introduction: Women and Oral Culture

Melissa Ames and Sarah Himsel Burcon

Origins of Gendered Communication

Throughout the centuries the binary between orality and literacy has fascinated scholars and philosophers — all of whom have helped to construct and reconstruct this very binary. This dichotomy has acted as a foundation for various views concerning which medium of communication has been favored at a given time in history. Eric Havelock, and later Walter Ong, for example, argued that the transition from an oral to a literate culture in ancient Greece (from about the 6th century B.C.E. through the 4th century A.D.) produced changes in human cognition. Ong traces the history of this shift in his seminal text, *Orality and Literacy*, where he distinguishes between "primary orality," or "the orality of a culture totally untouched by any knowledge of writing or print," and "secondary orality," the orality of "high-technology culture, in which a new orality is sustained by ... electronic devices that depend for their existence and functioning on writing and print" (11). Ong begins with Plato's belief that writing was a "mechanical, inhuman way of processing knowledge, unresponsive to questions and destructive of memory" (24). Plato, then, regarded writing in a skeptical manner. Many years later, with the invention of the Gutenberg Press in 1436, the printed word was made available to the masses. This invention played a crucial role in the orality/literacy binary switch: given the implications of such an invention, literacy now occupied the favored position in this binary split, a position it still occupies today.[1]

As might be expected, this binary, like all binaries, has carried with it gendered implications. Women have historically been defined in relation to the oral culture, in large part due to their exclusion from education, and therefore, from literary endeavors, while men have been aligned more with literary culture. Ong identifies a possible reason for this configuration that links print texts to education or knowledge more generally:

> Print creates a sense of closure not only in literary works but also in analytic philosophical and scientific works. With print came the catechism and the "textbook." ... By contrast, the memorable statements of oral cultures ... tended to be of a proverbial sort, presenting not "facts" but rather reflections ... inviting further reflection by the paradoxes they involved [131–132].

When something appears in print, then, it seems more accurate and closer to the "truth" than something that is merely spoken. Therefore men, who have historically been the writers and readers of literature, have been more aligned with "truth," while women, who have had restricted access to such texts, have been aligned with more "reflective" materials.

The conflation of women with oral culture and, therefore, with the lower portion of the binary, has been scrutinized by scholars in recent years. While this project does not claim that women *are always* or *should be* aligned with the oral culture, it does trace this historical tendency and analyzes the negative connotations surrounding this conflation of women with orality. At the same time, the essays contained here seek to disrupt that very hierarchal binary that privileges traditional print literature/communication over non-traditional oral performance/communication. This collection aims to do this by updating existing theories of orality in the light of technological advancements that have altered communication practices on a large scale. Although these shifts in communication practices affect both genders, this anthology looks particularly at how the last century of technological inventions have specifically affected women's means of communication. One key argument running through this text is that the use of oral communication — either spoken, or appearing as dialogue in a novel, for instance — can be in actuality a strategic, empowering, and subversive act working against the mandates to participate in androcentric normative print culture.

Women's Communication as Marginalized, Restricted, and Silenced

The issue of gendered communication has for at least three decades been considered a feminist concern, as Deborah Cameron points out in her book *The Feminist Critique of Language.* Cameron begins her text with an ostensibly simple question: "Why is language a feminist issue?" (1). Of course, there is no single, simple answer to this question. However, one answer she offers deals with speech and silence, a theme that is considered at length in this present anthology. Cameron argues:

> A claim that women are "silent" or "silenced" cannot mean that they are always and everywhere literally silent.... It cannot even mean that there are no linguistic activities associated with women more than with men, for in fact there are many ... "gossip," keeping teenage diaries, and writing letters or cards to family members are among those that come to mind [3].

Cameron continues that these genres — diaries, letters, and so forth that have been linked with women — provide "a clue to one possible meaning of women's silence" because they "are not prestigious, and some (e.g., gossip) are actually disparaged" (3). Furthermore, Cameron notes, these are "private uses of language, confined to the space of home, family and immediate community.... In the public domain, and especially the domain of official culture ... the genres associated with women have little currency" (3). It is often noted that women have been excluded from many forms of public discourse in which men have always participated, religious and political discourses among them. Therefore, along with the literacy/orality binary, the public/private binary is at issue. In both cases, the upper portion of the binary is privileged while the lower is denigrated,[2] the result being that women have been "othered" due to the perpetuation of stereotypes initiated by these binary pairs.

It may have been the case that women were aligned with the genres of diaries and letters, but it is certainly not the case that one can homogenize all writings by women — regardless of race, class, ethnicity, and sociocultural environment — into one group that fits into the category of "women's writings." An in depth discussion of autobiography — the umbrella genre that includes forms such as diaries and letters — is important here in that several of the texts analyzed in this collection have an autobiographical component: for example, one chapter is devoted to field research on salsa; another chapter studies author Julia Alvarez's life experiences as encapsulated in one of her novels; three chapters delve into non-fictional accounts delivered through letters and diaries; and one chapter offers an analysis of the closet drama through an autobiographical lens. Felicity A. Nussbaum contributes to this conversation, arguing that "one of the commonplaces of feminist criticism is the frequent claim that diaries and journals are an intrinsically female form, and that women's experience particularly lends itself to the diffuse for its expression" (152). Critic Estelle Jelinek, for example, claimed that women's autobiographies are "fragmented, interrupted, formless, and even when basically linear are anecdotal and disruptive" (qtd. in Nussbaum 153). Nussbaum, however, counters that this outlook "fails to account, on the one hand, for the large number of diaries and journals written by men, and on the other hand, for many women's autobiographies ... that display narrative closure" (153). Sidonie Smith and Julia Watson similarly point out that "first-stage theorists of women's autobiography" prompted "[p]rovocative questions" such as: "To what extent is women's autobiography characterized by the frequency of non-linear or 'oral' narrative strategies, unlike the master narratives of autobiography that seem to pose stable, coherent self-narratives?" and "To what extent is it characterized by frequent digression, giving readers the impression of a fragmentary, shifting narrative voice, or indeed a plurality of voices in dialogue?" and "Is the subject in women's autobiography less firmly bounded, more 'fluid'?" (10). They note, that this logic was questioned later, given that women of color were "rendered invisible in these accounts" of some sort of "uniform" women's autobiographical writing (Smith and Watson 10).

Smith and Watson maintain that after this initial period of homogenizing women's autobiographical writing into a single "type" of writing specific to women, in later years (the late 1980s), women's autobiographical studies underwent a change with the advent of new theories concerning women's writing. For example, in *A Poetics of Women's Autobiography* (1987), Smith argued that, in an androcentric society, autobiographical writing has not been granted to women. Thus, women, who were "[h]istorically absent from both the public sphere and modes of written narrative" found it necessary to "tell their stories differently" (Smith 12). Francoise Lionnet's *Autobiographical Voices: Race, Gender, Self-Portraiture* (1989) argued for a theory termed *métissage*, in which "marginalized subjects voice their lives" (Smith and Watson 12). Lionnet contended that "as historically silenced subjects, women and colonized peoples create 'braided' texts of many voices that speak their cultural locations dialogically" and continued that *métissage*, or "viewing autobiography as a multi-voiced act," stresses "orality and the irreducible hybridity of identity" (Smith and Watson 12). Crucial to this collection, *Women and Language,* is the discussion of polyvocality. The argument here is that multiple voices — in the form of orality, literary writings in which the oral culture is stressed, and computer mediated culture — are used as a means to challenge gender ideologies. Specifically, these communication strategies are used strategically by women in order for them to (re)write their experiences.

Language and Identity: Gendered Communication as Performance

Often when a discussion concerning "women's writings" surfaces, Virginia Woolf's notion of the "woman's sentence" is invoked. *In A Room of One's Own*, Woolf contrasts her fictional author, Mary Carmichael, to the celebrated

19th century writer Jane Austen in order to speculate on the question of whether there exists such a thing as a "woman's sentence." Woolf notes that in Carmichael's imagined novel, "The smooth gliding of sentence after sentence was interrupted" (80), which meant that Carmichael's novel was nothing like Austen's. But Woolf remarks that it is acceptable that Carmichael "broke the sentence" and indeed, even "the sequence" (81) because she did so "not for the sake of breaking, but for the sake of creating" (81). In these much quoted phrases, and in *A Room of One's Own* in general, Woolf attempts to demonstrate that women have long lacked the material resources, time, and space to create, and therefore women wrote differently from men, who were afforded these resources. Woolf's essay was published almost a century ago but she was hopeful that, given these resources—"a room of her own and five hundred a year"—women would create better texts than her fictional Carmichael within "a hundred years' time" (94). Now that nearly a century has passed, it is time to question whether women's texts have, indeed, "broken the sequence" of androcentric writing.

Sara Mills points out in her critique of Woolf that

> as with everything which is labeled masculine/male or feminine/female, these terms have very little to do with biological sex difference, but a great deal to do with assertions of power. In defining the female sentence we are not in fact defining a sentence at all, but defining females; this is just part of an ideological enterprise; we do not define males to anything like the same extent.... Defining the feminine sentence as lacking rationality, coherence, assertiveness and so on is an attempt to set up a particular subject position for females in the real world [76–77].

Mills is rightly arguing against a fixed definition of women. Certainly, while arguing for a "woman's sentence" appears essentialist at first glance—as it seems to be grounded in the belief that women and men have innate differences linked to their biological makeup—one can also argue, as does Rachel Blau DuPlessis, that

> To break the sentence rejects not grammar especially, but rhythm, pace, flow, expression: the structuring of the female voice by the male voice, female tone and manner by male expectations, female writing by male emphasis, female writing by existing conventions of gender—in short, any way in which dominant structures shape muted ones [32].

It is the last portion of this quotation that is crucial. Rather than arguing for an exclusively female form of writing (and therefore prefiguring the French Feminists' desire to do so, as will be discussed later), Woolf is really, it seems, arguing against "dominant structures [shaping] muted" voices. That is, at the same time that Woolf argues against women writing *as* men, she also invites women to write without considering their gender. Toward the end of her essay Woolf makes this explicit, once again appealing to her Mary Carmichael for assistance: "... [Carmichael] had ... mastered the first great lesson; she wrote as a woman, but as a woman who has forgotten that she is a woman, so that her pages were full of that curious sexual quality which comes only when *sex is unconscious of itself*" (93, emphasis added).

The questions now become: can/should women write in an androgynous fashion? And does their identity as "women writers/communicators" matter? These questions—and possible responses—appear throughout the pages of this text. To sort out these questions and the varied answers, we begin with the premise that gender itself is not fixed; rather, it is an unstable, constructed category and always in flux. Judith Butler presented the now evident view shared by many feminists that "gender is a performance with clearly punitive consequences" in which "those who fail to do their gender right" (178) are "regularly [punished]" (178). Butler stresses that gender performances require a "*stylized repetition of acts*" (179, emphasis in original) which means, simply, that one's gestures, body language, and movements "constitute the illusion of an abiding gendered self" (179) when, in fact, there is no such thing.

What, then, does this mean for "women's writings/communication"? It is Butler's contention that "one is a woman ... to the extent that one functions as one within the dominant heterosexual frame and to call the frame into question is perhaps to lose something of one's sense of place in gender" (xi). Part of the goal of this collection is to question this frame in order for women to (re)claim communication practices, whether these be gossip, garrulousness, or a less stigmatized tie to the oral culture. With the understanding that so much of communication in general is gendered and that the performance of that constructed gender expression is learned socially, this collection wrestles with the notion of an "authentic" voice, the idea of "women's writing," and with the criteria that would determine whether or not any product under either banner would be classified as "feminist."

The Questioning of (and Quest for) "Authentic" Voices, "Women's" Writing, and "Feminist" Texts

The debate over whether a voice can be authentic, let alone authentically female, has been documented at length elsewhere. Much of the early linguistic research studying differences between men and women's voices and communication practices is now viewed as essentialist. This would include studies relying on either the deficit framework,[3] which suggests that women lack beneficial communication strategies that men often master; or the dominance theory,[4] which suggests that women's communication is stifled in part because of men's linguistic capabilities to control communication settings (Cameron 14–15). Despite the criticism these studies have inspired, the mass of data collected on such communication differences (be they innate or constructed), is hard to overlook, and many of the essays here, specifically those in the first part of this text, return to this research either to recount, refute, question, or complicate it.[5]

A similar debate fuels the discussion of the second part of this book: do women (or can they) write differently than men? Is there really such a thing as female or feminine writing? Many scholars have argued that there is. For example, in *Feminist Stylistics,* Sara Mills claims that there are distinct linguistic differences in the writing crafted by women. Decades earlier, as discussed previously, Virginia Woolf noted some of these differences, not attributing them to *all* women but *some*, arguing that certain women writers were able to craft "a new type of sentence which [was] looser and more accretive than the male sentence" (Cameron 65). Writing in between Mills's and Woolf's time period, the French Feminists suggested that such writing, which they termed *écriture feminine,* could be done strategically and could be used for a feminist and/or political means.[6] Although the potential utility of this type of writing has interested many, its utopianism has caused it to be criticized by various scholars (Cameron 9). The concept itself, women's writing, has been devalued because it suggests universality between all women and, therefore, all women's writing. This accusation of minimalizing the differences among women is not a new one to be associated with the French Feminists nor is it unfamiliar to second wave feminists in general (the larger group of contemporary feminist thinkers of which they were a part).

This collection seeks to interrogate the notions of feminine voice and women's writing. For example, Chapter 2 deals with the authorial debate surrounding the Old English poem *The Wife's Lament,* specifically the arguments concerning whether or not scholars can determine if it was, indeed, written by a woman based on the writing style alone. Chapter 6 also explores the idea of an authentic voice and attends to how the war diaries written by a Vietnamese woman were published posthumously and marketed specifically as an authentic voice, one contrasted to the rhetoric concerning the war in Vietnam which prescribed pure heroics, sacrifices, and loyalty to the Party — all dictates more likely to have been associated with the writing of men than women. The question of what makes a voice authentic is therefore complicated when, as seen in this chapter, others co-opt that voice for their own purposes (in this case for economic profit and political reinforcement).

That writing can be productive, that it can accomplish tasks beyond itself, is also a common motif within this collection. Many have argued that this is exactly what a feminist text would do: be productive. Various essays in this collection tease out what it would mean for a text to be feminist. Chapter 7, "When Talk Meets Page," draws upon Elizabeth Grosz's definition that in order to be feminist a text must "render the patriarchal or phallocentric presumptions governing its contexts and commitments visible," "problematize the standard masculinist ways in which the author occupies the position of enunciation," and

> facilitate the production of new and perhaps unknown, unthought discursive spaces — new styles, modes of analysis and argument, new genres and forms — that contest the limits and constraints currently at work in the regulation of textual production and reception [22–23].

It is particularly this last point, that such texts would facilitate new discursive spaces, styles, genres, and forms, that binds many of the diverse arguments in this book together.

As many of the essays analyze texts or communication practices that could be classified as feminist, this collection attends to the various functions of different communication practices appropriated by women. For example, the first part relies heavily on gossip scholarship which well covers the various tasks gossip accomplishes, such as information acquisition, group acceptance, social control, healing talk, aggressive play, and reputation monitoring (Goodman and Ben-Ze'Ev 4, 15; Spacks x, 34, 57, 64; Dunbar 123). Chapter 1 traces gossip's association with women and discusses its role in both uniting and fracturing communities and social relationships. Chapter 2 switches to a male perspective and analyzes how the gossip of men, via lettered communication, provided solidarity between its participants through the reinforcement of norms shared by their social group, all the while acting in a way that "othered" those not belonging to that group — in this case, women. Chapter 12 considers gossip as a mechanism through which women, through their kin-keeping activities, access information needed to cope with their social worlds, to solve problems, and to deal with the people around them.

Other parts of this collection attend to how various functions of female communication may be considered more than just functional, but even subversive and hence possibly feminist. Continuing with the focus on gossip, Chapter 1 builds off Alexander Rysman's claim that gossip itself can be considered a transgressive activity because it "develop[s] social ties outside the institution of male dominance" (176). Other chapters look specifically at actions, more so than words, and how certain performative behavior draws attention to, or overcomes, gendered norms. Chapter 5, for example, focuses on the manipulation of clothing and costuming, and Chapter 9 emphasizes female performance during salsa dancing to highlight gendered norms. And a variety of the analyses of print literature housed in Part II address the ways that women strategically use writing to further feminist agendas or to explore feminist themes. This part suggests that when one historically does not have (or has not had) access to the official written language (which is clearly seen in Part I's focus on women's forced indoctrination into gossip culture), oral communication arises as an alternate strategy. The strategic ways that such orality is translated onto the page — and the way that it transforms various written genres — is well explored here (see specifically chapters 7 and 8). Technology's ability to foster spaces that can transgress gendered communication is explored in the second half of this text. For example, Chapter 12 discusses women's appropriation of the landline telephone, the mobile phone, and email, and Chapter 13 argues that teenage girls reconfigure instant-messaging spaces, experientially and semiotically, to meet their own personal demands, interests, and goals.

Navigating Through the "Spaces" in This Volume

As a whole this collection rests upon the belief that "language shapes the representation of self" (Gluck 9). This collection is divided into four parts, each dedicated to exploring how women utilize language in various forms (spoken, written, non-verbal, mediated) to shape these representations of self or purposely shape them differently than cultural norms would dictate. The essays in this collection are arranged so that the analysis of this phenomenon can be traced through two different trajectories, both temporally aligned to some degree. The collection begins with a discussion of oral communication and then shifts to written communication and communication mediated through technological apparatuses. Each part is also arranged chronologically, tracing developments in each realm of communication. For example, the first part traces not only the history of the word gossip, but its association with women, and how it alters when gossip itself moves from the mouth to the page[7]; the second part analyzes the writing of women across literary genres stretching from 10th century poetry to 20th century novels; and the fourth part traces communication debates and trends as technological devices from the landline telephone to the Internet blog became dominant fixtures in the cultural landscape.

Part I, Spoken Spaces: The Historicization, Evolution, and Gendering of "Gossip," begins with Giselle Bastin's chapter, "Pandora's Voice-Box: How Woman Became the 'Gossip Girl,'" which provides a historical context for the gendering of the term gossip. The notion that woman is considered a leaky vessel prone to spreading disorder and chaos is linked to etymological associations of the term "gossip" with "midwife." Although gossip was traditionally considered a female activity, research abounds on how both sexes have participated in the activities at nearly equal rates throughout the centuries. In "Just Like a Woman: Misogynistic Gossip in the Correspondence Between John Chamberlain and Dudley Carleton," Emily Ross studies the gendered communication between two men as showcased through letters from the 17th century. This essay analyzes instances of gossip present in their communication, exploring the relationship between gossip, misogyny, and stereotypes. The third chapter, "'Paper cannot blush': Martha Fowke, an 18th Century Abandoned Woman," continues with an analysis of letters housing gossip, only in this instance they are those housing the self-gossip of their female writer. In this essay Earla Wilputte analyzes female letter writing practices during the 18th century by specifically examining the poet Martha Fowke's 1723 autobiographical letters which document the breakup of her love affair. Wilputte explores how letter writing permitted an abandoned woman to actively re-insinuate herself in another's mind through her imaginative language and imagery.

Part II, Literary Spaces: The Convergence of Orality and Print in Women's Writing, continues to look at the written work of female authors and attends to the way different genres allow for different gendered practices. In Chapter 4, "Delete as Appropriate: Writing Between the Lines of Female Orality in *The Wife's Lament*," Miriam Muth examines the steps by which phallocentric criticism has appropriated the surviving voices of female speakers from early medieval cultures by examining the *The Wife's Lament*, a tenth century Old English poem. Lindsay Yakimyshyn's "Voicing the Feminine and the (Absent) Masculine in *The Concealed Fancies*," analyzes performative gender found in scripted closet dramas of the 17th century, looking particularly at Jane Cavendish and Elizabeth Brackley's *The Concealed Fancies*, written during the English Civil War. Hanh N. Nguyen and R. C. Lutz also analyze a text crafted by a woman during war time in their essay, "The Wartime Diaries of Dang Thuy Tram: Extolling and Gendering the Heroine's Voice in Postwar Vietnam and Beyond." This chapter examines the diaries of Tram Thuy Dang, a 25-year-old doctor who treated injured soldiers in the war zone of Northern Vietnam during the Vietnam War. Although this text is written in diary format, a genre stereotypically associated with women, Nguyen and Lutz argue that much of the content within these diaries did not align with what one would expect to have been written by a woman during this time period. Chapters 7 and 8 focus their analysis on 20th century American novels that are often classified as feminist. Melissa Ames's "When Talk Meets Page: The Feminist Aesthetic of Adapted Narration and Language Play" analyzes literary works such as Zora Neale Hurston's modernist novel *Their Eyes Were Watching God* and Margaret Atwood's experimental postmodern novel *The Handmaid's*

Tale, focusing specifically on their orality. Ames reads these literary works against the theoretical writings of the French Feminists to suggest that despite their different formats, their shared feminist stylistics point to a productive commonality often overlooked. In "Blurred Boundaries and Re-Told Histories: Julia Alvarez's *How the García Girls Lost Their Accents,*" Sarah Himsel Burcon examines Julia Alvarez's 1991 work, *How the García Girls Lost Their Accents,* and demonstrates how Alvarez both *records* and *revises* stories/histories by strategically employing memory and storytelling. Burcon analyzes the non-normative stylistics of Alvarez's novel, focusing on the effects its reverse chronological narration has on the reader.

Part III, Performative Spaces: Constructing and Instructing Gendered Behavior, moves away from the focus on the written word and turns to less traditional forms of communication. Aleysia Whitmore's "Bodies in Dialogue: Performing Gender and Sexuality in Salsa Dance" starts off this part with an analysis that highlights the need to scrutinize body language and physical performance as a form of communication. This essay explores salsa dance, revealing the ways in which it too is gendered much like oral communication. While Whitmore studies gender performance on the physical dance floor, Diana York Blaine studies gender performance on the mediated small screen. Her chapter, "Tell Me, Does She Talk During Sex? The Gendering of Permissible Speech on *Dr. Phil,*" demonstrates that, rather than considering woman an active agent, Dr. Phil idealizes the silent female and reinforces a gendered hierarchy in which women are lauded for being the supporter of their aggressive husbands. This essay shows not only how gender is performed — as Dr. Phil performs his role as relationship counselor and the couples act as his raw material to mold — but it also shows how gender instruction and socialization occur (often problematically) through the medium of television. Analyzing another screen — that of the computer — Ashley M. Donnelly's chapter "Read My Profile: Internet Profile Culture, Young Women and the Communication of Power" offers a theoretical analysis of how Internet "profile culture" teaches young women to communicate, arguing that the communication that takes place within these sites limits genuine discourse and alters young women's concepts of what it means to communicate their sense of gender and agency.

Part IV, Technological Spaces: Transforming "Talk" in the 21st Century, the final part of this collection, offers an investigation into how advanced technology contributes to changes in gendered communication.[8] In "Women, Kin-Keeping, and the Inscription of Gender in Mediated Communication Environments," Julie Dare contrasts early cyberculture theories, which constructed computer-mediated environments as liberating and potentially gender-neutral spaces, with empirical evidence that reveals how online communication channels actually reinforce gendered communication practices, particularly in relation to women's traditional kin-keeping role. In contrast to Dare's findings, Koen Leurs and Sandra Ponzanesi's essay, "Gendering the Construction of Instant Messaging," analyzes the use of Instant Messaging among teenage girls and finds that the cultural stereotype of girls as friendly gossips gets resisted and transgressed in these spaces and that female IM users are able to construct a perfomative, mediated self that transcends traditional gender restraints. The final chapter in this collection takes on many of these issues and demonstrates their importance across cultural boundaries by analyzing the text-based interactions among a group of young mothers on a Brazilian blog. In "Gender Blogging: Femininity and Communication Practices on the Internet," Adriana Braga suggests that this specific blog documents both a change in the traditional perspective towards femininity and at the same time a lack of direct action to change personal circumstances in any way that might be considered feminist. Braga ends her discussion with a call to action that echoes the women on this site, although their call to action relies on the next generation while Braga urges more immediate action.

This collection suggests that even in the 21st century all communication practices are tied in some ways to the cultural norms put in place by patriarchy. While the format the communication employs — the medium in which it is relayed — does influence its ability to subvert these cultural norms (as some communication practices do allow more or less strategic gender performance than others, and some inhibit or allow expression of self and affect more readily than others), there is no magic communication forum that frees the speaker completely from the constructed gender communication practices of his or her culture. And although technological progress does allow for increased communication in general, and more diversified communication in particular, technological apparatuses in and of themselves do not have the power to undo the cultural training that influences communication patterns.

NOTES

1. For a more in-depth discussion of this binary, as this is an admittedly reductive account, see the work of Eric Havelock, Walter Ong, and Marshall McLuhan.

2. But at the same time, Cameron notes, "The generalization that women across cultures are excluded from public and highly valued forms of speech ... has been contested in recent feminist scholarship, and on this subject there is much still to know" (Cameron 4). Furthermore, silence can also be a form of power: "in situations where one is required to 'confess all' by a priest, therapist or officer of the law, for instance-silence is a strategy of resistance to oppressive power" (Cameron 4).

3. Mary E. Crawford's *Talking Difference* addresses this framework.

4. See Deborah Tannen's *You Just Don't Understand: Men and Women in Conversation* for an example of this research.

5. Although the findings in such studies are too numerous to list, some noteworthy

reported communication differences include: a greater rapidity of thought in female communication versus men (shown linguistically by pronoun use) (Jespersen 238); women's tendency to shy away from offensive communication practices and vocabulary to the extent that they will actually "invent innocent and euphemistic words and paraphrases" (Jespersen 233); women's tendency to laugh and smile more regularly than men during conversation, with women being much more likely to laugh on cue to men's jokes in comparison to men's lack of willingness reciprocate in similar situations (Dunbar 182); or even men's tendency to appropriate local accents while women tend to more readily retain a more standard, or proper, dialect (Dunbar 184).

6. For more information on the theories of the French Feminists, see Hélène Cixous's "Castration or Decapitation?" or her *Reader;* Luce Irigaray's *The Sex Which Is Not One;* or Monique Wittig's *The Straight Mind.*

7. This collection is not the first to analyze written and technological communication forms as a type of gossip. Patricia Spacks has analyzed the gossip contained in 18th century published letters, the link between biographical writing and gossip, and literature's ability to transform "gossip's preoccupations" and to dramatize "its operations" (69, 119, 261). Concerning the latter, Ned Schantz has argued that the novel in particular works "in the mode of gossip," fixated on the private lives of people, and therefore participates "in disreputable feminine discourse" (17, 4).

8. The debates concerning how technology, and specifically, the advent of the Internet, has affected gendered communication is well documented elsewhere. It is often argued "that the virtual world, like the real one, is male dominated, while women remained second-class netizens as measured by their overall rates of active participation (posting) in many discussions" and that cyberspace itself is not a very "woman-friendly" environment (Spacks 6). This collection interrogates these claims.

Works Cited

Benstock, Shari, ed. *The Private Self: Theory and Practice of Women's Autobiographical Writings.* Chapel Hill: University of North Carolina Press, 1988. Print.

Butler, Judith. *Gender Trouble.* New York: Routledge, 1999. Print.

Cameron, Deborah, ed. *The Feminist Critique of Language: A Reader.* 2nd ed. New York: Routledge, 1998. Print.

Cixous, Hélène. "Castration or Decapitation?" *Signs: Journal of Women in Culture and Society* 7.1 (Autumn 1981): 41–55. Print.

_____. *Hélène Cixous Reader.* 1979. Ed. Susan Sellers. New York: Routledge, 1994. Print.

Crawford, Mary E. *Talking Difference.* London: Sage, 1995. Print.

Dunbar, Robin. *Grooming, Gossip, and the Evolution of Language.* Cambridge: Harvard University Press, 1996. Print.

du Plessis, Rachel Blau. *Writing Beyond the Ending.* Bloomington: Indiana University Press, 1985. Print.

Gluck, Sherna Berger, and Daphne Patai. *Women's Words: The Feminist Practice of Oral History.* New York: Routledge, 1991.

Goodman, Robert F. and Aaron Ben-Ze'Ev, eds. *Good Gossip.* Lawrence: University Press of Kansas, 1994. Print.

"Gossip, *n.*" *Oxford English Dictionary Additions Series.* 1997. *OED Online.* Oxford University Press. 23 Mar. 2000.

Havelock, Eric. *Preface to Plato.* Cambridge: Belknap Press of Harvard University Press, 1982. Print.

Irigaray, Luce. *This Sex Which Is Not One.* 1967. Trans. Catherine Porter and Carol Burke. Ithaca, NY: Cornell University Press, 1985. Print.

Jespersen, Otto. *The Feminist Critique of Language: A Reader.* 2nd ed. Ed. Deborah Camerson. New York: Routledge, 1998. 225–241. Print.

McLuhan, Marshall. *Understanding Media: The Extensions of Man.* 1964. Cambridge, MA: MIT Press, 1994. Print.

Mills, Sarah. *Feminist Stylistics.* London: Routledge, 1995. Print.

Nussbaum, Felicity. "Eighteenth-Century Women's Autobiographical Commonplaces." *The Private Self: Theory and Practice of Women's Autobiographical Writings.* Ed. Shari Benstock. Chapel Hill: University of North Carolina Press, 1988. 147–176. Print.

Ong, Walter J. *Orality and Literacy.* London: Routledge, 1982. Print.

Rysman, Alexander. "How the 'Gossip' Became a Woman." *Journal of Communication* 27.1 (1977): 176–180. Print.

Schantz, Ned. *Gossip, Letters, Phones: The Scandal of Female Networks in Film and Literature.* Oxford: Oxford University Press, 2008.

Smith, Sidonie, and Julia Watson. *Women, Autobiography, Theory.* Madison: University of Wisconsin P, 1998. Print.

Spacks, Patricia Meyer. *Gossip.* Chicago: Chicago University Press, 1995. Print.

Tannen, Deborah. *You Just Don't Understand: Men and Women in Conversation.* New York: Morrow, 1990. Print.

Wittig, Monique. *The Straight Mind and Other Essays.* Boston: Beacon Press, 1992. Print.

Woolf, Virginia. *A Room of One's Own.* San Diego: Harcourt, 1929. Print.

Part I

Spoken Spaces: The Historicization, Evolution, and Gendering of "Gossip"

1

Pandora's Voice-Box: How Woman Became the "Gossip Girl"

Giselle Bastin

The numerous studies about gossip from the last thirty or so years have tended to confirm one particular assumption over and over: gossip has traditionally been categorized as a "feminine" pursuit more than a masculine one. Everybody gossips, it would seem, but women are supposedly "better" at it, and certainly more drawn to gossiping as a social and recreational function.

As recently as 2006, Clare Birchall, in her detailed study about gossip and conspiracy theory, asserted that the "gradual feminization" of the term gossip in the centuries leading to Dr. Johnson's 1755 dictionary certainly "consolidated gossip's negative status" (97). And just as gossip and women have assumed an almost inviolable link in popular consciousness, this connection has assumed also an almost unconscious association for scholars in the field of gossip studies. It was not until Alexander Rysman published his important essay, "How the 'Gossip' Became a Woman" (1977) in a volume of essays in the *Journal of Communication* largely devoted to studies of gossip in a range of contexts, that someone tried seriously to investigate the origins of the cultural connection between women and gossiping. Rysman argues that the slow etymological journey of the word "gossip" from "god-parent" to "female tattler" reflects a deep, cross-cultural suspicion that "[w]omen [talking] together can make trouble for men" (176). What Rysman helped introduce to the field of gossip studies was the question of how it was that a seemingly innocuous noun such as gossip could become one that is gendered in highly complex ways. While Rysman is correct in suggesting that the word gossip had been "a positive term applied to both sexes" prior to the nineteenth-century, it has since then become a pejorative term applied mainly to women. Rysman's study, though providing an excellent overview of the etymological transformation of the word from medieval times to the nineteenth century, stops short of critiquing how women have been throughout history consistently situated as "the gossip" because of a biological predisposition to waste words and meddle in the lives of others with their chatter. What is missing in so much of the scholarly — and popular — discussion about gossip is an analysis of how and why garrulousness has so long been associated with female sexuality and corporeality.

Certainly, there has been much written on how gossiping is a female past-time, and much on so-called feminine uses of speech, yet there has been a reluctance to make explicit the link between gossiping as a gendered, sexualized act situated at the corporeal level.

It must be admitted that the range of sources drawn on here tend, on the whole, to assume a certain universality of both the "feminine" and "the gossip," and the examples cited do stem from a predominantly Western construction of the gendering of gossip. Despite the potential for an exploration of the gendering of gossip as a non-essentialized category, commentary from across the ages has been drawn to the notion that woman and gossip are essentialized categories rather than categories constructed in different cultures at different times. This problematic nature of gossip studies merely reflects, however, the embedded assumptions in much critical discourse about gossip as a feminine past-time over the epochs.

As will be shown, the idea of the woman as gossip is embodied in the ancient myth of Pandora who, as a feminine figure and cultural archetype, literally opens that which should remain closed. Gossiping becomes the verbal equivalent of Pandora's shameful spillage and rupturing of the (masculine) borders of order and containment. Pandora's "box," with all the sexual punning that this term engenders, becomes Pandora's voice-box in the sense that the two primary female openings of the mouth and vagina have been seen, I would argue, to conspire in a rupturing of social order. Moreover, it is necessary to consider this gendered relationship in terms of the structural bias against gossip which has been used to perpetuate and legitimate gossip's (and women's) relegation to the margins. Furthermore, I shall contend that the idea of "village gossip," embodying as it does a mode of talking characterized by its local qualities and effects, has been expanded into the "global village gossip," where international media content is thought by many to have been detrimentally feminized: all news, it seems, is gossip now.

Categorizing Gossip

In order to arrive at an understanding of how woman became the Gossip, it is useful first to survey the field of gossip studies as it has taken shape over the last forty years in Western historical and anthropological discourse. There have been many attempts in recent decades to define gossip, with most definitions falling under three categories identified by social historian Irit Rogoff: firstly, "Anthropologizing," which looks at gossip as "the discourse of 'others'" and "the communicative habits of tribes"; secondly, "Moralizing" where "exhaustive efforts" are made to "vindicate gossip from its morally inferior position and earnest attempts to find some purpose in its activity"; and thirdly, the "Sociological" view that deals with "celebrity" and assumes that "gossip is a by-product of mass culture" and is "refracted through the apparatuses of mass, popular culture" (58–59). The last category has attracted much attention for the way that it suggests that gossip has somehow feminized serious news coverage; that it is seeping (indeed, it is often thought of as "infecting" or "contaminating") traditional forms of objective, dispassionate news reportage. This idea is not new. Henry James's character Basil Ransom in the 1885 novel *The Bostonians* states with some dismay about his own century: "the whole generation is womanised; the masculine tone is passing out of the world; it's a feminine, a nervous, hysterical, chattering, canting age" (283).

Despite four decades of scrutiny from anthropologists (most notably by Max Gluckman in his 1963 essay "Gossip and Scandal"), it took some time for theorists to concentrate on the ways that the term gossip came to be associated with women. It was Rysman's brief 1977 study of women and gossip that re-situated gossip as a gendered discourse. It was followed by what is perhaps the most quoted study of gossip and its uses in literature: Patricia Meyer Spacks's 1985 text titled simply *Gossip*. Spacks's central thesis is that gossiping is a predominantly female pastime because women are "[b]y tradition talkers," a view shared by the evolutionary linguist, Robin Dunbar (Dunbar 149). Following Spacks, Maryann Ayim argued that gossip is a discourse of the marginalized and powerless, one that is "used to question, criticize, and eventually reject the principles and values of the powerful" (94). Ayim adds: "Viewed in this way, gossip is a clear threat to the social order, and therefore one should expect social sanctions against it. This is one reason for the sense of uneasiness or anxiety that society might harbour towards gossip" (94). Rysman puts forward this proposition also when he argues that gossip has been posited as transgressive because it is seen as a female activity that "develop[s] social ties outside the institution of male dominance" (176).

Yet, despite the recuperative project of recent decades which has seen a re-evaluation of gossip's positive uses, most commentary on gossiping and women has, nevertheless, been notable for its negativity. The ancient connection between female sexuality and verbal incontinence has largely been lost in modern folklore, yet the insinuation that the two remain related is still present in modern perceptions of the gossip. Many references to women and gossiping draw a clear link between feminine loquacity and feminine sexuality, but the link is offered as a given: women have insatiable lusts, *ergo,* they indulge in a communicative act which is equally unbridled and dangerous.

The Midwife and the Witch

When Samuel Johnson in his dictionary identified two meanings for the word gossip, one being "a tippling (drinking) companion," and the second, that of "female companions present at a birth," he tapped into a crucial element that connected the noun gossip with its verb form by identifying the word as meaning "A person, mostly a woman, of light and trifling character, especially one who delights in idle-talk; a newsmonger, a tattler" ("Gossip"). Henry Kingsley in his 1859 Australian novel, *The Recollections of Geoffry Hamlyn,* uses the term in this latter context: "On going in, they found the mother asleep, while her gossip held the baby on her knee; so the doctor saw that he was not needed ..." (376). The reference here to the woman "gossip" as midwife is present also in a seventeenth-century reference in the *Oxford English Dictionary* to the "midwife, and all the gossips present at their mothers' labours" ("Gossip"). This marks the entry into language of a connection between woman's access to the private world of childbirth and knowledge of the untidy doings of the bedroom. The last part of the excerpt from *Geoffry Hamlyn* issues a faint warning as to why the gossip has become a problem: it is because the doctor can see that he is *no longer needed.*

After the Middle Ages, a term that initially meant "God-related" came to denote a potentially dangerous woman who had access to intimate local information, and herein lies an early, albeit camouflaged, reference to gossip as a feminine term. According to overtly radical feminist readings of the European witch-trials of the fifteenth to eighteenth centuries, the midwife's reputation suffered because she, along with all the women present at the lying-in, became "privy to many family secrets which husbands may well have preferred to remain hidden" (Tebbutt 21). As keeper of female secrets and sometimes apothecary of women's (and men's) ailments, the midwife was systematically victimized throughout the Middle Ages and her traditions and knowledges all but eliminated. Mary Daly, a participant in the feminist recuperative studies of the 1970s, took the position that the knowledge and powers of healing which were considered the domain of the midwife threatened the "supremacy of the clerics," their influence and involvement in village affairs posing a threat to local male authority (63).

The persecution of the midwife was given official status in the fifteenth-century treatise, the *Malleus Maleficarum* (1486),[1] a text in which the authors singled out midwives as being particularly prone to acts of witchcraft. Accusations aimed at midwives were spread, ironically, through what today would be called gossiping. The verbal evidence mounted against these "gossips," which led to the deaths of so many, was gathered under the mantle of institutional dictum: local, private whispers fed into the structures of state-led systems of control. The belief that midwives were thought to couple with the devil meant that they bore the anger of a society bewildered and fearful of the mysterious process of childbirth, an event which commonly ended in tragedy. So the midwife, as overseer of this female event and keeper of female secrets, was blamed and often persecuted for her part in and knowledge of private affairs. The midwife, by profession, was responsible for delivering babies and tending to female physiology in such a way that her actions embodied the delivery of "new artefacts"; she dabbled in the dark, mysterious — literally the *underbelly*—of human existence. Together, the midwife and the witch are symbolic of gossip itself. They are women in possession of information which does not serve the interests of people whom the gossip may indict, and the outcome of this is that they must be silenced or at least made to suffer for the threat they pose to public order.

Today, the words gossip and midwife may not together conjure images of threat and social disorder, but the terms can be found being used in conjunction as recently as 1945 in the opening pages of Katherine Anne Porter's novel *Ship of Fools*. Here, reference is made to an intimately connected group of people who meet each day before work to drink lemonade and watch the local activity:

> They had all grown up together in the several generations, married each other's cousins or sisters or aunts, knew each other's business, told all the gossip they heard, and heard all the gossip they had told repeated to them; had assisted indeed with the intimacy of midwives at the making of each other's histories [Porter 14].

So, the midwife, with her etymological link to the noun gossip, was vulnerable to accusations of witchcraft; the gossip was hunted down in state-led campaigns to have her and her like eradicated. A perusal of interpretations of medieval and Renaissance historical documents reveals that woman became the Gossip through a complex congruence of socio-historical, medical, religious, and philosophical beliefs that posit the feminine as inferior. As excessive and wasteful, prone to sin, women were "naturally" more inclined to enact transgressions of moral law, and one of the most notable of these was their propensity to talk too much about the lives of men.

The Lips of Destruction

In sifting through examples from European history and literature of the evils of feminine verbosity, one encounters a common thread which binds many tracts on the subject, and this thread is a preoccupation, bordering on an obsession, with the relationship between feminine loquacity and feminine sexuality. Women's language has long been connected with the female reproductive system, and their bodies are considered in myth as "The source of all evils" (Lamberton 101) as are, indeed, their tongues. Women have been designated as the main culprits of spreading rumor and gossip because they are physiologically incapable of retaining anything. As "open," "leaky," "wasteful" repositories, vulnerable to contracting and spreading disease, women have been made the "natural" culprits for utilizing a form of communication that is viewed as potentially destructive. Melanie Tebbutt notes a nineteenth- and early twentieth-century connection between "loose talk" and "sexual laxity" (23). Aaron Ben-Ze'ev refers to the ancient Jewish prohibition against all forms of gossip, "the assumption apparently being that loose talk may easily become loose living. Just as sins of the heart may lead to vicious activities, idle talk about sex may turn into loose sexual conduct" (19). Warner, too, says of this connection: "The seduction of women's talk reflected the seduction of their bodies.... Eve sinned by mouth: she bit into the apple of knowledge, she spoke to the serpent and to Adam" (31). Paul Corcoran has also argued that Eve's misdemeanor in the Garden was not one of offering the apple to Adam, but of having a conversation with the serpent in the first place: it was a woman's chatter that brought an end to man's paradise (175). While Eve's misdemeanor was deemed a transgression of the patriarchal order within Judeo-Christian thinking, it is her predecessor, the ancient Greek goddess Pandora, who takes line honors as the first to have unleashed destruction on the world.

Pandora's Insatiable Curiosity

As the myth tells us, Pandora was the first woman in the world, a woman created by Zeus to be the bane of all men as punishment for Prometheus's theft of fire from the gods. Created from earth and water, Pandora was provided with knowledge of weaving (arts) by Athena and beauty by Aphrodite.

Most importantly, Hermes bestowed upon her speech, which, in her possession, became cunning and flattery, and provided her with "a shameless mind ... and a treacherous nature" (Radford Reuther 92). Worse still, Hermes put into her heart "lies and wheedling words" (Grant 109).

Pandora brought with her a box which she then opened, despite being warned by Zeus not to do so, and from the box sprang all the evils and sins of the world. In the box only Hope remained as the sole comfort of Man after the folly of Woman had brought about the ruination of Paradise. This myth, with its Christian parallel to Eve and her misdemeanour in the Garden as it is told in Genesis 1: 1—2:9, embodies the connection often made between women and their essential weakness of will—a connection between curiosity and the feminine. As Sarah Pomeroy asserts, Pandora's box "may be a metaphor for carnal knowledge of women, which was a source of evil to men" (4). The cultural archetype of Pandora exemplifies the notion that there is something about women and their curiosity that drives them, with a lustful passion, to interfere in matters which should not concern them. This is an idea uppermost in the mind of the ancient Roman writer, Juvenal, who, in the second century, warned his countrymen in his vicious Sixth Satire of the predisposition women have for destructive idle chatter. For Juvenal, the stuff of nightmare is the thought of women gathering together to converse:

> She knows all the news of the world, what's cooking in Thrace or China, just what the stepmother did with her stepson behind closed doors, who's fallen in love, which gallant is all the rage, she'll tell you who got the widow pregnant, and in which month; she knows each woman's pillow-endearments, and all the positions she favours.... She's on to the latest gossip and rumours as soon as they reach the city-gates, or invents her own [142].

Western theological and scientific thought have colluded over the centuries to produce a system of knowledges that stipulate women's "natural" inferiority to men (Gould 155), but how female speech and genitalia came to be considered as analogous is harder to trace. Many commentaries imply that the vaginal and oral openings of the female body conspire to devour and engulf men. They suggest, too, that the curiosity and lusts of women need such constant sustenance that there is a serious risk that the bodies and reputations of men will be sapped and destroyed in the fulfilment of these needs. Sandra Gilbert and Sandra Gubar claim that "There is, of course, a long masculinist tradition that identifies female anatomy with a degrading linguistic destiny" (82). They cite as evidence one of William Faulkner's characters who views all women as "articulated genital organ[s]" (qtd. in Gilbert and Gubar 82). Lamberton draws readers' attention to the Panofskys' study of Pandora's Box in which:

> the history of the visual arts of that Hesiodic myth is explored so brilliantly in its evolution from one elusive allegorical expression to another—all relentlessly pointing to the idea that the authors equally relentlessly refuse to articulate: the female genitals are the source of all evils [Lamberton 101–102].

Laura Mulvey in her essay "Pandora: Topographies of the Mask and Curiosity" offers other significant readings of Pandora's "box," suggesting that the box is no simple container of the evils of the world, but rather a container which acts as a metonymic representation of the female body. The metonymy of the box, sometimes depicted as a jar, is suggestive of the secrecy and concealment of the female body, and of female genitalia in particular. Mulvey cites the example of a Dutch engraving from the mid-seventeenth century which depicts the pyxis as a fig-leaf, "lowered to the part, which [Pandora] covers, from which has flowed so many of the miseries and anxieties that afflict man" (63). Mulvey mentions also another example found in the Panofskys' study of Pandora of a drawing by Paul Klee, dating from 1936, *Die Busche der Pandora als Stilleben*, "representing the ominous receptacle ... as a kantharis-shaped vase containing some flowers but emitting evil vapours from an opening clearly suggestive of the female genitals" (63). With this in mind, it is perhaps unsurprising that the Latin translation for *pudenda*, which means literally female genitals, is "something to be ashamed of" (Goldenson and Anderson 207).

Pandora's box is a metonym for feminine representation, also, in that once opened it has no inside or outside. Woman's (voice) box conflates borders of inside/outside (and by inference, private/public), thereby disrupting systems of categorization in the symbolic. Mulvey quotes Gaston Bachelard on the metonymical representations of boxes:

> [Chests and small caskets are] objects that may be opened. When a casket is closed, it is returned to the general community of objects; it takes its place in exterior space. But it opens! For this reason a philosopher mathematician would say it is the first differential of discovery. From the moment the casket is opened the dialectics of inside and outside no longer exist [qtd. in Mulvey 56].

Mulvey's study of Pandora focuses on a similar concern in that she argues:

> Inside/outside polarization is not derived from the connotations implicit in the male/female binary opposition but from something else: a disturbance, iconographically represented in images of the female body, symptomatic of the anxieties and desires that are projected onto the feminine within the patriarchal psyche [57].

Gossip becomes a discourse that negates and conflates the dialectics of inside and outside in its movement between the private and public realms. Importantly, the spatial and feminine corporeal metaphor allows for a way of interpreting responses to gossip's movement between the private and public realms.

The key to establishing how gossip has come to be gendered as feminine lies, also, in the perception of how gossip circulates. Certainly, the liberal humanist project which seeks to ground gossip as a style of language that women use in specific ways to achieve particular ends suggests that gossip is restricted to a linear, two-way directional flow. Such a view reflects ancient charges that gossip is a form of intended malice produced by women. By situating gossip as a discourse of the margins and of the marginalized, however, an opportunity arises to observe instead how gossip embodies the multi-directional properties of all borders. Such a metaphor is helpful in explaining how responses to gossip have been shaped.

The anthropologist Mary Douglas's pioneering 1966 study, *Purity and Danger: An Analysis of the Concepts of Pollution and Taboo* became a pivotal source for late twentieth-century psychoanalytical studies of the taboos which surround physical and social bodies. Her work provided a model in which to explore gossip's status as a product of women's physical bodies and gossip's relationship to the social body. Douglas notes how concepts of disorder and formlessness are both powerful and dangerous as they pose a threat to all bounded social systems. The physical body as bounded system, she asserts, can stand in for any social bounded system, and that social pollution — represented as any "flow" which transgresses and traverses the orifices/margins of the physical body — poses a threat to the unity and integrity of the social body. She writes:

> The body is a model which can stand for any bounded system. Its boundaries can represent any boundaries which are threatened or precarious.... We cannot possibly interpret rituals concerning excreta, milk, saliva and the rest unless we are prepared to see in the body a symbol of society, and to see the powers and dangers credited to the social structure reproduced in small on the social body [Douglas 115].

All margins are dangerous, she contends, and "[a]ny structure of ideas is vulnerable at its margins" and the "threatened boundaries of [the] body politic [is mirrored in care] for the integrity, unity and purity of the physical body.... The anxiety about bodily margins expresses danger to group survival" (Douglas 124).

Douglas's model can be used to develop a corporeal metaphor in order to consider how the female physical body (more than the male physical body), with its two primary orifices (the mouth and vagina), has been constructed within Western philosophical discourse as a major threat to (masculine) notions of social integrity. Douglas places notions of pollution into four categories:

> Four kinds of social pollution seem worth distinguishing. The first is danger pressing on external boundaries; the second, danger from transgressing the internal lines of the system; the third, danger in the margins of the lines. The fourth is danger from internal contradiction, when some of the basic postulates are denied by other basic postulates ... [122].

Any threat to external and internal boundaries, and the margins of these same boundaries — any flouting of the primacy of these boundaries *at all*— must be monitored, repressed, and subdued in the interests of conserving the bounded social body. The surveillance of borders and boundaries proves difficult given the provisionality of all borders. As Elizabeth Grosz says:

> The boundary between the inside and the outside, just as much as between self and other and subject and object, must not be regarded as a limit to be transgressed so much as a boundary to be traversed.... Boundaries do not so much define the routes of passage: it is movement that defines and constitutes boundaries. These boundaries, consequently, are more porous and less fixed and rigid than is commonly understood, for there is already an infection by one side of the border of the other ... [131].

Douglas asserts that all forms of social pollution which pose a threat to the integrity and unity of the social body must be policed or contained through ritualised strategies of control. In gossip's case, this has eventuated in centuries of derision and admonition about how destructive it is and why practitioners of gossip are weak-willed spreaders of evil and dirt. Gossip has earned its reputation as dangerous and threatening within a Cartesian system of thinking that posits Woman as "body" in relation to Man as "mind"; as her body, Woman cannot be separated from that body in her production and circulation of knowledges. The long association between women's mouths and vaginas, as constituting the condition of femininity, also points to the paradoxical nature of how gossip is perceived. Women's mouths (which should, ideally, remain closed and silent) work in conjunction with the genitals (which, when open, constitute the source of all men's pleasure — and pain) and together combine to bring about the destruction of men. The broken surfaces of the female body compromise the social bounded body. The body, Julia Kristeva declares, "must bear no trace of its debt to nature: it must be clean and proper in order to be fully symbolic" (102).

The fascination and fear evoked by the image of women's unbridled tongues, found in commentary from the Old Testament through to William Faulkner, suggest that the clue to understanding gossip's gendered status might lie in understanding more fully the construction of feminine corporeality in Western philosophical discourse. How is it that female physiology has so often been blamed for behavior deemed feminine? How has gossip become so reviled that it has invoked such a complex range of sanctions and taboos against it?

It becomes necessary to move beyond liberal humanist accounts of gossip, and even the feminist recuperative project of establishing gossip's virtues, and to formulate another way of tracing this ancient association. Denunciations of gossip echo through the centuries and "constitute an unconscious dimension of our cultural heritage" (Gatens xi) and reflect assumptions "embodied in history, *internalized as second nature*" which become, as a result, says Bourdieu, "forgotten as history" (qtd. in Gatens, xi). Douglas's theories about how societies regulate and outlaw forms of threat to the social bounded system have been useful in establishing a corporeal metaphor for gossip. The feminine form, postulated as incomplete and open, is thought to imperil and destabilize the bounded (male) body politic just as gossip's movement between the private and the public is perceived to threaten the integrity of these realms. As a feminized discourse, gossip reflects and constitutes a range of competing bodies (bodies of knowledge, authority, and power) as it presses on external boundaries, traverses internal lines, operates in the margins of those lines, while at the same time revealing the internal contradictions of the socio-symbolic order.

The paradox of gossip is that it contains the properties of all discourses in that it conflates the dialectics of inside and outside, resisting, even, borders of its own definition. As the contaminating source which hovers in and around the margins, on the *rim*, of other discourses, gossip is symbolic of Pandora's box in that its openings mark it as transgressive according to a system of logic which must define as "Other" any source of threat to its continued existence. Thus, Douglas's theories about the rituals and taboos surrounding any form of social pollution which unsettle social order can be ascribed to the dangerous and powerful discourse labelled as gossip.

Women, then, had to become labelled as gossips because they have been caught between a rock and a hard place. Traditionally, women have been the midwives who have delivered new facts into the world and have been privy to the hushed secrets of people's lives; there is fear, too, in the notion that the gossip's knowledge of private affairs always has the potential to "leak" into the public sphere, thereby blurring the distinction between the private and the public. As Mary Leech says, echoing Spacks, gossip is marked by its "incalculable scope" (311). It is an intriguing form of communication in that it both defines communities and has the capacity to fracture communities. It is a form of communication that is deemed trivial and inconsequential, but the amount of vitriol flung at it over the centuries would suggest that it is anything but inconsequential. Gossip, as anecdotal evidence might suggest, is not something that only women do: it is not a biological weakness that women intrinsically possess. Rather, it is a convenient label attributed to what women are *presumed* to be doing when they talk together. Such an association lingers on into the present in works such as Cecily von Ziegesar's hugely successful *Gossip Girl* series (2002). Beyond the alliterative qualities of the title of this book (and television) series, and while seemingly stemming from the tenets of "girl power" politics in popular culture, von Ziegesar's novels nonetheless feed into the popular historical association between females and dangerous, subversive activity. And while modern forums like *Gossip Girl* supposedly celebrate gossiping because of the outlet it offers women otherwise cut off from official avenues of public discourse, there is a lingering suspicion that female garrulousness defies the so-called natural order and poses the ultimate form of danger to the social bounded body. Gossip is considered excessive and wasteful, and particularly voluble and aberrant in women when times are lean or when the social bounded system is under threat from outside sources. As society enters a new era of lean and fragile economic times, expressions of excess—linguistic and bodily—come under renewed scrutiny. Perhaps this is why von Ziegesar's gossip girls remain so thin while doing all that gossiping. Communal anxiety about gossip necessitates a silencing of the source of the unease—the witch and her sorcery, the midwife, the gossip girl, the *god-sip*. Rysman, I would argue, could have added a coda to his study "How the 'Gossip' Became a Woman" to suggest that she did so because she had, as it turned out, very little say in the matter.

NOTE

1. The *Malleus Maleficarum* (1486) was a compendious treatise drawn up by two Dominican Inquisitors to assist in the tracking down of witches. It dictated the means by which one can identify a witch, and detailed the methods to extract confessions. The word *maleficarum* is the feminine derivation of the word *maleficorum,* its use in the title of this document reflecting the assumption that women are far more likely to be witches than men.

WORKS CITED

Ayim, Maryann. "Knowledge Through the Grapevine: Gossip as Inquiry." *Good Gossip*. Eds. Robert F. Goodman and Aaron Ben-Ze'ev. Lawrence, Kansas: University of Kansas, 1994. 85–99. Print.

Ben-Ze'ev, Aaron. "The Vindication of Gossip." *Good Gossip*. Eds. Robert F. Goodman and Aaron Ben-Ze'ev. Kansas: University of Kansas, 1994. 11–24. Print.

Birchall, Clare. *Knowledge Goes Pop*. Oxford: Berg, 2006. Print.

Corcoran, Paul. "Silence." *Disclosures*. Eds. Paul Corcoran and Vicki Spencer. Aldershot: Ashgate Publishing, 2000. 172–201. Print.

Daly, Mary. *Beyond God the Father: Towards a Philosophy of Women's Liberation*. Boston: Beacon Press, 1973. Print.

Douglas, Mary. *Purity and Danger: An Analysis of the Concepts of Pollution and Taboo*. London: Ark Paperbacks, 1984. Print

Dunbar, Robin. *Grooming, Gossip and the Evolution of Language*. London: Faber and Faber, 1996. Print.

Gallop, Jane. "Snatches of Conversation." *Women and Language in Literature and Society.* Eds. Sally McConnell-Ginet, Ruth Borker and Nelly Furman.New York: Praeger Publishers, 1980. Print.

Gatens, Moira. *Imaginary Bodies: Ethics, Power and Corporeality.* London: Routledge, 1996. Print.

Gilbert, Sandra M., and Gubar, Susan. *The Madwoman in the Attic: The Woman Writer and the Nineteenth-century Literary Imagination.* New Haven and London: Yale University Press, 1979. Print.

Gluckman, Max. "Gossip and Scandal." *Current Anthropology* 4.3 (1963): 308–316. Print.

Goldenson, Robert, and Anderson, Kenneth. *The Wordsworth Dictionary of Sex.* London: Wordsworth Editions Ltd., 1986. Print.

"Gossip." *The Oxford English Dictionary.* 2nd edition. 1976. Print.

Grant, Michael. *Myths of the Greeks and Romans.* New York: Mentor Books, 1962. Print.

Grosz, Elizabeth. *Volatile Bodies: Towards a Corporeal Feminism.* Sydney: Allen and Unwin, 1994. Print

James, Henry. *The Bostonians.* New York: Dial Press, 1945. Print.

Juvenal. *The Sixteen Satires.* Trans. Peter Green. London: Penguin Books, 1967. Print.

Kingsley, Henry. *The Recollections of Geoffry Hamlyn.* Adelaide: Rigby Books, 1975. Print.

Kristeva, Julia. *Powers of Horror: An Essay on Abjection.* New York: Columbia University Press, 1982. Print.

Lamberton, Robert. *Hesiod.* New Haven: Yale University Press, 1988. Print.

Leech, Mary. "Feminist Figurations: Gossip as a Counter Discourse." *Qualitative Studies in Education* 10.3 (1997): 305–314. Print.

Mulvey, Laura. "Pandora: Topographies of the Mask and Curiosity." *Sexuality and Space.* Ed. Beatriz Colomina. Princeton: Architectural Press, 1992. 53–72. Print.

Panofsky, Dora, and Erwin. *Pandora's Box: The Changing Aspects of a Mythical Symbol.* New York: Bollingen Foundation, 1962. Print.

Pomeroy, Sarah B. *Goddesses, Whores, Wives, and Slaves.* New York: Schocken Books, 1975. Print.

Porter, Katherine Anne. *Ship of Fools.* London: Secker and Warburg, 1945. Print.

Radford Reuther, Rosemary. *Womanguides: Readings Towards a Feminist Theology.* Boston: Beacon Press, 1985. Print.

Rogoff, Irit. "Gossip as Testimony: A Postmodern Signature." *Generations and Geographies in the Visual Arts: Feminist Readings.* Ed. Griselda Pollock. London and New York: Routledge, 1996. 75–86. Print.

Rosnow, Ralph L., and Fine, Gary Alan. *Rumor and Gossip: The Social Psychology of Hearsay.* New York: Elsevier Scientific Publishing Company, 1976. Print.

Rysman, Alexander. "How the 'Gossip' Became a Woman." *Journal of Communication* 27.1 (1977):176–180. Print.

Tebbutt, Melanie. *Women's Talk? A Social History of Working-Class Neighbourhoods, 1880–1960.* Aldershot, England: Scholar Press, 1995. Print.

von Ziegesar, Cecily. *Gossip Girl.* London: Bloomsbury Publishing, 2002. Print.

Warner, Marina. *From the Beast to the Blonde: On Fairy Tales and Their Tellers.* New York: Farrar, Straus and Giroux, 1994. Print.

2

Just Like a Woman: Misogynistic Gossip in the Correspondence Between John Chamberlain and Sir Dudley Carleton

Emily Ross

According to early modern diatribes against gossip, gossip was an activity engaged in predominantly by women,[1] particularly those of the lower classes.[2] However, while lower class women may well have gossiped, little of their speech has been preserved — other than within the conduct literature which satirized it. The same patriarchal prerogatives which condemned women's speech discouraged women's literacy, with the ironic result being that the majority of the early modern gossip which has survived was written by upper class men.

Of all early modern correspondents, John Chamberlain is one of the most renowned. A large number of his letters are extant, many written to his friend Sir Dudley Carleton. As Chamberlain and Carleton are the protagonists of this chapter, a short introduction of each is appropriate. John Chamberlain (1554–1628) seems to have lived all his life in London, as a gentleman of leisure. He is not known to have attained any qualifications or held a profession, and may have lived on inheritance from his father (McClure 4, 8). Chamberlain's primary pen-pal, Sir Dudley Carleton (1573–1632), was a career civil servant, holding a number of high status bureaucratic positions overseas (Ambassador to Venice 1610–1616, Ambassador to the Hague 1616–1624) and in England (Vice-Chamberlain of the Royal Household 1625–1626, Secretary of State 1626–1632) (Lee 5, 10, 17, 21).

Although Chamberlain and Carleton were rarely in the same country and so only occasionally met, the correspondence between them lasted thirty years (McClure 11). Their correspondence is exceptional not only because of its longevity, but also because both halves of it survive, meaning that their letters can be read together as a form of conversation. While it might be assumed that putting the letters in sequence would reconstruct a dialogue between the men, with each text becoming in effect a "conversational turn" (Ochs and Capps 7), in actuality their interaction is transactive rather than dialogic: Chamberlain responds to gossip about Carleton's world by offering gossip from his own world, and so forth. Jörg Bergman describes this pattern of gossip exchange as a "seriality of stories" (135). It would be interesting to examine correspondence between women from the same period to see whether this same pattern was present. However, almost all of the female-authored letters available for study were written to male recipients (presumably for similar patriarchal reasons to those discussed above), so the opportunity for such a comparison has not yet arisen.

Gossip stories pass on more than news about people; they are embedded with the "norms, laws, morals, scripts, traditions, and other rules" of groups to which gossip participants belong (Baumeister et al. 113). Chamberlain and Carleton were both members of the male educated elite, and their letters may be read for evidence of the values held by that class. In Norman McClure's view, Chamberlain wrote about "all that was uppermost in the minds of Englishmen" and "his predilections and prejudices were [...] those of his day and of the men with whom he was intimate" (2, 18). While McClure may be overstating his case by eliding Englishmen with members of the upper class, and no such claim has been made for Carleton, it seems plausible to hypothesize that prejudices circulating in early seventeenth English society might make an appearance in their letters.

While gossip creates solidarity between participants through the reinforcement of norms that they share with their social group, this solidarity comes at the expense of defining those that do not share those norms as outsiders (Wert and Salovey127–29). Nikolas Coupland terms this stigmatizing mechanism "othering," which he defines as "the process of representing an individual or a social group to *render* them distant, alien or deviant" (5, italics in original). Othering manifests as prejudices such as homophobia and racism or, in the case of this discussion, misogyny. The exchange of misogynistic gossip reconfirms men's shared values about gender, enabling them to "other" women as an out-group against which they can define their own masculinity (Heale 247).

In Coupland's work, he identified five predominant "discourse strategies" used in representations of the "other":

1. Suppression and silencing
2. Homogenization
3. Pejoration
4. Displaying liberalism
5. Subverting tolerance [9].[3]

Coupland's fourth and fifth strategies describe linguistic behavior in a politically correct environment, in which a speaker is aware that overt prejudice is unacceptable and so disguises or counteracts it. These tactics are therefore not applicable to the seventeenth century context, but I did find instances of prejudice being communicated covertly using methods which I will group under the heading Euphemization. Following the lead of Fairclough and Riggins, I will also discuss the role of Cultural Discourses in the othering process.

Suppression and Silencing

The distinction between silence and suppression is a matter of degree rather than of category. Out-group members may be discriminated against by being un-represented or under-represented, selectively represented, or misrepresented. The former two cases relate to the frequency that representations are present, and will be discussed in this part. The latter two cases relate to the quality of those representations which are present, and will be discussed under the homogenization and pejoration sections.

In terms of the Carleton-Chamberlain correspondence, women are unrepresented in individual letters and under-represented across the published collections as a whole. Of the approximately 660 named persons mentioned in the index to Maurice Lee's collection of Carleton's letters (90 letters in one volume), only 9 percent are female. In comparison, in McClure's larger and more comprehensive collection of Chamberlain's letters (479 letters in two volumes), women feature more frequently: 21 percent of the approximately 2640 names in his index are female. Because Chamberlain's letters provide a much larger pool of representations than Carleton's, most of the examples in this article will be drawn from his texts.

While the remainder of this chapter will focus on the ways that women are being othered when they *are* represented, it is clear from these statistics that non-representation is the most dominant means of exclusion. Some of the possible explanations for such a low level of representation of women include the gendered division of public and private, editorial intervention, and/or acquaintance gender (i.e. a male letter-writer may have more male than female friends, and so write more frequently about men).

In early modern England, patriarchal discourses promoted a gendered division of labor, allocating the public sphere to men and the private sphere to women, through such statements as "the dutie of the husband is to [...] seeke liuing: and the Wiues dutie is to keep the house" (Dod and Cleaver 167–68). This ideology was reinforced through segregationary measures prohibiting women from holding public office, denying them the same legal rights as men, and limiting their access to literacy, property, and other means to improve their own fate. Although the public-private binary was artificial and never unanimously implemented, these patriarchal discourses and prohibitions worked to create a society in which women were on the whole relegated to the domestic space. Therefore, men's activities were more likely to be of national and international import, and were more often reported by Carleton and Chamberlain.

This bias in favour of gossip about men may have been exacerbated (or even created) by editorial selection. Certainly editing may account for the greater degree of under-representation of women in Carleton's letters. Lee states in his introduction that the "small fraction" of Carleton's letters that he chose to publish are those of "general interest," and that he has omitted much of Carleton's correspondence about friends and family (4). On the surface, this decision makes good sense: Carleton's family and friends would probably not have been familiar names to Lee's audience who would, however, have recognized the public figures mentioned in the letters Lee elected to publish. Carleton may have self-censored his gossip for the same reasons: Chamberlain would be less likely to know the wives and daughters of Carleton's foreign associates, so Carleton might be less inclined to pass on gossip about them. However, this rationale soon becomes tautological: publishing gossip about men *because* men's business is more important than women's and men are more well-known contains the judgment that men's business *is* more important and perpetuates the relegation of women to the background and to anonymity.

The third possibility is that Carleton and Chamberlain may have gossiped mainly about men because, as stated earlier, as men, they were more likely to have male than female associates. Certainly, the exclusion of women from public office would have ensured that all of Carleton's business colleagues would have been male, although women would have been present at court and would have taken part in some of the state occasions that he reports on. On the other hand, it might be anticipated that Carleton would have more female associates than Chamberlain because he was married, whereas Chamberlain was not. However, on the whole, Carleton discusses the news of others rather than himself and his wife, just as Chamberlain's letters reveal little about their author. This is consistent with Sally Johnson's finding that male self-talk involves very little personal disclosure. Alternately, Chamberlain's bachelor status may have made him more, rather than less, able to have female friends. He seems to have been on good terms with the female relatives of some of his male associates; including Carleton's sister Alice, to whom he wrote a number of letters (McClure 16).

Homogenization

Homogenization occurs when people are categorized into groups on the basis of a single shared feature of their identity (ethnicity, gender), and that single feature becomes a label used to represent the whole (Coupland 10). There are three components of homogenization: labeling, attribution, and simplified or selective representation.

One of the most recognizable features of othering is "labeling which symbolically dehumanizes the referent" (Jaworski and Coupland 675). Whereas in-group members are often named individually, out-group members tend to be labeled by the feature that they have in common (Riggins 8). This is certainly true of the Carleton-Chamberlain correspondence. A select few female acquaintances are referred to by name,[4] or by the names of the men they are related to,[5] but on the whole women are labeled in terms of their marital status (e.g., as wives or widows).[6] While these labels may seem benign and value neutral, this categorization of women according to their familial role is obviously linked with the relegation of women to the domestic space, and to discourses about a woman's worth as a marital, reproductive, and sexual commodity.

Stereotypes of out-groups tend to characterize their members as embodying those qualities most disapproved of by the in-group (Wert and Salovey 128). Usually attribution involves superimposing a stereotype onto all individuals in a category by generalizing a quality to the group as a whole. For example, Chamberlain writes to Carleton that "our pulpits ring continually of the insolence and impudence of women."[7] Occasionally, this works in reverse, with a judgment applied to an individual being generalized from them to the group. For example, Chamberlain wrote to Carleton that Sir John Bennett was negotiating a match between his son and Sir Roger Ashton's widow, but that meanwhile the widow was openly socializing with another man, Tom Hatton. Chamberlain ends this piece of gossip by extending his condemnation of Sir Roger Ashton's widow to widows generally: "I know not what to say to the widowes of this age, nor what privilege they pretend."[8]

When representations of out-group members are simplified or selective, individuality and diversity are suppressed, and instead "dominant groups" representations articulate just those dimensions of a minoritised group's experience that suit their own agendas" (Coupland 14). In alignment with patriarchal ideologies which prohibited women from holding public office and relegated them to the household, Chamberlain and Carleton predominantly gossip about how well women conform to the domestic roles prescribed for them.

Although out-group members are generally assumed to be homogenous and able to be represented in simplified or selective ways, those out-group members known personally may be allowed more individuality (Riggins 5). For births, marriages, and deaths involving women with whom Chamberlain is unfamiliar, he is interested only in listing dates and names (or, more frequently, labels): formulaic data points such as might be entered in a family Bible.[9] The individuality of the persons involved is minimal, and may be further reduced by listing, which has the effect of making individuals seem identical and interchangeable. For example, Chamberlain wrote to Carleton that 1601 had been a "great yeare of wiving and childing," listing off four marriages and five pregnancies/births.[10]

In contrast, Chamberlain's gossip about the same events within the lives of persons who are deemed of greater interest (either because of familiarity, high status, or controversy) shows greater diversity. Instead of births, marriages, and deaths being reported *fait accompli,* these life markers devolve from historical co-ordinates into clusters of subsidiary events rich with individual detail. The birth events cluster includes reports that women are pregnant,[11] have miscarried,[12] or gone to "lie downe" (i.e., into confinement),[13] and the labor itself may be commented on.[14] After the birth, new mothers are churched,[15] and their children christened.[16] The marriage events cluster is similarly diverse and protracted. For example, Chamberlain's gossip about the high status and controversial marriage of Lucy Percy (daughter of the Earl of Northumberland) and Lord James Hay (future Earl of Carlisle) charts the progress of the couple's courtship and Northumberland's resistance to it over nine months,[17] culminating in a description of the wedding and wedding-supper in November 1617.[18] The death events cluster includes concern for people's health, with speculation about ill health being particularly intense for high status individuals.[19] The announcement of a death may be an opportunity for a gossiper to pass judgment on the life of the deceased,[20] or to comment on the stateliness of the funeral.[21] Deaths were also accompanied by legal arrangements with which women might be involved, such as dispersal of inheritance,[22] and wardship issues.[23]

Pejoration

Gossipers who criticize high status targets may protect their own reputations by using subtler forms of othering, such as euphemization. However, gossipers whose targets are perceived as having violated important social norms can use more direct forms of othering, such as pejoration, without incurring criticism themselves (Baumeister et al. 113–14). Pejoration involves devaluing members of social groups, by "invoking generally tabooed group labels" and by "adding explicitly negative attributes" (Coupland 13). Examining these labels and attributes can provide insight into which social discourses are being evoked (Fairclough 114).

As discussed above, the vast majority of the women mentioned by Carleton and Chamberlain were depersonalized and homogenized by being labeled with everyday familial terms such as wives or widows. However, for some women, the labels used are more value-loaded, impugning the status and sexual virtue of the women so designated.

One pejorative term that both Carleton and Chamberlain use for women is "wenches." According to the OED, the associations of the term are with women who are young (n. 1a.), lower class (n. 1b., 3), and "wanton" (n. 2). Carleton uses the term to designate specifically young women in one instance,[24] and Carleton and Chamberlain both use the term to refer to lower class women or servants,[25] but at other times the term is used to infer character rather than characteristic. Carleton reports that Sir Francis Bacon has married a "young wench,"[26] and Chamberlain writes in a similar vein that John Moore has "fallen to the world" and married a "wench."[27] On one occasion each, Carleton and Chamberlain use the phrase "boys and wenches,"[28] counterposing the neutral, male diminutive against the sexualized, class-loaded pejorative which is, by implication, being applied to the whole female gender.

While "wench" is a label with negative associations rather than the designation for a social group, other labels explicitly categorize women according to their perceived sexual role. Terms which Carleton and Chamberlain use for sex workers, "courtesan" and "whore,"[29] become pejorative when applied to other women because these labels attribute the characteristics of sex workers (specifically, promiscuity) to their targets. For example, Carleton described the costumes of the women participating in the *Masque of Blackness* as "too [...] courtesanlike."[30] While Chamberlain does not use the terms "courtesan" or "whore" pejoratively, he uses the label "concubine" to refer to the mistresses of married men, with the application of the pejorative term to the woman serving to shift all the blame onto her and away from her lover.[31]

Euphemization

Successful denigratory gossip requires that all participants share the same low opinion of the target. Low status out-groups can often be homogenized and pejorated overtly, because gossipers can safely assume that other participants share their negative view. However, when a gossiper is uncertain whether other participants will accept the person or group they have chosen to criticize as a valid target, strategies of euphemization may be used. There are two noticeable types of euphemization in Carleton and Chamberlain's correspondence: tactics of disavowal and tactics of indirection. In all the cases noted below, euphemistic gossip relates to the sexual reputations and/or activities of the targeted women.

Tactics of disavowal serve to deny the gossiper's culpability for the prejudices they pass on, through attributing statements or the views that statements contain to someone else (Bergman 77, 99; Riggins 11). Carleton and Chamberlain regularly attribute information to anonymous others, particularly when the truthfulness of the gossip is uncertain. For example, Chamberlain wrote that Sir Michael Stanhope's Lady had a daughter "as is saide" by Sir Eustace Hart.[32] Attributing views to others can also serve to protect the gossiper's own reputation. In a letter about acts of vandalism against some Venetian sex workers, Carleton reports that one had her windows broken and another had "both her water gate and back door set on fire in one night (I mean honestly, not as Ned Wimarke will take it when you tell him the story)."[33] The parenthetical comment ensures that Chamberlain will not miss the joke but protects Carleton's moral superiority by projecting its lewdness away from himself and onto Wimarke.

Tactics of indirection conceal the barb of a gossiper's criticism behind wordplay. Here the gossiper is relying on his recipient to read meaning back into a text from lexical clues. Sometimes the intended meaning is inferred. For example, Chamberlain commented on Lady Haddington's death that "they say (howsoever she lived) [she] went away vertuously."[34] The word "howsoever" is noncommittal, but the sentence structure sets up a contrast between Haddington's virtuous death and her (by implication) sinful life. At other times, the intended meaning is presented figuratively. For example, Chamberlain reported that Sir William Webbe's horse won the Garterly race, and Webbe is himself "newly mounted on a well ridden fillie," having recently married one of the daughters of Sir Strickland.[35] Chamberlain's purpose in terming Sir Webbe's bride a "fillie" punningly links his two pieces of news about Webbe, but also sets up the sexual double entendre of "mounted" and "well ridden." Euphemistic wordplay of this nature might be passed on intact through quoting. For example, Chamberlain wrote that the French King had returned to his mistress, purportedly replying to the Queen's protests that "though shee as his wife shalbe still his *panis quotidianus* [daily bread],[36] yet he must have a collation [meaning both a comparison and a meal consisting of delicacies ("collation" n. 2, n. 9)]."[37] The metaphor is of consumption, with the two women being read as sexual objects for the king's satisfaction. It is notable that Lady Haddington, Lady Webbe, and the French King's mistress are all upper class targets, which may be why euphemistic tactics are being used.

Cultural Discourses

Misogynistic discourses are a key means by which women are othered. A discourse is a set of representations about an aspect of society. Discourses are not derived from reality; rather they socially construct the reality they purport to reflect. Discourses are ideologically loaded, and present views of reality which favour dominant groups while disenfranchising out-groups (Fairclough 18; Riggins 2).

For the purpose of this essay I have identified five misogynistic discourses which were present in seventeenth century society and which appear in Carleton and Chamberlain's correspondence. For the sake of brevity, I will give only a few examples of each. While these discourses are presented separately for the purpose of clarity, they are tightly interlinked and reinforce one another, while at the same time being internally inconsistent and contradictory.

1. *A Woman's Appearance Determines Her Worth*

This discourse is particularly overt in Chamberlain's gossip about women and small-pox. On the one hand, he writes that women who had caught small-pox were at risk of losing the value of their appearance: for example, that Mistress West, "one of our prime and principall bewties," had the small-pox and was in danger of being "quite undon" because "her goode face is the best part of her fortune."[38] However, Chamberlain condemns a woman who took precautions not to endanger her looks: reporting that the recently married Sir John Smith had smallpox and his bride, Lady Isabella, "forgetting her late promise for better or worse in sicknes and in health is fled to save her faire skin."[39] The same double-edged reasoning appears in Carleton's attitude towards cosmetics. Carleton wrote in 1603 that the newly arrived Queen Anne had a "comely personage" and that amongst her ladies there were "many very fair and goodly ones"; however, he simultaneously disparaged her ladies' use of cosmetics as not being "*in rerum natura*" [i.e. not natural].[40]

2. *The Dowry a Woman Brings with Her at Marriage Determines Her Worth*

The commodification of women is at its most literal in gossip about dowries. Chamberlain wrote that Mistress Diana Drury "since the death of her brother is become a goode marriage worth ten or twelve thousand pound,"[41] and he disparages the bride-to-be of Sir Calistenes Brooke as "a widow [...] of no great goode report for wealth or otherwise."[42] In some instances, the importance of the dowry so surpasses the individuality of the woman that her name is omitted, although the exact amount of the dowry is carefully recorded.[43] However, wealth might not cancel out all other factors. Chamberlain appends the news that Master Sherly had married the Lady Umpton with the comment that "for mine owne part as poore a man as I am I wold not buy such another of the price."[44]

3. *A Woman's Ability to Reproduce Determines Her Worth*

In a society structured around patrilineal inheritance of property and title, fecundity was an essential quality in a wife. Chamberlain was doubtful about a match between Master Hopton and Sir Arthur Capell's widowed daughter because the woman in question was "above thirtie yeares old, and never had but one child her daughter," which made the marriage a "hasard" for Mr. Hopton.[45] Despite women taking the most obvious role in reproduction, child-bearing is sometimes still viewed from a male perspective. Chamberlain observes that Henry Howard's son has died but "he is younge enough to have more."[46]

Meanwhile, although high fertility was a prized trait, the terminology that Chamberlain uses to talk about pregnancy tends towards the animalistic. He talks about women "breeding,"[47] and having "great" or "swollen" "bellies."[48] However, the discrepancy discussed above between the treatment of unfamiliar and known out-group members is apparent here. Chamberlain is more complimentary about the pregnancies of upper class women of his acquaintance, writing that Winifred Wallop, is "prettily forward with child."[49]

4. *A Woman's Virtue Determines Her Worth*

As discussed in terms of attributing traits to stereotypes, patriarchal discourses attempted to didactically impose prototypes of the "ideal" woman. Women who did not conform to the role proscribed for them might be punished by having their virtue impugned. For example, when a woman refuses to marry Carleton's nephew, Chamberlain tries to console Carleton by blaming the woman's choice on her "naturall malignities," and suggesting that the nephew was lucky to "dodge" a woman who could "so easilie depart from her first love."[50]

While the prototype was most often used to rebuke women who did not conform to it, Chamberlain does occasionally praise a woman as an epitome of virtue.[51] However, as with physical appearance, over-concern with one's own qualities might be interpreted as a form of vanity. Chamberlain wrote satirically that Sir Rowland Lytton's daughters were "compleat women for learning, language and all other rare qualities, yf you may beleve their servants, that set them out as yf they were to be sold."[52]

5. *A Woman's Sexual Behavior Determines Her Worth*

Although all the discourses discussed here were in circulation in early modern society, the greatest misogynistic preoccupation was concern with a woman's sexual reputation. All of the pejorative and euphemistic examples mentioned earlier relate to this theme. While out-group members on the receiving end of prejudice have a purely negative experience, in-group members engaging in othering behavior may experience a more ambivalent mix of "desire and derision" (Bhabha 67), combining devaluation with eroticization (Riggins 5). This observation seems particularly apt for sexual gossip which both interprets women as sexual objects and condemns them for being so, enabling gossipers to engage in titillating voyeurism while retaining the moral high ground. Because of the high level of interest in sexual matters and the tangle of motives involved, it is unsurprising that discourses around sex seem particularly self-contradictory.

On the one hand, gossip about a woman's sexual honesty could cause considerable harm to her reputation and occasionally even lead to her death at the hands of a jealous husband.[53] However, a woman could also incur criticism for protesting against such defamation. Carleton described how the King of Denmark "made a sign with his two fingers" to the young Lady of Nottingham's seventy-year-old husband. As Carleton notes that the lady was pregnant and "jealous of her credit," it can be assumed that the sign made was that of the cuckold's horns. For "reveng[ing] herself with a railing letter" to the King of Denmark, the Lady of Nottingham was banished from court.[54]

Different standards of behavior were required of in-group as opposed to out-group members, granting sexual license to men while denying it to women. Carleton wrote that one of the court's women had "lost her honesty" after "being surprised at her business on the top of the terrace."[55] Whereas in other gossip (about marriages for example), the female party to a transaction may be omitted or unnamed, in gossip about sexual transgression the reverse is true: the woman is the active party and the man is either present only as an accessory or absent entirely.

Even women who were victims of abuse were condemned for their participation in sexual activities. For example, in 1612, Chamberlain reported that "a younge mignon of Sir Pexall Brockas [...] whom he had entertained and abused since she was twelve yeares old" was made to do penance at St Paul's Cross.[56] Although Chamberlain acknowledges that the woman had been "abused," he shows his support for the state's decision to punish her for her participation (even if involuntary) through his choice of the words "mignon" (which he uses in another context to mean extramarital lover)[57] and "entertained" (suggesting pleasurable activity).

Conclusion

The intent of this chapter was to explore instances of misogyny within the correspondence of Carleton and Chamberlain, and a great deal of evidence was found for the types of othering strategies previously identified by Coupland, Fairclough, and Riggins. However, in order not to make the same errors of reasoning described above of attending to only one feature of individual lives, over-emphasizing the similarity between individuals, and consigning all members sharing that feature into a labeled out-group (in this case, misogynistic men), it is important to end this with some provisos.

Even though the letters of both men provide evidence of misogyny, it is important to emphasize that they were not unique in their chauvinism; the prejudices they evince were ubiquitous in early modern England at the time that they were writing. Most of the examples in this article were drawn from Chamberlain's letters, which may give the impression that he was more sexist than Carleton. However, Chamberlain gossips about women more frequently than Carleton, and his gossip is more normative than Carleton's, which suggests that the opposite was true.

While this study has exposed the misogyny present in the Carleton-Chamberlain correspondence, the letters discussed above represent a very small portion of their writing. This lack of representation is, in itself, indicative of misogyny, with exclusion being the most dominant means by which women were disempowered. But even though the Carleton-Chamberlain letters are riddled with overt and silent misogyny, they nonetheless provide a wealth of interesting commentary on other aspects of early modern culture, including many aspects relevant to women's lives.

Women were not the only targets of Carleton's and Chamberlain's criticism; other out-groups, such as Catholics, also come in for ridicule. One of Carleton's sisters and one of his nieces were Catholic and Chamberlain wrote to Carleton about his efforts to reason with them, which suggests that Carleton may have asked him to attempt to intercede with them on his behalf. However, the sister and niece refused to forswear their faith. In one letter, Chamberlain criticized Carleton's niece for being "foolishely obstinate" and for spending "whole dayes and nights" at a lodging which is the "rendez-vous and all the revell of the men."[58] Here anti–Catholicism and misogyny combine, with religious nonconformity read as feminine disobedience and borderline promiscuity.

Finally, although othering women through misogynistic gossip served the purposes of the patriarchy in the instances discussed above, the strategies described were equally available to other groups. In fact, the prevalence of misandristic gossip amongst women was one of the rationales given in attempts to extinguish the practice. Satires of gossiping women, such as Samuel Rowland's *A Crew of Kind Gossips* (1613), show groups of women exchanging complaints about their husbands and sharing strategies to thwart them: the wife of a miser has learned to be sullen and to scold; the wife of a contradictory husband has taken up domestic violence; the wife of a drunk plays pranks on him and trips him up; and the wife of a gambler gets revenge by mocking his sexual inadequacy. While such satires are clearly caricatures, evidence from court testimonies suggests that women gathering together did indeed complain about "the violence, infidelity, meanness, or drunken profligacy of bad husbands" (Capp 376). William Gouge's description of gossips' meetings closely echoes such portrayals, and he blames the actions of rebellious wives on the "euill counsell of wicked Gossips" (336). It seems, therefore, that gossip could be a means of resisting misogyny as well as of perpetuating it.

NOTES

1. See, for example, Adams 150.
2. See, for example, Rowlands.
3. In Coupland's article the order of the first three is: 1. Homogenization, 2. Pejoration, 3. Suppression and Silencing.
4. See Chamberlain to Carleton, 14 November 1618, Chamberlain 2: 184.
5. See Chamberlain to Carleton, 9 September 1613, Chamberlain 1: 476.
6. For one example, see Chamberlain to Carleton, 17 May 1602, Chamberlain 1: 147.
7. Chamberlain to Carleton, 12 February 1620, Chamberlain 2: 289.
8. Chamberlain to Carleton, 11 March 1613, Chamberlain 1: 438.
9. For examples, see Chamberlain to Carleton: 28 November 1618, Chamberlain 2: 187; 12 December 1618, Chamberlain 2: 193.
10. Chamberlain to Carleton, 27 May 1601, Chamberlain 1: 124–25.
11. See Chamberlain to Carleton, 20 October 1621, Chamberlain 2: 401.
12. See Chamberlain to Carleton, 5 October 1611, Chamberlain 1: 306.
13. See Chamberlain to Carleton, 1 January 1620, Chamberlain 2: 278.
14. See Chamberlain to Carleton, 29 January 1612, Chamberlain 1: 414.
15. See Chamberlain to Carleton, 5 October 1611, Chamberlain 1: 305.
16. See Chamberlain to Carleton, 25 February 1613, Chamberlain 1: 430.
17. Chamberlain to Carleton: 22 February 1617, Chamberlain 2: 55; 8 March 1617, Chamberlain 2: 58; 24 May 1617, Chamberlain 2: 77; 5 July 1617, Chamberlain 2: 85; 9 August 1617, Chamberlain 2: 94; 11 October 1617, Chamberlain 2: 99.
18. Chamberlain to Carleton, 8 November 1617, Chamberlain 2: 114.
19. See Chamberlain to Carleton: 30 March 1603, Chamberlain 1: 188.
20. See Chamberlain to Carleton, 12 December 1618, Chamberlain 2: 193.
21. See Chamberlain to Carleton, 19 December 1618, Chamberlain 2: 195.
22. See Chamberlain to Carleton, 11 August 1612, Chamberlain 1: 377.
23. See Chamberlain to Carleton, 31 October 1617, Chamberlain 2: 109.
24. Carleton to Chamberlain, 2 August 1616, Carleton 209.
25. Carleton to Chamberlain, 19 April 1603, Carleton 31; Chamberlain to Carleton, 19 September 1601, Chamberlain 1: 130.
26. Carleton to Chamberlain, 11 May 1606, Carleton 84.
27. Carleton to Chamberlain, 13 June 1617, Carleton 237; Chamberlain to Carleton, 10 January 1609, Chamberlain 1: 281
28. Chamberlain to Carleton, 30 March 1615, Chamberlain 1: 591
29. Carleton to Chamberlain, 20 March 1612, Carleton 122; Chamberlain to Carleton, 23 August 1599, Chamberlain 1: 85.
30. Carleton to Chamberlain, 7 January 1605, Carleton 68.

31. See Chamberlain to Carleton, 20 December 1623, Chamberlain 2: 533–34.
32. Chamberlain to Carleton, 30 April 1616, Chamberlain 1: 626.
33. Carleton to Chamberlain, 20 March 1612, Carleton 122.
34. Chamberlain to Carleton, 12 December 1618, Chamberlain 2: 193.
35. Chamberlain to Carleton, 9 September 1613, Chamberlain 1: 476.
36. Trans. Kyle Gervais.
37. Chamberlain to Carleton, 16 July 1606, Chamberlain 1: 231.
38. Chamberlain to Carleton, 14 November 1618, Chamberlain 2: 184.
39. Chamberlain to Carleton, 30 January 1619, Chamberlain 2: 208.
40. Carleton to Chamberlain, 4 July 1603, Carleton 34–35. Trans. Kyle Gervais.
41. Chamberlain to Carleton, 23 November 1616, Chamberlain 2: 40.
42. Chamberlain to Carleton, 28 February 1602, Chamberlain 1: 187.
43. See Chamberlain to Carleton, 24 November 1614, Chamberlain 1: 558.
44. Chamberlain to Carleton, 8 December 1598, Chamberlain 1: 57.
45. Chamberlain to Carleton, 21 December 1622, Chamberlain 2: 468–69.
46. Chamberlain to Carleton, 12 January 1614, Chamberlain 1: 570.
47. See Chamberlain to Carleton, 15 October 1602, Chamberlain 1: 165–66.
48. See Chamberlain to Carleton: 5 October 1606, Chamberlain 1: 234.
49. Chamberlain to Carleton, 19 September 1601, Chamberlain 1: 130.
50. Chamberlain to Carleton, 5 June 1624, Chamberlain 2: 560–61.
51. See Chamberlain to Carleton, 8 January 1620, Chamberlain 2: 282.
52. Chamberlain to Carleton, 22 April 1606, Chamberlain 1: 227.
53. See Carleton to Chamberlain, 14–16 September 1623, Carleton 309–10.
54. Carleton to Chamberlain, 20 August 1606, Carleton 90.
55. Carleton to Chamberlain, 7 January 1605, Carleton 68.
56. Chamberlain to Carleton, 12 February 1612, Chamberlain 1: 334.
57. Chamberlain uses this term in another context to mean extramarital lover. Chamberlain to Carleton, 13 June 1600, Chamberlain 1: 97–98.
58. Chamberlain to Carleton, 26 April 1602, Chamberlain 1: 140–41.

Works Cited

Adams, Thomas. "The Taming of the Tongue." *The Works of Tho[mas] Adams*. London: Tho. Harper [and Augustine Mathewes] for Iohn Grismand, 1629. *STC* (2nd ed.). 143–54.

Baumeister, Roy F., et al. "Gossip as Cultural Learning." *Review of General Psychology* 8.2 June (2004): 111–21. Print.

Bergman, Jörg R. *Discreet Indiscretions: The Social Organisation of Gossip*. New York: Aldine de Gruyter, 1993. Print.

Bhabha, Homi K. *The Location of Culture*. London: Routledge, 1994. Print.

Capp, Bernard. *When Gossips Meet: Women, Family, and Neighbourhood in Early Modern England*. Oxford: Oxford UP, 2003. Print.

Carleton, Dudley. *Dudley Carleton to John Chamberlain, 1603–1624: Jacobean Letters*. Ed. Maurice Lee. New Brunswick, NJ: Rutgers UP, 1972. Print.

Chamberlain, John. *The Letters of John Chamberlain*. Ed. Norman E. McClure. 2 vols. Philadelphia, PA: The American Philosophical Society, 1939. Print.

"Collation, *n*." *The Oxford English Dictionary*. 2nd ed. 1989. *OED Online*. Oxford University Press. 5 Mar. 2010.

Coupland, Nikolas. "'Other' Representation." *Handbook of Pragmatics 1999*. Eds. Jef Verschueren, *et al*. Philadelphia: John Benjamins Publishing Company, 1999. 1–24. Print.

Dod, John, and Robert Cleaver. *A Godlie Forme of Householde Government [...]*. 2nd ed. London: Thomas Man, 1612. *STC* 5386.

Fairclough, Norman. *Media Discourse.* London: Edward Arnold, 1995. Print.
Gouge, William. *Of Domesticall Duties [...].* 2nd ed. London: Iohn Haviland for William Bladen, 1622. *STC* 12119.
Heale, Elizabeth. "Misogyny and the Complete Gentleman in Early Elizabethan Printed Miscellanies." *The Yearbook of English Studies* 33 (2003): 233–47. Print.
Jaworski, Adam, and Justine Coupland. "Othering in Gossip: You Go out You Have a Laugh and You Can Pull Yeah Okay but Like..." *Language in Society* 34 (2005): 667–94. Print.
Johnson, Sally. "A Game of Two Halves? On Men, Football and Gossip." *Journal of Gender Studies* 3.2 July (1994): 145–54. Print.
Lee, Maurice. "Introduction." *Dudley Carleton to John Chamberlain, 1603–1624: Jacobean Letters.* Ed. Maurice Lee. New Brunswick, NJ: Rutgers UP, 1972. 3–25. Print.
McClure, Norman E. "Introduction." *The Letters of John Chamberlain.* Ed. Norman E. McClure. Vol. 1. Philadelphia, PA: The American Philosophical Society, 1939. 1–25. Print.
Ochs, Elinor, and Lisa Capps. *Living Narrative: Creating Lives in Everyday Storytelling.* Cambridge, Mass: Harvard UP, 2001. Print.
Riggins, Stephen Harold. "The Rhetoric of Othering." *The Language and Politics of Exclusion: Others in Discourse.* Ed. Stephen Harold Riggins. Thousand Oaks, California: Sage Publications, 1997. 1–30. Print.
Rowlands, Samuel. *A Crew of Kind London Gossips All Met to Be Merry Complaining of Their Husbands, with Their Husbands Answer in Their Own Defence [...]* London: S.L., 1663. Wing (2nd ed.) R2078A.
_____. *Tis Merrie When Gossips Meete [...].* London: W. W[hite] for [J.] Deane, 1613. *STC* (2nd ed.) 21210.5.
"Wench, *n.*" *The Oxford English Dictionary.* 2nd ed. 1989. *OED Online.* Oxford University Press. 5 Mar. 2010.
Wert, Sarah R., and Peter Salovey. "A Social Comparison Account of Gossip." *Review of General Psychology* 8.2 (2004): 122–37. Print.

3

"Paper cannot blush": Martha Fowke, an 18th-Century Abandoned Woman

Earla Wilputte

Clio's *Letter to Hillarius*

Seneca defined the epistle as "talking on paper," while the medieval description was *sermo absentis ad absentem*— speech of an absent speaker to an equally absent listener (qtd. in Henderson 157, 172). In the eighteenth century, the relation between speaking and letter writing continued; poet William Walsh echoed the opinion of the age when he advised that "the style of letters ought to be free, easy, and natural: as near approaching to familiar conversation as possible" (qtd. in Jones 21). The familiar letter was an intimate discourse, revealing the writer's heart by providing a "window in the bosom" (Jones 21); such intimacy therefore rendered it as inappropriate for a woman to write to a man as to speak with him clandestinely. The danger in a woman's writing was that she might reveal too much of her heart in an unguarded moment. In 1721, Eliza Haywood cautioned in her "Discourse Concerning Writings of this Nature" (that is, epistles to men) that "Paper cannot blush," and without the guardianship of virtue's "natural Bashfulness," women could "take great liberty in expressing themselves" in letter form (6). Poet Martha Fowke— popularly known as Clio, daughter of Sappho— unlike most women of her time, and despite Haywood's warnings, was wholly uninhibited about writing down, circulating, and publishing expressions of her innermost thoughts. Although she expressed her fear to lover Aaron Hill that her letters to him might be discovered, that fear did not prevent her from continuing to write and send them. In so doing, Fowke, like many heroines of mythical proportion before her, demonstrates how letter writing permits the passionate woman a space in which to explore, express, and exploit her own and her lover's passions. For Fowke it is also an opportunity to clearly present an unimpeded image of her mind to Hill so that he could appreciate her as both a woman and a poet.

In her October 1723 autobiographical letter to Hill Martha Fowke delivers a passionate outpouring of her feelings for Hill while recounting for him her love life before she met him. At the time of her writing, she is thirty-four years old, a published poet "well known in London literary circles" (Guskin 62)—some cattily remarked "too well known" (Johnson, "Thomson," 368)—and three years married to London lawyer Arnold Sansom. Her relationship with the married Hill probably began soon after they started corresponding in June 1721.[1] As Phyllis Guskin notes, "We do not know when or how [Fowke's] relationship with Hill came to an end" (39) but by 1723 the affair appears to be over. Fowke writes "Clio [...] a Letter to Hillarius" to Hill in an effort to win him back.

While eighteenth-century conduct books insisted that a woman "feign an Insensibility, smother the rising Sighs, dress up her Face in Smiles, [and] wear a composed Serenity in her Countenance, when all the Furies are at work within her," Haywood noted "O hard Condition! which [...] forbids us to complain" (16). Fowke is unwilling to do anything so repressive. She conflates the physical artifact of her little volume written for Hill with her body, urging him "to thy Arms receive / My Life and me" (Sansom 60), and concludes, "let the Fulness of this Book impart / A little Emblem of my crouded Heart" (Sansom 140). Fowke knows that her physical body, separated from Hill's, must be brought back to his imagination to re-engage his passion for her. Elizabeth Cook comments on how the epistle can stand in for a woman's body: "on the model of the abandoned lover's epistolary complaint established by the *Heroides*, writing a letter can be understood as the attempt to construct a phantasmatic body that in some measure compensates for the writer's absence" (26). Fowke's substitution of her book for her body—her volume being an object that he can hold in his hands, privately reading her feelings for him, while even the turning of the pages intimates a sexual act—is an attempt to make him remember and relive their relationship.

The Power of the Letter

Fowke always associated the art of writing with seduction—from penning love letters as a teenager for her father to gain him mistresses (Sansom 66), through her 1720 poetic collaboration with William Bond writing *Epistles of*

Clio and Strephon (Sansom 125), to her receiving letters from Aaron Hill before she met him (Sansom 131). "What artful Methods the Poetick find / To steal themselves into the Reader's Mind," Clio commented to Strephon (Fowke 39). Fowke uses her long autobiographical letter to Hill to steal into his mind in a way unavailable through oral discourse and physical presence. She incorporates the rhythms and flow of speech by interrupting her life history with interjections of love and longing for Hill. She knows that reading evokes empathy, and that as Hill reads her words he will feel as she feels. To read her letter will be to put himself in the position of saying her words himself or imagining her voice saying them (Culler 74).

Fowke's letter begins and ends with passionate expressions of her love and pain as well as resentment of Hill for being incapable of appreciating the caliber of her emotion for him. "Oh! if you have a Heart, why did it not beat with Clio's Anguish? why was it silent when mine was torn to death with Love and Sorrow? Oh! insensible *Hillarius*, will it be to your Glory that you have pierc'd to Death the most faithful of all Women?" (Sansom 58). Fowke contrasts her suffering and inability to act with Hill's lack of feeling and his distinctively masculine actions — the "Glory" of seducing and "pierc[ing her] to Death." While her passion is ongoing, moving from love to anguish, Hillarius's passion is quick and destructive and seemingly founded (as Clio's diction suggests) in sexual conquest.

Fowke's separation from Hill causes her complaints to rise to an anguished cry by the end of her letter. All that remains for her to do is wish for the softer passion of pity from the absent Hillarius — a passion emphasizing his position of superiority without any real compassion for her suffering.

> Oh! would to Heaven, ever-most-charming *Hillarius*, would to Heaven and you, I were here to end my Life; never was I fonder of resigning it; never was I more unable to support it; your Absence kills me. Oh! I am undone without you, and more miserable than Envy can wish me. I am lost to myself, and to the World, nor am I of much value to you. What would inrich another is no Treasure to you; yet can you not restore it, nor can I take it back. My soul is sweetly lost in your dear Bosom, nor can ever find itself again; the God that created it, will, I hope, never divide it from you, whatsoever becomes of this miserable Body which loves to Adoration. When it lies in Dust, sigh your Pity over it; and give it one of those Moments I now languish for; sure I shall be proud in Death, and happy [Sansom 132].

Here is the cry of the abandoned woman: abandoned in that her lover has left her, but also in that she reveals her passions so openly and shamelessly. Lawrence Lipking notes that in the figure of the abandoned woman from Sappho, through Heloise, the Portuguese Nun, and onward, there is no disguise of emotion:

> And that is why [she] commands such threatening and fascinating power. No feelings are too strong or too shameful for her to express. Hysteria, carnality, self-loathing, infatuation, fury, abasement, longing — these are her daily bread. Even in her quiet moments she lives at a pitch of despair obliterating everything that does not feed her passion [20].

This, of course, was not the behavior of a socially respectable eighteenth-century woman. Unrestrained female expression was regarded as reprehensible. Haywood, in her "Discourse Concerning Writings of this Nature," voices the social disapproval of such abandonment, making clear that she feels there is nothing to be gained by so thoroughly revealing one's vulnerability and sacrificing one's pride.

> [I]n a Case like this, Pride only is becoming; and tho the Heart weeps Blood — the Eye-balls start — each Limb, with Tremblings, loses its nervous Use — and inward Horror shakes the whole Fabrick like an Earthquake; a noble Mind will struggle thro the Pangs, if not *conceal, disguise*, under some other Name, the unconquerable Dart, affect, at least a generous Disdain, and seem to scorn the Scorner [21].

Fowke constructs her letter so that Hill does not witness her physical suffering, but does experience her emotional suffering. Removed from him physically yet stealing into his mind by expressing her pain, Fowke's writing legitimizes her emotions for Hill with a power that even Haywood could comprehend.

> There is certainly an Influence in an artful, tender, and passionate Way of Writing, which more sensibly affects the Soul, than all the Tongue can utter: Words, tho never so moving, and with never so great a Grace deliver'd, we may avoid list'ning to, or they may slide from our Memory, when Letters will remain perpetual *Monitors*. Tho we know each Line is an Arrow aimed at our Virtue or our Peace; our Curiosity, or our Inclination, seldom fails engaging us to peruse them [Haywood 6–7].

Though "Paper cannot blush" and so may compromise a woman's femininity, it can allow her freedom from shame as there are no biological or social impediments to restrict her written words. The letter form also surmounts the problems of interruption and loss of train of thought that orality and presence might precipitate. A speaking woman, Haywood indicates, can be ignored or her words forgotten. The epistle permits the woman writer both the time and the space in which to develop her points; she can carefully construct and revise her thoughts, as well as (seemingly) spontaneously confess her feelings. Michael McKeon notes that "the letter becomes a passport not to the objectivity of sense impressions but to the subjectivity of mind" (414). The physicality of the letter concretizes a woman's words and, more importantly, conveys her mind to the reader in a way not possible in person. Finally, as Haywood points out, the recipient's curiosity compels him not only to read the letter but also to come back to it as a material artifact whereas a woman's speech would not necessarily command an auditor's attention at all.

Redefining Virtue

Fowke's letter, in addition to expressing her love for and grief over Hillarius, presents a progress from a philosophical discourse to a quasi-medical discourse on the passions. Despite her past mistakes with men, she makes no apologies for her conduct, insisting that, in her own way, she has been virtuous; but her definition is equivocal. From her description, one knows that her virtue is not aligned with the chastity demanded of eighteenth-century women.

> Oh need I say what Virtue is! 'tis to adore *Hillarius*, and him divinely as I do,without Reserve or Interest; to sacrifice the mean Incense of the Crowd to the heavenly Passion to live for him alone, to languish for him amidst the Praise and Adoration of the World: This is Virtue, to love the Virtuous, and truly Noble. I look down with Contempt on the mean Mortals who confine Virtue to the narrow Compass of the Body: Sure it is seated in the Soul, or rather your divine Breast is its Treasury [Sansom 93].

For Fowke, virtue is based on sensibility, that intense emotional responsiveness in the form of unreserved love to someone worthy of that response. Her ability to look down on the "mean Mortals" who define virtue physically gives the impression that she is godlike in her superiority to them; her mind and morality are formed on a grander scale. Neither her virtue nor her passions can be confined to the physical realm. The polarity evident in her passage on virtue — the vulgar crowd's anger versus her heavenly passion; her languishing versus Hillarius's being adored; the body versus the soul — emphasizes the chasm between Fowke's divine love for Hill and the pettiness of the world concerned with chastity. Like Aphra Behn, who had suggested that female honor, based as it is in virginity, is an artificial value, Fowke professes that real virtue is not constrained by the physical: it is "seated in the Soul"; that is, it is an abstract, spiritual concept. She regards her contemporaries' definition of virtue as hypocritical. For Fowke, virtue must be newly defined to accommodate the realities of human nature, and especially female nature.

Speaking of another lover, whom Fowke had rejected after he offered her a settlement to become his mistress, she notes that her scornful refusal only seems like virtue. "Alas! there requires little Virtue to refuse the Half of Mankind. 'Tis a Justice to ourselves, 'tis a Love for ourselves" (Sansom 93). There is, she says, a great difference between virtue and a lack of desire. A woman is not morally virtuous if she turns down a lucrative offer when she has no feeling for the man or desire for his money. There is no real virtue, struggle, or sacrifice in denying herself what she doesn't want. She tells Hillarius, "I [...] give you a true Draught of my Soul, which I think is not without some little Virtue, even what the World calls so; 'tis possible indeed there was Want of a violent Passion, such as I now burn with for you" (99). Her phrase—"even what the World calls so"—suggests that her lack of "a violent Passion," that is, absence of physical desire, denotes socially prescribed virtue. But being defined by lack or absence connotes something negative and inferior and makes it evident that Fowke finds nothing particularly laudable in being without that physical passion. She further admits, "I cannot value myself too much upon [turning down a settlement to become a mistress], for I fear it might be partly the Want of a proper Address in him" (Sansom 99). Ever honest with herself and Hill, she suspects that it was the man's mercantile-minded and unromantic proposal, not propriety, which led to her rejection of him.

The Mind/Body Conflict

In addition to using her letter to redefine feminine virtue, Fowke also recasts Platonic love from its emphasis on the spiritual bond between lovers to "a bold defence of infidelity based on the 'Platonic' argument that unfaithfulness to individual lovers can be justified as fidelity to love itself" (Davis 34) or, as she states in a later published poem entitled "The Innocent Inconstant," "Restless and tired, my Wishes still remove, / Nor can I clip the Wings of Flying Love" (Clio 100–1). More than a libertine dedication to the passions, Fowke's Platonism is a reverence for the soul's self-expression, complemented and enacted by the body. Instead of a denial of physicality, Fowke insists that the soul and mind be as equally addressed and engaged in relationships as the body. She expresses some distaste for the men who fail to achieve similarly enlightened or elevated ideas of love. Of the Duke of B[eau]fort she writes:

> From a Patron, he grew a Lover, and as passionate a one as he could be. But [...] he was too general, and sought the Body more than the Soul. We could not agree in our Sentiments. I found him a coarse dull Lover. He desired me to instruct him in *Platonick* Love; but he was a strange Scholar, and I grew weary of him [Sansom 94].

Likewise, regarding the earlier lover who wanted her as a mistress, Fowke comments, "Whilst he was talking in this Manner, my Soul felt a just Disdain to hear its Body bargaining for" (99). In both quotations Fowke emphasizes for Hill that she wants a lover who can appreciate her for her mind as well as her body. The epistolary form again serves her well as it can present her mind to Hill without the distraction for him of her physical self.

Intrigued by the mind-body relationship, Fowke concentrates with an almost physician-like intensity on the languishing bodies of lovers who become lovesick over her. She attempts to delineate for Hill how she has only come to understand the lovers' suffering for her through her own suffering for Hill. In at least five cases that she describes — the young Huguenot, her sea-faring cousin, her brother's friend, a young Gentleman, and a "Mr. T---ds"— the frustrated passions of these men subject their bodies to a battery of physical symptoms ranging from sleeplessness, pallor, and fever, to emasculation. "He was naturally, [...] bold and assur'd, but was now grown silent, tender, and a kind of Coward" (Sansom 111) she writes of her brother's military friend; and of another she notes, "His Health began to languish, the Roses and the Lillies faded away, and at last he grew pale as the dying *Adonis*" (119). While Fowke pities these men and sometimes attempts to counsel them —"When he was well enough to bear it, I advised him against his inconsiderate Passion" (119)— such efforts are obviously ignorant of the real pain these men undergo. She recognizes in hindsight that she was a poor physician for their souls having not been in love herself. Her earlier attempts to apply reason and logic to those afflicted with love demonstrate to Hill that she has never felt genuine love for anyone before him. It is in her recounting of her cousin's lovesickness that she makes that point explicit: "I was then a Stranger to [these soft, yet fatal Errors], and perhaps had not Pity enough for them" (Sansom 104). Her personal inexperience of love had rendered her an ineffectual human being, lacking compassion for the suffering of others. Now, however, having been abandoned by her adored Hillarius, she does understand her former lovers' pain and can easily empathize (in verse, no less):

> *When the poor trembling Heart to Grief resign'd,*
> *In Silence mourns, and can no Language find:*
> *Far worse than Death these bitter Moments prove,*
> *Extended on the Rack of doubtful Love.*
> [...]
> *While pale Despair, and ever-trembling Fear,*
> *Pours Death into the Soul, and stabs the Ear.*
> *The cold and dewy Limbs confess the Pain,*
> *And the Mind bleeds thro' every breathing Vein* [104].

In her verse, Fowke quickly makes the transition from sympathy for her cousin who physically pines for her and becomes deranged by jealousy, to an anatomization of her own lovesickness for Hill. The attention that her cousin's body elicited is now focused on the personified passions — Love, Grief, Despair and Fear — that torture her body — Heart, Ear, and Limbs. Most significant, though, is the physiological interaction of mind and body, the mind "bleed[ing] thro' every breathing Vein" (104), the spiritual love which commences in the mind or soul being diffused throughout the body by the blood so that there is a corporeal experience of a spiritual, loving affliction. Fowke's poem within her letter emphasizes the very real physical torment that unrequited love can exert on the body; the poetry erupting out of the prose like uncontrolled pain. That these intense feelings must be revealed to Hillarius in poetry rather than mere prose is demonstrative not only of the degree of her love for him, but of their aspiration toward the sublime: "a relation to what exceeds human capabilities of understanding, provokes awe or passionate intensity, gives the speaker [as well as the auditor/reader] a sense of something beyond the human" (Culler 76).

Love-Melancholy and Pregnancy

The spiritual ideals of Platonic love are reinterpreted in Fowke's descriptions of her suitors' love-longing into dangerous threats to both the body and mind. The sublimation of physical desire, "lovesickness," is regarded by Fowke as it was by contemporary medical texts:

> an excessive and degrading passion that could result in chronic melancholy, mania or even death. [...] [A]bstinence was considered a cause of sickness, rather than spiritual ecstasy, in that it allowed for the accumulation of seed, or sperm, to infect [the] body and derange reason [Dawson 9].

According to theories of Platonic love, however, the dangers of abstinence pertain only to the man. Fowke refuses to make the pains of unrequited love gender-specific; rather, she would concur with Robert Burton in his *Anatomy of Melancholy* that if the passion of Love-Melancholy continues in any person, male or female, "*it makes the blood hot, thick and black; and if the inflammation get into the brain, with continual meditation and waking, it so dries it up, that madness follows, or else they make away themselves*" (214).

In addition to examining the languishing bodies of her lovesick suitors, Clio focuses again and again on her own blood in the veins, reminding Hillarius through this imagery that he and she have been intimate, and exchanged blood and souls in their sexual relationship. Her passions — love, admiration, grief, jealousy, joy, desire, hope, fear, anger, and revenge — all have Hillarius as their object and focus, but they are very much preying upon herself: her mind, heart, veins, breast and soul. Fever and fire, in conjunction with the blood, are also continually appealed to in the lyrical poems with which she ends her long letter.

> Thy Body is a perfect Mind.
> Ev'ry bright, transparent Vein,
> Surely does a Soul contain;

Mine, at least, is there I'm sure,
From the Transports I endure
[Sansom 135].

More poems follow: "Nor Rules nor Reason can my Love restrain; / Its godlike Tide runs high in ev'ry Vein" (Sansom 136); "In my blood thy Beauty reigns, / *Hillarius* beats in all my Veins" (Sansom 139). Fowke is not being merely poetic in her imagery; she is also alluding to contemporary scientific notions. For her, Hill's body "is a perfect Mind" because both of their souls flow through his veins; but her "Spirits waste" because they have been separated from her and are now denied access to him. Her letter is an attempt to reconnect her spirits with his. According to Thomas Willis's seventeenth-century theory of the nervous system,

> [t]he animal soul had [...] a double location: in the blood (vital fluid) circulating, as Harvey had shown, through the heart and vessels; and in the "animal liquor," or nervous fluid, present in the brain and flowing through the nerves [...]. [T]he aspect of the soul inherent in the blood was comparable to a flame; that within the nerves was like the light rays, issuing from such a flame. [...] The corporeal soul performed various functions, above all activating the blood (metabolic activity) and the nerve juices (nervous activity). In addition, there was a third aspect, an outgrowth of the "vital flame," involved in sexual activity and reproduction [qtd. in Porter 56–7].

Similar to lovesickness with its thick, hot blood, in pregnancy it was believed that the menses stopped flowing because the blood was settling in the womb and breasts to warm and nurture the fetus. Fowke's couplet regarding Hillarius "beat[ing] in all [her] Veins" could be an allusion to the theory of the homunculus or "little man" (most famously referred to in *Tristram Shandy*)[2] that flows through a woman's bloodstream before settling in her womb for its nine-month rest. It is this connection between the "vital flame" in the blood involved in reproduction, the increased heat in Clio's blood and heart, and her statements of Hillarius being within her very veins that bolster the theory that Fowke may have been pregnant while writing this little volume for Hill. Phyllis Guskin notes that because Eliza Haywood observed in 1724 that a child had recently been born to the Sansoms, "Fowke may have written her autobiography while she was pregnant" (31); and Christine Gerrard comments that "Fowke's morbid frame of mind and frequent references to imminent death might be explained by the possibility that she was in the late stages of pregnancy when she wrote *Clio*." Also citing Haywood's 1724 claim of Fowke's recent delivery, Gerrard goes so far as to admit that "[i]t is tempting to speculate that the child was Hill's" (87). More than simply utilizing the trope of the abandoned woman, Fowke may indeed be communicating to Hill through her language and descriptive references to her physiology that she is carrying his child. Her heightened alarm and the emotional gamut she experiences over his absence; her references to her blood and veins; her fear that she has become "poor, old, and miserable" (Sansom 138); and her very need to write her life and clarify her past to Hill, all point to the possibility that she is expecting his child and feels she may die because of it. But she never explicitly articulates this in her letter. Unlike speaking face-to-face, Fowke's epistle's literary space allows Hill the time and reflection to literally read between the lines and arrive at his own conclusion.

"The Image of the Mind"

The last lover that Clio devotes special attention to in her letter is the married "Mr. H[ope]" who devotes himself entirely to her: "the sweet Object was more mine than I could wish. His Soul, his Time, his Wishes were devoted to me, and he only lived in beholding me; never were two Hearts more sweetly joined" (Sansom 128). Hope is the feminized lover of the Platonic tradition; in fact, he is described as the perfect male counterpart to the passionate eighteenth-century woman who does not, like men do, have "Business" to "defend" her from thoughts of love. Fowke describes him as a kind of angel: "His Face was spread over with Love and Softness: I have often thought of him like some rosy Bed, which invites the Traveller to rest" (128).

The detailed description of Hope serves as a very pointed criticism of Hill's weaknesses, particularly his abandonment of Fowke. Where Fowke begins her letter by asking Hill, "Are you not afraid, oh! too assured Charmer, a Day may come, when the neglected *Clio* may return this Coldness, and transplant herself to some kinder Bosom?" (58), her concluding pages remind him of this possibility in the persons of Hope, and later, John Dyer. Like Hill, Hope first made an immediate physical impression on her with his singularly good looks. Her homey image of him "like some rosy Bed" (Sansom 128) is particularly comforting: a suggestive combination of eroticism and rest. While not an overtly passionate image, it is certainly a pleasant one connecting Hope with the physical senses — the eye-appealing color, the tactile softness and comfort, and the scent of flowers. As well, the imagination is captured as the phrase plays upon connotations and allusions such as the Homeric "rosy-fingered dawn," and the image of the bridal bed strewn with rose petals, both suggestive of sexual intimacy.

Fowke's language describing her relationship with Hope is not particularly passionate (though she does use words like "aching," "pleasing Anguish," "Misery"), but the style and structure cleverly suggest that Hope is still competitively present in her failing relationship with Hill, making an intriguing emotional triangle involving Hope's memory. Whenever Fowke comments upon Hope's physical attractions she adds that they are not quite as alluring as Hill's, but she suggests that they are sufficient for her; and, while Hope did not achieve for her those "divine Transports" Hill induces, neither did he cause her "the bitter Anguish ... those cruel Torments that now sink me to the Earth" (Sansom 128). It is worth noting that Samuel Johnson defines "Transport" as "Rapture; ecstasy" and an "Ecstatick violence of passion," that is, to be beyond rational consciousness; but it also suggests sexual orgasm, believed necessary for becoming pregnant.[3] Fowke may be hinting to Hill, in a backward compliment, that her other Mr. H. is not responsible for her pregnancy because only Hill could "transport" her. Fowke's critique of Hill becomes explicit when she compares Hope's assiduity and devotion to her with Hill's tormenting absence. In her most bitter admonishment of Hill she writes, "[Hope] had none of those exalted Views that now tear my divine *Hillarius* from me"; that is, neither Hope's marriage nor business prevented him from devoting "his Love, [...] his Interest, his very Soul" to Clio (Sansom 128).

She and Hope were "two Lovers" and "two Hearts" but Fowke repeatedly uses three terms to describe Hope's devotion to her. She begins by giving pairs of Hope's traits—"Form and Manner," "Love and Softness"—then parallels her feelings with his—"uncommon Tenderness for him, [...] respectful Passion for me"—before moving to patterns of three: "His Soul, his Time, his Wishes"; "all Love, and Tenderness, and mine"; "his Love, [...] his Interest, his very Soul." These linguistic multiples emphasize Hope's ardor while suggesting how far Hill falls short and how he is now, in her letter, being relegated to a third-party voyeur of her relationship with Hope. "Never did two Lovers live a more harmonious Life. It was a Kind of Heaven we possessed, our Hearts wore no mean Disguise, but seemed made for one another" (Sansom 128).

Just before the letter breaks down into a death wish to release her from her love for Hillarius, Clio's memories of Mr. Hope reveal the other passions by which she is afflicted, most notably anger and resentment at the way Hillarius has treated her. Though not as conflicted as Alexander Pope's abandoned Eloisa who oscillates regularly between desire for and rejection of Abelard,[4] Clio's passions are barely within her control as she attempts to stifle her bitter anger and growing hatred beneath her grief and love for Hillarius. Her "Last Will" poem that formally concludes her letter gives the impression that Fowke is playing her last emotional card. She surreptitiously introduces one more lover—poet and mutual friend, John Dyer—who is entrusted to deliver her will to Hillarius. She describes the bearer of her "Will" as "The second Jewel"; "Next to thyself most noble and sincere" (Sansom 148). She concludes her letter with her focus firmly on Dyer as she bequeaths the young man, her masculine surrogate, to Hill's care, before one last reference to Hill himself:

> He [Dyer] knew my Passion, and he sweetly knew
> To keep its Brightness, yet to sooth it too;
> His Youth and undesigning Breast defend,
> And wear to Death itself this valued Friend.
> No more, what have I else intitled mine,
> My Life, my Soul, my Muse, my Friend, are thine.
> To thee I make my only Treasures o'er,
> Yet if you grieve, am richer than before
> [Sansom 148].

By concluding her little volume to Hillarius with her last will and testament that leaves him her Life, Soul, Muse and Friend, Fowke underscores that she is, first and foremost, a poet. As she prefaces her self-history with her most famous poem, "Clio's Picture" to stand "in the place of a portrait frontispiece" (Guskin 32), she stresses, "let the Muse perform the Painter's Art, / And strike the Picture of my Face and Heart" (Sansom 55). Fowke insists on being recognized through her words rather than her physical attractions because as a poet she wants to be identified for the powers of her mind rather than her physical presence: "Poetry's call'd the Image of the Mind, / On mine the Soul and Body both are join'd" (Sansom 55). For Fowke, her history in the form of a long and self-revelatory epistle to Hill, a combination of direct prose and emotional outbursts of poetry, represents her whole self that she wants communicated first to her lover, and then to posterity. "[A]lthough on the one hand she is writing a private letter, on the other clearly Fowke is alert to aspects of public print, arranging the dedication to look as it would if set in type" (Guskin 32). Though she concludes her "little Book" (Sansom 146) with anticipations of her death —"your Absence kills me. [...] I now flatter myself I have not long to live; [...] I am sad to Death" (132)— she takes some comfort in that she gives over her "only Treasures" to Hill in the form of her letter.

Haywood's "Discourse" warns that letter-writing can "plunge, not only [a woman's] Reputation, but [her] Peace of Mind, into a Sea of Troubles" (1):

> When therefore a Woman, by her own Indiscretion, has rendred herself incapable of maintaining the Conquests which her Eyes had gain'd, the wisest thing she can do, is to sit down contented with the loss, lest by the vain Attacks she makes to recover it, she discovers her own Weakness the more, and provokes the Insults of the disdainful Repeller [...] there is nothing a Woman can do more to the prejudice of her Peace of Mind, her Honour, and her Reputation, than the encouraging a Correspondence of this kind: nor can any Motives whatever, that shall induce her to it, be reconciled to Reason, or to Prudence [25, 29].

Fowke was not a woman "to sit down contented with [...] loss"; nor did she feel that repressing her pain and desire so that she could appear like a reputable woman was an option for a writer like her. She concludes that she "would, if possible, restrain the Fondness of my Soul; but [...] it has overflowed in this little Book, [...] all my Passions flow down this immortal Stream" (Sansom 146). She embraces the one advantage of being an abandoned woman—expressing herself without restriction—and works to actively re-insinuate herself into the mind and heart of Aaron Hill through her evocative language and imagery. Much to the chagrin of eighteenth-century pragmatists like Eliza Haywood, Martha Fowke's letter-writing disguises nothing about her feelings, and, it does not blush.

Notes

1. See all five of Aaron Hill's letters to Martha Fowke Sansom (the first dated 21 June 1721) as well as his poems to her, collected by Guskin in "Appendix A" of Sansom, 168–190.

2. See Laurence Sterne, *The Life and Opinions of Tristram Shandy*, Volume 1, chapter 2, 6 for Tristram's description of the "Homunculus," "the miniature human figure which early microscopists believed they saw in a spermatozoon" (note 1, 549).

3. "It was commonly agreed that conception [...] happened only if both partners had an orgasm, causing them to release seed. [...] Sexual pleasure for both woman and man, was then, essential if they wanted to have children" (Hobby xx).

4. See Pope's poem, "Eloisa to Abelard," inspired by the letters between the nun Heloise and her priest-lover Peter Abelard, which, Pope says, "give so lively a picture of the struggles of grace and nature, virtue and passion" (298).

Works Cited

Burton, Robert. *Anatomy of Melancholy*. Ed. A. R. Shilleto. Vol. 3. New York: AMS Press, 1973. Print.

Clio [Martha Fowke]. "The Innocent Inconstant." *Miscellaneous Poems and Translations. By Several Hands*. Ed. Richard Savage. London: Printed for Samuel Chapman, 1726. Print.

Cook, Elizabeth. *Epistolary Bodies: Gender and Genre in the Eighteenth-Century Republic of Letters*. Stanford: Stanford University Press, 1996. Print.

Culler, Jonathan. *Literary Theory: A Very Short Introduction*. Oxford: Oxford University Press, 1997. Print.

Davis, Karen E. "Martha Fowke: 'A Lady Once Too Well Known.'" *English Language Notes* 23.3 (Mar. 1986): 32–6. Print.

Dawson, Lesel. "'New Sects of Love': Neoplatonism and Construction of Gender in Davenant's *The Temple of Love* and *The Platonic Lovers*." *Early Modern Literary Studies* 8.1 (May 2002): 4. 1–36. Web. 15 June 2008.

[Fowke, Martha]. *The Epistles of Clio and Strephon (1720)*. New York: Garland Publishing, 1971. Print.

Gerrard, Christine. *Aaron Hill: The Muses' Projector 1685–1750*. Oxford: Oxford University Press, 2003. Print.

Guskin, Phyllis J. Introduction. *Clio: The Autobiography of Martha Fowke Sansom (1689–1736)*. Newark: University of Delaware Press, 1997. 15–50. Print.

Haywood, Eliza. "A Discourse Concerning Writings of this Nature, by Way of Essay." *Letters from a Lady of Quality to a Chevalier*. London: William Chetwood at Cato's Head, in Russel-Street, Covent-Garden, 1721. 1–29. ECCO. Gale. Killam Library, Dalhousie U. Halifax. 12 Sept. 2009.

Henderson, Judith. "Humanism and the Humanities: Erasmus's *Opus de conscribendis epistolis* in Sixteenth-Century School." *Letter-Writing Manuals and Instruction from Antiquity to the Present.* Eds. Carol Poster & Linda C. Mitchell. Columbia: U of South Carolina P, 2007. 141–177. Print.

Hobby, Elaine. Introduction. *The Midwives Book; or, The Whole Art of Midwifry Discovered (1671).* Jane Sharp. New York: Oxford, 1999. xi–xxxv. Print.

Johnson, Samuel. "Thomson." *Johnson's Lives of the English Poets.* Vol. 2. London: Oxford University Press, 1949. 365–377. Print.

_____. "Transport." *A Dictionary of the English Language.* Vol. 2. 2nd ed. London: W. Strahan, 1756. ECCO. Gale. Killam Library, Dalhousie U. Halifax. 16 July 2010.

Jones, Wendy L. *Talking on Paper: Alexander Pope's Letters.* ELS No. 50. Victoria BC: University of Victoria, 1990. Print.

Lipking, Lawrence. *Abandoned Women and Poetic Tradition.* Chicago: University of Chicago Press, 1988. Print.

McKeon, Michael. *The Origins of the English Novel, 1600–1740.* Baltimore: Johns Hopkins University Press, 2002. Print.

Pope, Alexander. "Eloisa to Abelard." *The Twickenham Edition of the Poems of Alexander Pope: The Rape of the Lock.* Vol. 2. London: Methuen & Co., 1954. 297–327. Print.

Porter, Roy. *Flesh in the Age of Reason: How the Enlightenment Transformed the Way We See Our Bodies and Souls.* London: Penguin, 2004. Print.

Sansom, Martha Fowke. *Clio: Or, A Secret History of the Life and Amours of the Late Celebrated Mrs. S-n — m. Written by Herself, in a Letter to Hillarius.* Ed. Phyllis J. Guskin. Newark: University of Delaware Press, 1997. Print.

Sterne, Laurence. *The Life and Opinions of Tristram Shandy, Gentleman.* Ed. Ian Campbell Ross. Oxford: Oxford University Press, 1983. Print.

Part II

Literary Spaces: The Convergence of Orality and Print in Women's Writing

4

Delete as Appropriate: Writing Between the Lines of Female Orality in *The Wife's Lament*

Miriam Muth

Ic this giedd wrece bi me ful geomorre,
minre sylfre sith. [*Wife's Lament* ll.1–2a]
[I make this song that is wholly sorrowful to me,
of my own journey.]

The anonymous tenth century poem known as *The Wife's Lament* is written from the perspective of a woman pining for her lover. Banished to live in an earth cave, the woman recounts her past life, referring to a confusing succession of leaders and beloved men who have betrayed her (Klinck, *WL* lines 93–94). Leaving it unclear whether this is a tale of adultery involving several different figures or a betrayal by one man with many faces, she describes the dark and desolate wood in which she sits "the summer long day, weeping for the many hardships of her exile" (*WL* 37b–39a), and contrasts her life with the joy of "lovers living on earth" who may lie in bed together, while she "walks alone at dawn" (*WL* 33b–35). Finally, her tone shifts to one of general reflection on men hiding their sorrow, and she pictures her beloved sitting isolated and "set about by storms under a stony cliff" (*WL* 47), in a familiar Anglo-Saxon topos of exile.

From the nineteenth century onward, this originally untitled piece of alliterative poetry has been entitled *The Wife's Lament* and has been packaged and preserved in a surprisingly diverse range of ways. As this chapter shows, the debate surrounding the text has cast it as a mystery to be solved, a problematic work that falls short of modern readers' expectations regarding Anglo-Saxon genre and gender roles. As a result, critical attention has frequently bypassed the content of the text and the unmediated first-person voice of the tenth century female narrator. Rather, the focus has been on that which the text does not contain: explanatory context, clearly defined characters, a didactic message, and a consistent adherence to genre.

In attempting to create a location for this displaced text, a genre for this idiosyncratic poetic voice, and a wider explanatory context within which to pin down the ambiguous causes of the speaker's sorrow, the large majority of criticism on the poem has either ignored, refuted, or reframed a rare fragment of individualized female characterization. In place of a moderating narrator, the poem depicts a first person speaker who addresses her emotional response directly to the reader rather than placing her experiences in a social, ancestral, or didactic context. As will be further discussed below, this absence of conventional framing is what makes the voice of the speaker stand out so clearly across the centuries. What has emerged most visibly in critical editions of the poem, however, is the refusal of modern textual readings to contemplate the uncertainty generated by this female voice from the past.

This authoritarian approach has been exacerbated by the anonymous authorship of the poem. It may not be necessary to know whether, in the words of Virginia Woolf, the "Anon." who created the female speaker of the poem was herself a woman in order to comprehend the speaker as a representative of a female voice (50). Nonetheless, the anonymous authorship of the work has left the poem far more open to radical editing and inventive reinterpretation by a masculinist critical tradition than comparable works by named Old English authors, all of whom are male. Cases in point are the works of Aelfric and Alfred, both of whose works have remained strikingly unaltered in modern editions. The first step to understanding this process of appropriation and rediscovering the ambiguity and openness of the text is to consider the title. Here, modern scholars such as Anne Klinck and Elaine Treharne can be seen presenting the text in a form that is strikingly mediated and influenced by the controversial decisions of early editors. Thus, modern editions of the text routinely title the poem as *The Wife's Lament*, often failing to mention that this title was only added to the text in the nineteenth century. This means that before readers even begin the poem, editors like Klink have independently answered two questions that the text leaves open concerning the genre of the text and the social status and situation of the speaker (Klinck 93).

As a result of this added title, the woman in the *Lament* is outwardly defined by her marital status, although this is never clarified in the poem. Meanwhile, the male speakers of the originally untitled Anglo-Saxon poems now known as *The Wanderer* and *The Seafarer* have come to be defined by their occupation. The influence of the "wife" in the title has been so pervasive that even Marilynn Desmond, offering a feminist approach to the text, writes with ease about the speaker's "husband," despite having concluded only four sentences previously that "none of these terms [describing the men in the poem] specifically denotes a husband, and most are only seldom used to refer to a man's position in his marriage" (586).

Interestingly, there is only one other example of an Old English poem being named after the speaker's status: *The Husband's Message*— a poem often regarded as a companion piece to the *Lament* (Klinck 100–02). In this poem, a man in exile sends an engraved letter to his beloved, which speaks of his love for her and promises a return to the happiness they shared together if she journeys across the sea to meet him. While the link between the two works — namely the shared theme of lovers separated by exile — is superficially convincing, it does not stand up to closer investigation. *The Husband's Message* clearly describes his beloved as living "hung about with jewels" in a luxurious city (Klinck, *HM* 14), whereas the speaker in the *Lament* describes her lover as having "commanded her to live in this earth cave" (*WL* 27–28). She also makes it clear that it is she who is initially in exile, rather than her lover. These decisive indications of the speaker's situation show that the wife in the *Lament* cannot be the wife of *The Husband's Message.*

In this context, the accepted titles of both works must be regarded as critically anachronistic. This anachronism is particularly marked in the case of the *Lament,* however, since the poem never refers to a husband, but refers instead to "friendship" and "lordship" (*WL* 6, 25). "Friend" and "lord" are two potentially separate categories, neither of which would necessarily denote husband. In contrast, the "husband" of *The Husband's Message* is a more convincing title for a poet whose speaker describes a past life together and refers to the vows they made to one another in legalistic language (*HM* 16). It appears, then, that the theory of the two works as companion pieces is based primarily on the evidence of *The Husband's Message* and that the *Lament* has remained cast as an auxiliary to the other text. This acceptance of an outdated title is in keeping with the wider approach to the text as a negotiable quantity, which has been regarded as open to editorial emendation even in its most defining characteristics.

This form of authoritarian intervention by editors and critics has been directed primarily at the role of the speaker — a role that has been contested on all levels. A cursory reading of the text in literal translation reveals a number of details about the speaker: readers know that she must be a woman, because of the feminine endings used in words such as *sylfre (WL* 2a), which can be translated as 'own'; that she is inhabiting an earth cave of some kind in the wood; and that she is lonely and mourning a personal loss she has experienced on account of some man in her past.

Over the past two centuries each of these defining features of the speaker's self-identification has in turn been questioned and reinterpreted. As Desmond has pointed out, one of the key motives for these alterations has been an unwillingness on the part of modern critics to contemplate a female narrator in the Anglo-Saxon corpus (574). Along with the enigmatic poem *Wulf and Eadwacer*, the *Lament* is one of only two surviving Anglo-Saxon poems featuring a female speaker. In this context, the poem appears to represent a voice that was already marginalized in the speaker's own society: that of a female exile. Instead of drawing this voice back into the center of critical debate, however, critics such as Benjamin Thorpe, Rudolph Bambas, and Jerome Mandel have chosen to query the text and suggest instead that the unexpected female speaker is the result of scribal or editorial errors. This theory is based on the assumption that the use of feminine grammatical endings in the text is the result of scribal error, implying a surprisingly systematic failure of the scribal copying process. First suggested by early editor Thorpe in 1842, the theory remains surprisingly current. Interestingly, having posited a male speaker, Thorpe entitled the poem *The Exile's Lament*, no longer referring to the speaker's marital status but to his situation (441). This highlights the extent to which the identification of the poem with marriage was linked in the editor's mind with the speaker being a woman and became irrelevant once he had identified the speaker as male.

The argument for a male speaker is particularly surprising because the female gender of the speaker is one of the few tangible facts that emerges from the poem. While she uses gendered terms denoting status such as *hlaford* 'lord' (*WL* 6a); *leodfruma* 'leader of my people' (*WL* 8a) and *felaleofan* 'much beloved' (*WL* 26a), to describe the man, or men, she has dealt with, she refuses to reveal whether he is a lover, a husband, a lord, or even an individual person. However, the speaker's use of female adjectival and pronominal endings in phrases of self-description such as *bi me ful geomorr**e** / minr**e** sylfr**e** sith* 'it is wholly sorrowful to me / my own journey' (*WL* 1b–2a, emphasis added) is less ambiguous and leaves no doubt that she is a woman.

Other alternative readings have also focused on diminishing the possibility of the speaker as a living woman. In 1983 William Johnson published one of the more recent readings of the poem as a death song (Green 80), interpreting the "earth cave" in which the speaker lives as a grave. This interpretation disregards the other contexts in which the Anglo-Saxon word "earth cave" is used to mean a barrow. A striking example of this arises in the Anglo-Saxon life of Saint Guthlac, who is described as living in an "earth cave" or barrow in the fens. Another popular interpretation of the poem has been based on Christian allegory, presenting the speaker as the mournful Christian Church longing to be reunited with her beloved Christ (Swanton 270–271).

Here too, the argument is focused on making sense of the poem's trajectory as a whole, glossing over the fact that the "beloved" of the poem deceives and betrays the speaker, inferring an unlikely image of Christ concealing murderous thoughts from the Church (*WL* 20b–21a). Other details of the poem, including the initial description of the family of the woman's beloved as treacherous (*WL* 12) and the speaker's envy of joyful lovers at dawn (*WL* 34), make this a highly unlikely devotional text. These apparent contradictions show the extent to which critics such as Swanton have been prepared to ignore decisive elements of the text in order to avoid a literal reading.

What all of these theories have in common is an overall reception of the text as a problem to be solved. As will be discussed below, the spotlight this type of criticism has cast on the so-called problems of the text reflects back on the critics themselves, revealing the outline of a totalizing, masculinist approach to reading Anglo-Saxon literature. Thus the underlying assumption driving the many interpretations discussed above is that the speaker cannot be read as a living woman. This, however, is a claim so flimsy that it dissolves under even the slightest investigation. Take, for example, the argument of Rudolf C. Bambas. Bambas explains that according to Anglo-Saxon poetic conventions "the only matters worth celebrating in verse are the affairs of heroic war chiefs" (303). Operating under this assumption, he concludes that a female speaker is therefore a practical impossibility.

Given the fact that so few Anglo-Saxon texts survive, Bambas's claim must be based directly on those scant and randomly selected texts still extant, making any generalizing conclusions somewhat tautological. In essence, Bambas's line of argument is that because so few texts with female speakers have survived, such texts did not exist, meaning that those texts that do exist are not rare examples of less common form, but the results of scribal error. According to this logic, any unusual textual forms at all would be subsumed into the form and genre of the majority, despite that majority itself being based on a very small sample of works.

Genre—*The Wife's Lament* as a "Deviant Elegy"

The literary context of the *Lament* has been as unnecessarily controversial as the poem's social and narrative context. The decision of early editors to cast this poem as a lament is not in itself surprising, nor is it even controversial. The speaker is clearly suffering great sadness, and she does indeed sorrow after what she has lost, describing "the pain of exile" (*WL* 5), and "the trials I have suffered" (*WL* 3). In the context of Anglo-Saxon literature, however, the word "lament" has taken on a more specific meaning, as it has become associated with a genre described as the Anglo-Saxon elegy. Here, elegy is taken to mean not simply works written in a classical elegiac meter, or those concerned with lamenting the dead, but rather what Klinck describes as Anglo-Saxon works characterized by "a sense of separation: a distance in time and space between someone and their desire" (225).

Only a handful of these works remain, the most famous including *The Wanderer*, *The Seafarer*, and *The Ruin*, as well as the more enigmatic *Deor* and *The Husband's Message* (Klinck 30). Alongside these poems with male speakers, there is one additional Anglo-Saxon elegy, besides the *Lament*, which contains a female speaker: the similarly controversial *Wulf and Eadwacer*. All these works have been broadly referred to as Anglo-Saxon elegies, based on their shared theme of sorrowful loss. It is primarily the first two, however, on which current expectations of Anglo-Saxon elegies have been constructed. Thus *The Wanderer* and *The Seafarer* share the central themes of "exile, solitude, the wintry sea, the remembered delights of the hall, [and] the contrast between earthly and heavenly values," which, as Klinck notes, have come to be considered the archetypal themes of Anglo-Saxon elegies (32).

The Wanderer and *The Seafarer* also share a number of literary features that post-nineteenth century scholarship presents as typical of Anglo-Saxon literature: both works are narrated by male speakers who speak of a past in which their status within Anglo-Saxon society was defined by the homosocial bond between their lord and themselves as his loyal subjects. This is clearly a strong element in both works — which depict lonely male travelers who describe themselves as exiled from the joys of society and kinship. Both speakers yearn for the joys in hall and love of their lord experienced in a past life that they have now lost. Both also speak of their loneliness as an oppressive and devastating fate, describing it as *wræclaestas*, 'an exile's journeys' (*Wanderer* 5a), and *geswincdagum*, 'days of hardship' (*Seafarer* 2b). This emphasis on a yearning for the communality is defined by an enacted loyalty between a group of warriors. In this process, the individual is identified by the role he plays in battle, presenting a wholly masculine perspective of social interaction. The two genre-defining elegies are thus united in presenting masculine experiences of Anglo-Saxon life.

It is therefore perhaps not unexpected that a poem dealing with a woman's reaction to a personal tragedy does not correspond to the expected criteria of the elegy genre, despite its elegiac tone. The *Lament* clearly adopts the tone of a lament, reflecting as it does on loss, yet it is perceived as deviant in that it fails to affirm any of the social ideals described above. It does not contribute to a consistent narrative that exemplifies the bond of loyalty between a warrior and his lord — indeed, it does not speak of political or social practices at all. Instead, the frame of reference remains entirely personal throughout, beginning with the speaker's description of her own sorrow and concluding with the depiction of her beloved's sorrow. This personal frame of reference is no coincidence; as a woman, the speaker cannot inhabit the role of loyal warrior assumed to be genre-defining by critics such as Levin Schücking (11). After all, the reader cannot be reassured of her conformity to Germanic ideals of warrior loyalty, as her gender would preclude her from being a warrior. Consequently, she would also never have participated in the elaborate social rituals in which loyalty in battle was sworn, quantified, and rewarded by the giving of gold when the battle was done.

Since the reader cannot be reassured as to the acceptable Anglo-Saxon virtues of loyalty this woman possesses, both the modern critic seeking Anglo-Saxon archetypes and presumably the contemporary Anglo-Saxon reader as well, must be somewhat disquieted by the indefinability of this woman's status and the personal rather than political nature of her allegiances. This uncertainty hinges on the words with which the men in the speaker's life are described as *hlaford* 'lord' (*WL* 6), and *felaleofan* 'much beloved' (*WL* 26), both words that could refer as much to a lord as to a lover, or indeed a husband. As a result of her undefined status this woman cannot be an authority but remains an exile whose lack of social context undermines her respectability. Lacking social prestige, the speaker is automatically precluded from fulfilling the third and most striking characteristic of Anglo-Saxon elegies as defined by the famous final passages of *The Wanderer* and *The Seafarer*: that of gnomic wisdom.

This literary feature, in which the speaker concludes his monologue by proffering advice on overcoming hardship and turning to God for inspiration, is a prominent characteristic of classical Anglo-Saxon elegy and stands in contrast to the emphasis on pagan Germanic loyalty in other parts of *The Wanderer* and *The Seafarer*. The same dichotomy can be found shaping other Anglo-Saxon works, most famously *Beowulf*, in which the anonymous poet creates a distance between him or herself and the pagan hero, Beowulf, by inserting Christian references, such as those in which Beowulf's first attacker, the monster Grendel, is described as a descendant of Cain. The Christian frame of reference serves to incorporate guiding elements of the poet's Christian world view into the very text of a poem based on older pre–Christian stories, a textual combination that critics such as Richard North have read as an archetypal expression of the contradictions between Christian and heroic ideals of good life and rule (North 195).

It is on the basis of works such as these that a canon of Anglo-Saxon literature has been retrospectively projected onto the surviving corpus. This canon, framed within the context of spiritual debate, systematically marginalizes any texts that might obfuscate the clear opposition between the pagan

Germanic warrior and the devout early Christian monk that interested the learned men of the nineteenth century

In the *Lament*, however, even the most challenging editorial interventions have failed to dissolve the uncertainties that characterize the speaker. The non-negotiable kernel of pointed literary ambiguity has remained preserved within the opacity of the speaker's imagery. This technique culminates in the final passage of the poem, in which the image the speaker creates of her beloved — sitting in desolation beneath a stormy cliff— subverts the genre of elegy by failing to deliver the didactic wisdom the preceding lines promise (*WL* 45–48). Where other elegies conclude such generalized observations as "always a young man must be sad" (*WL* 42), with advice and consolation for all, the *Lament* proceeds to turn it instead into an extended image of loneliness (*WL* 45–48), which is just as likely to be a curse as it is to be a fact, a fear, or even a gleefully satisfying revenge fantasy. This equivocal end encapsulates the irreconcilable elements of revenge, indignation, and fractured identity within the speaker and the refusal of the author to resolve the contradictions of the poem.

Considerations and Conclusions

The conclusions one can draw from this study are just as revealing with regard to the editors and critics as they are with regard to the text itself. Despite the varied and extensive criticism on the *Lament*, the poem remains ambiguous with regard to its narrative and implied context. Put simply, none of the theories expounded above have been able to fully convince the majority of readers and critics. As a result, what has emerged most clearly from critical debate is the fact that this is a poem that defies classification and tells a story that is not coherent on a narrative level.

Critics such as Patricia Belanoff have described the "polysemous" nature of the vocabulary within the poem and the poem's exclusive focus on experiential elements of the speaker's life rather than contextualizing details such as place names. Given this emphasis, it should come as no surprise that the *Lament* expresses an emotional state rather than a plot-based narrative (Belanoff 202). In this context, there is indeed a mystery surrounding how one is to read the poem, but that mystery is not the question of "what is this poem about?" Clearly, the poem is about the speaker's distress, framed in a deliberately oblique context. For the modern reader, the real mystery is what lies at the root of the many desperate attempts by modern critics to re-interpret the poem's content.

This observation is not as flippant as it appears. Given the amount of critical smoke obfuscating this short, 53-line poem, it is valid and necessary to ask: who started the fire and why did they do so? This line of questioning brings the critical response to the poem into sharp focus, offering a revealing history of repressive reception. Hence the most striking element of all the interpretations previously discussed is the extent to which they base their understanding of the text on outside factors, ranging from social and political context to literary genre. While these are valid components of an analysis, they can only be helpful as complements to the evidence of the text itself, and this is where these approaches have failed.

Not all the theoretical readings of the *Lament* have been as overtly dismissive of the textual evidence as that of Bambas. Nonetheless, the credence given to his theory of a scribal error in grammar reveals how far twentieth century criticism was prepared to go in misunderstanding this poem, with most recent support coming from Jerome Mandel in 1987 (154). Both Bambas and Mandel present the text as misleading and mysterious and in doing so obscure those aspects of the speaker's self-identification that are taboo in that they contradict established ideas of Anglo-Saxon literary culture. As Julia Kristeva writes in "About Chinese Women," the narrative and literary problems that critics invite readers to dwell on often serve to protect a narrative taboo that is still being observed. Kristeva draws this conclusion from her efforts to expose the Freudian focus on the Oedipus myth as a smokescreen to distract attention from a myth that threatens patriarchal discourse: that of Klytemnestra (151). Klytemnestra's murder of her husband Agamemnon threatens the passive acceptance of male sexualized authority in the homes of Ancient Greece — a gendered hierarchy that is one of the unspoken premises of how the Renaissance was later to interpret the ideal of the Greek demos (Kristeva 151).

This reclaiming of the myth can be applied to the *Lament* on quite a simplistic level if one considers further the work of writers, such as Barrie Ruth Straus. Straus has attempted to redress the masculinist bias underlying much critical discussion by casting the *Lament* not as a lament, but as the curse of an empowered female voice, resembling the strong women of the Norse sagas (Straus 284). At first glance, this appears to be a reading that empowers the speaker, who is no longer presented as a suffering victim but as a potent enemy, condemning her treacherous beloved to a terrible fate. If scholars are truly interested in divesting the text of critical authoritarianism, however, they must resist such a reading. Thus the martial vocabulary with which Straus entitles her essay, "Women's Words as Weapons," already indicates a reading intent on perpetuating the myth of Anglo-Saxon literature as heroic, even when faced with a poem as personally mournful as the *Lament.* It seems that in offering readers an alternative framework of strong women within which to resolve the uncertainties of the poem, Straus colludes in what must be regarded as the most oppressive assumption of all: that this text is an enigma to be solved in order to suit current perceptions of Anglo-Saxon literary norms.

Underlying this authoritarian suppression of the multivalent text is what Kristeva might describe as the taboo that is still being observed: that of a narrative content based on ambivalence and subjectivity and therefore resistant to fully conclusive historicist interpretation of any kind, including those that empower women. The dangers of such texts are immediately apparent, if we regard them as the bomb with which the myth of the learned poet of the Anglo-Saxon *comitatus* can be exploded.

It is surprisingly simple to read the *Lament* as containing an element of many of the theories outlined above: an elegy with a female speaker; a speaker in whose eyes the different masculine roles of lord, husband, and lover she has been confronted with blur into one. Put more radically, she might be a woman whose existence is so cut off from society and miserable that it is hard to tell whether she is alive or dead. Rather than being contradictory, all of these elements are in fact complementary to one another. If one accepts the poem as an individualized expression of anger and sorrow rather than a description of the underlying events, then the emotions of the speaker constitute the main content of the text. The same can be said of the final passages of the poem, which subvert the expectations of elegiac works, by replacing the wise reflection one might find in *The Wanderer* and *The Seafarer* with a far more ambiguous image of suffering. In this context, again, one need not decide between reading the image of the sorrowful man presented in these lines as knowledge, curse, or even wishful thinking, since all of these elements are so clearly present in the work. Having suffered at the hands of this man, the speaker gains some satisfaction from envisioning her treacherous friend in a scene of classic Anglo-Saxon desolation.

Scholars cannot know that the *Lament* was written by a woman. Although female literacy was strikingly high in Anglo-Saxon society, those authors who are named in their works are all men (Brown 45). It would therefore be rash to assume female poets behind the anonymous works that have survived — although that too would tell its own tale of marginalized women's voices. What can be said with more certainty of the poet, however, is that he or she was trying to create a female voice that would represent a type of experience otherwise almost entirely absent from the surviving Anglo-Saxon corpus. The *Lament* is one of only two surviving Anglo-Saxon works with female speakers and it is quite telling that these two works have sparked such critical controversy over the years.

That is not to say that the many critics who have attempted to interrogate and "redress" the texts have done so solely because these texts have female speakers, although that is clearly one of the reasons. Rather, one can conclude more broadly that the Anglo-Saxon poets who wrote *Wulf and Eadwacer* and the *Lament* present both their female speakers and the stories they tell in ways that modern criticism has been unable to accept as a straightforward part of the Anglo-Saxon corpus.

Thus, these female speakers do not identify themselves through their names, or even through their status; rather, they are socially anonymous throughout their texts. This stands in striking contrast to the traditions of Anglo-Saxon heroic poetry, for example, in which the names of the male warriors are emphasized alongside the names of their fathers, drawing attention to their status and heritage. Instead, these women identify themselves through their experiences and express their emotional responses to these experiences in the form of direct address in the absence of adjudicating narrators. The men these women interact with are equally ill-defined. Despite the fact that the speaker's situation results from the man's actions, she makes no attempt to explain the situation and the motives underlying the manner in which this man or these men have shaped her life.

In all of these aspects of the poem, the *Lament* defies not only modern totalizing readings but also what scholars expect from historical Anglo-Saxon texts: a corpus dominated by military or devotional works whose sometimes contradictory values are embodied in canonized works with male protagonists, including the epic *Beowulf*, *The Battle of Maldon*, *The Wanderer*, and *The Seafarer*. Many modern scholars' expectation continues to be for Anglo-Saxon texts to resemble these canonical works in expressing status, wisdom, and a sense of continuity, while focusing on the role of the individual within society. In most cases that individual is a male representative of a profession, such as the seafarer, the warrior, the king, or else he is defined by his situation, as in the case of *The Wanderer* or "the last survivor" in *Beowulf*.

As discussed above, however, women are largely unrepresented in Anglo-Saxon literature, and given their apparently low social status, they would not have the authority to appear in socially representative roles, to boast of war or give lectures on how to live life. As a result, those writers creating or simply capturing the voices of female speakers are forced to show a more personalized experience of Anglo-Saxon society, less affected by the political and religious demands of masculine poetic traditions.

The result is the *Lament*, in which pronouncements on life and didactic or exemplary narratives and characterizations are replaced by the seemingly contradictory expression of how a situation of exile might be experienced by one particular woman. The woman in question is angry as well as sad and her ultimate frame of reference is her fractured history and the fruit of her own imagination rather than a divine or philosophical framework. This problematic, personalized emphasis is contained within the allusive self-description that arises throughout the text, which places the speaker slightly outside of herself, describing her own reflection as an exiled woman, rather than fully inhabiting the role of lonely exile and speaking from within it. A key example of this disenfranchised self-representation can be found in line 29, where the speaker exclaims *Eal ic eom oflongade*; here the woman claims literally 'I am afflicted by longing'; she does not actively yearn but is passively consumed by the feeling. The precedent for this is first set up in line one of the speaker's tale of woe, *bi me ful gemorre*, 'is wholly sad to me' (*WL* 1b). Again, the speaker is not sad, but something is saddening to her; she is not active but passive and therefore remains disconnected from her own emotions.

In a poem explicitly concerned with this sadness, such a displacement serves to fragment the voice of the speaker, who is at the same time an observer of the forces that lay hold of her emotions, and a passive recipient of them. This fragmentation is one of the strengths of the poem, because it leads to irreconcilable contradictions, between the speaker's sorrow, as expressed in the early parts of the poem, and her aggressive and confused ambivalence as expressed in the final image of the text: the man himself exiled. The fact that the speaker's expression does not seek to be unified and exemplary is the key to the interest the speaker continues to generate.

At the same time, the speaker's use of Anglo-Saxon words with a wide and ambiguous semantic range such as *hlaford* 'lord' draws out the semiotic potential of a language frequently confined within strict poetic and thematic mores. Further, the speaker's use of desolate landscape imagery indicating her mood makes it impossible to determine what exactly has happened to her, or indeed where she positions herself within the events of the poem. Rather than explaining her current situation, the speaker's passive self-references and ambiguous descriptions raise as many questions as they answer. This is not a shortcoming of the work, however. Ironically, the wide range of inventive and contradictory readings of the *Lament* illustrates how ultimately successful the speaker's insistent subjectivity has been in conjuring up confusing images of a fractured identity. An example of this is the theory of the speaker as dead; Johnson's conclusion that she must be dead (Green 71) is based primarily on the speaker's contrasting of her own "desolate hall" (*WL* 29a) with the mornings of lovers "living on earth" (*WL* 34a). This juxtaposition is well-suited to describing the experience of exile as a living death. Indeed the exiled woman would be regarded as "dead to the world." The same can be said of the final lines of the poem, in which curse, regret, and wishful thinking merge into one another in the speaker's mind.

Given the absence of any recognizable masculine perspective in the poem, the one interpretation that is directly at odds with the text is that which would deny the speaker to be a female voice. Thus a reading based on a masculine speaker would suggest consistent and unusual scribal error in the surviving text — always a dubious basis for any theory. More strikingly, it would also suggest that this text is the only Anglo-Saxon text in the corpus to present a male figure speaking of personal feelings and family relationships that go beyond the homosocial bonding of the lord's retinue in the mead hall. Given the female grammatical endings in the text, it appears more likely that the unusual emotional emphasis of the poem is a reflection of the speaker's female perspective. Indeed, the argument for a male speaker is so strained that it holds up an intriguing mirror to the masculinist face of twentieth century Anglo-Saxon scholarship, which goes to great lengths to portray the gender roles of the Anglo-Saxon world in its own image. Bearing this in mind, one can only conclude that the plethora of alternative readings concerning the *Lament* are the result not of misunderstandings but of a concerted effort to silence the tenth century speaker of the poem and to mold the multivalent text into hermeneutic unity.

Despite such attempts to muffle this woman's voice in murmurings about scribal error, however, this is still a text that unequivocally demands to be read on the speaker's terms, and such a reading must encompass the shifting meaning within the words and images themselves. As a result, the *Lament* remains one of a handful of Anglo-Saxon texts whose interpretation has not been signed and sealed in the canon, leaving it open to fresh readings by a generation of scholars less encumbered by the shadow of nineteenth century historical constructions of an Anglo-Saxon heroic ideal. The rewards for doing so are great, as readers are shown a voice that departs from the dutiful deference to God that shapes many other Anglo-Saxon poems, in order to show an altogether more vivid fragment of the brittle individuality forced upon someone excluded from the ideal of Anglo-Saxon communal life, both as a woman and as an exile.

Works Cited

Bambas, Rudolph C. "Another View of the Old English *Wife's Lament.*" *Journal of English and Germanic Philology* 62.2 (Apr. 1963): 303–09. Print.

Belanoff, Patricia A. "Women's Songs, Women's Language; *Wulf and Edawacer* and the *Wife's Lament.*" *New Readings on Women in Old English Literature.* Eds. Helen Damico and Alexandra Hennessy Olson. Bloomington: Indiana University Press, 1990. 193–203. Print.

Brown, Michelle P. "Female Book Ownership and Production in Anglo-Saxon England: the Evidence of the Ninth-Century Prayerbooks." *Lexis and texts in early English: studies presented to Jane Roberts.* Eds. Christian Kay and Louise Sylvester. Amsterdam: Rodopi, 2001. 45–68. Print.

Desmond, Marilynn. "The Voice of Exile: Feminist Literary History and the Anonymous Anglo-Saxon Elegy." *Critical Inquiry* 16.3 (Spring 1990): 572–90. Print.

Fitzgerald, Robert P. "*The Wife's Lament* and the 'Search for the Lost Husband.'" *Journal of English and Germanic Philology* 62.4 (Oct. 1963): 769–77. Print.

Immelmann, Rudolf. *Die Altenglische Odoaker-Dichtung*. Berlin: Julius Springer, 1907. Print.

Johnson, William C. "*The Wife's Lament* as Death-Song." *The Old English Elegies; New Essays in Criticism and Research*. Ed. Martin Green. Rutherford, Madison and Teaneck: Fairleigh Dickinson University Press, 1983. 69–81. Print.

Klinck, Anne L. *The Old English Elegies; A Critical Edition and Genre Study*. Montreal & Kingston: McGill-Queen's University Press, 1992. Print.

Kristeva, Julia. "About Chinese Women." *The Kristeva Reader*. Ed. Toril Moi. Trans. Sean Dean. Oxford: Blackwell, 1986. 138–59. Print.

Mandel, Jerome. *Alternative Readings in Old English Poetry*. New York: Peter Lang, 1987. Print.

North, Richard. "The King's Soul: Danish Mythology in Beowulf." *Origins of Beowulf: From Vergil to Wiglaf*, New York: Oxford University Press, 2006. Print.

Rickert, Edith. "The Old English Offa Saga II." *Modern Philology* 2 (Jan. 1905): 321–76. Print.

Schücking, Levin L. "Das Angelsächsische Totenklagelied." *Englische Studien* 51 (1918–19): 1–13. Print.

Straus, Barrie Ruth. "Women's Words as Weapons: Speech as Action in *The Wife's Lament*." *Texas Studies in Literature and Language* 23.2 (1981): 268–85. Print.

Swanton, Michael J. "*The Wife's Lament* and *The Husband's Message*: A Reconsideration." *Anglia* 82 (1964): 269–90. Print.

Thorpe, Benjamin. *Codex Exoniensis. A Collection of Anglo-Saxon Poetry, from a Manuscript in the Library of the Dean and Chapter of Exeter*. London: William Pickering, 1842. Print.

Treharne, Elaine. *Old and Middle English c.890–c.1450: An Anthology*. Oxford: Wiley-Blackwell, 2009. Print.

Woolf, Virginia. *A Room of One's Own*. Boston: Houghton Mifflin Harcourt, 1989. Print.

5

Voicing the Feminine and the (Absent) Masculine in *The Concealed Fancies*

Lindsay Yakimyshyn

As male dramatists dominated the public stage in sixteenth and seventeenth-century England, it seems appropriate that recent scholarship on early dramatic texts by women has focused on the genre of closet drama.[1] However, as women writers of the early modern period have gained critical attention, a new dramatic genre has emerged — the household drama. Whereas closet dramas are texts that are not intended for performance, the household dramatic genre provided a venue for women's texts to be performed. Hovering between the public and private realm, the household drama acts as a site for female agency. The simultaneous empowerment and voicelessness, the fusion of the public and the private, which constitutes the female author's ambiguous position in early modern English society, is exemplified in household theatre. From Mary Wroth's *Love's Victory* (ca. 1620) to Jane Cavendish and Elizabeth Brackley's *The Concealed Fancies* (ca. 1644), it is evident that early modern women's dramas were influenced by their household environment and that female dramatists engaged the spaces that were available to them.[2] As part of the influential Cavendish family, Jane and Elizabeth had access to the family's estates, Bolsover Castle and Welbeck Abbey. Through writing and (presumably) performing *The Concealed Fancies*, the Cavendish sisters employ the household playing space to elucidate and realize the feminine voice and to negotiate the complicated presence and absence of the masculine.

"Your tongue's at liberty!": The Stages of the (Captured) Cavendish Estates

The Cavendish sisters wrote *The Concealed Fancies* during the English Civil War, an event that had removed the sisters' father and brothers from the household. William, Charles, and Henry Cavendish had been fighting in the war, and were exiled at the time that Jane and Elizabeth would have written *The Concealed Fancies*. The absence of the patriarchal figures forced Jane, in particular, to take charge of the family households. As several critics have highlighted, the Cavendish estates, Bolsover Castle and Welbeck Abbey, were besieged at the time that Jane and Elizabeth wrote, and performed, *The Concealed Fancies*.[3] Although they were prisoners in their home, Welbeck, following its seizure by Parliamentary troops, the Cavendish sisters employed the setting to create a play which draws on the tradition of the courtly drama. Indeed, there is critical focus on the ironic imaginative freedom that Jane and Elizabeth's internment had afforded them. It is not the "brick and mortar" estates, though, which facilitated Jane and Elizabeth's creativity, nor is it only the capture of their family estates that inspired their dramatic work. The Cavendish family members were well-respected patrons of drama; it is because of their familial connection to literature and their access to drama that the Cavendish sisters were capable of composing an original drama which draws on the work of early modern dramatists.

Jane and Elizabeth's familiarity with literary and dramatic form is evident in their collective work, *Poems, Songs, a Pastorall, and a Play*, which includes *The Concealed Fancies*. William Cavendish, their father, "[had] been a great lover and admirer of the female sex" (Cavendish 206) and had promoted Jane and Elizabeth's education. *The Concealed Fancies* exemplifies the literary grounding and authorial permission that William had granted his daughters. He told Jane that she "hath the pen of a most ready writer," and Elizabeth that she "must write too" (qtd. in Turberville 45–46). The Cavendish sisters were able to gain rhetorical space through their father's aristocratic and literary position. In *Winter Fruit: English Drama, 1642–1660*, Dale B.J. Randall devotes a chapter to the Cavendishes, arguing,

> Why might the Cavendishes warrant a chapter of their own? Simply put, we rarely find so many members of a single family concerned with writing drama, and nowhere else do we find a playwright [Jane and Elizabeth's father, William] who was himself both a friend and patron of dramatists from Ben Jonson to John Dryden. Furthermore, the appearance of no fewer than three women dramatists in the family is a phenomenon worth special attention [313].

Of the Cavendish women, Margaret is the most famous. She married into the Cavendish family in 1645, shortly following the composition of *The*

Concealed Fancies, and became the most widely published female author of her time. Scholars have privileged her work over that of her stepdaughters, Jane and Elizabeth, likely because she had written multiple texts which were published during her lifetime, while the few dramas and poems that the sisters had composed were only circulated in manuscript form, and not easily available until 1931. Margaret, allegorized in *The Concealed Fancies* as Lady Tranquility, and her remarkable publications exemplify William's promotion of female authorship. Although several critics highlight the influence of Shakespearean texts on Margaret Cavendish's writings, she maintained that her work did not draw on other writers, and attributes any inspiration to her husband, referring to him as "the best lyric and dramatic poet of this age" (Cavendish 201).[4] Despite Margaret's claims, her work has explicit ties to Shakespeare's dramas, and the connections between Margaret's work and Shakespeare's dramas imply that she was intimately aware of the bard and his plays. By extension, then, it is likely that Shakespeare's plays were present in the Cavendish homes, and that Jane and Elizabeth, too, were highly conscious of his dramatic work.[5] Although Jane and Elizabeth likely drew from several sources for inspiration, particularly as their father patronized several writers and was himself an author, *The Concealed Fancies* is most strongly linked with prominent early modern playwright Ben Jonson.

William Cavendish had commissioned Jonson to write two royal entertainments, which were performed at Welbeck Abbey and Bolsover Castle. Jonson's *The King's Entertainment at Welbeck* and *Love's Welcome to Bolsover* were staged on May 21, 1633, and on July 30, 1634, respectively.[6] These courtly entertainments were grossly expensive, and focused on the dramatic element of spectacle. By the time that Jonson wrote *The King's Entertainment at Welbeck* and *Love's Welcome to Bolsover* for Charles I's visits to the Cavendish estates, the conventions of the masque had been well-established. The emphasis on marriage and costuming, and the integration of song in Jonson's entertainments at Welbeck and Bolsover reinforce the masque conventions, and these features are echoed in Jane and Elizabeth's drama. The allusions to allegorical figures in *The Concealed Fancies* also link the household drama to court entertainments, while foregrounding gender roles in marriage. Cupid and Hymen, for example, are invoked on several occasions by Courtley, Presumption, and Luceny. In particular, the two cupids in *Love's Welcome to Bolsover* and the marriage in *The King's Entertainment at Welbeck* may have served as inspiration for Jane and Elizabeth's household drama, which is centered on love, courtship, and marriage. Timothy Raylor notes,

> The governing metaphor of Caroline rule, reiterated in innumerable poems, masques, and portraits, was that ... mutual love was to thank for the peace and concord that England, alone among the states of Europe, enjoyed: the love of

> king and queen, of governor and governed, of humanity and nature. Such love was the controlling topic of Jonson's entertainment for the visit[7] [423].

The mutual love that Raylor suggests Jonson emphasized in *Love's Welcome to Bolsover* is evident in *The Concealed Fancies*, as the Cavendish sisters explore the balance of power in marital relationships. It is also apparent that, in the household drama, the "peace and concord" of the home is fully restored with the return of the patriarch; Jane and Elizabeth acknowledge the authority of the patriarch and assert that mutual love can only exist in the governed, restored household. Therefore, the Cavendish sisters had perhaps perceived the "governing metaphor" that was evident in Jonson's entertainments, and constructed their play to replicate the themes and ideas associated with it. The references to allegorical figures and the incorporation of song in *The Concealed Fancies* reinforce the link between the household play and Jonson's entertainments, which incorporate figures such as Doubt, Love, Joy, and Delight.

Although Jane and Elizabeth were only twelve and seven years old, respectively, when Jonson's *The King's Entertainment at Welbeck* was staged, the sisters were undoubtedly aware of the production and its spectacular features. Alison Findlay suggests, "Jane and Elizabeth may have wished to create a magnificent spectacle like those staged for the king and queen's visits" ("She gave you" 264). In Act 5, scene 2 of *The Concealed Fancies*, Courtley and Presumption's entrance, "coming down out of the sky" (28), is grandiose, and reminiscent of courtly dramas. S.P. Cerasano and Marion Wynne-Davies indicate that, in *The Concealed Fancies*, "the use of stage machinery to lower figures onto the stage and the disguises adopted by the two young noblemen are drawn from court masque conventions" (213). A production of *The Concealed Fancies* would likely have been incapable of recreating the same visual impact as Mildmay Fane's *Raguaillo D'Oceano* or Jonson's *The Masque of Blackness* given their elaborate set designs. The Cavendish sisters' play, though, does not call for an elaborate set, other than the machinery for the "godly" entrance. Rather, *The Concealed Fancies* places emphasis on clothing, and the costuming of their production was Jane and Elizabeth's attempt to re-create the spectacle of patriarchal courtly entertainments.

"I, a petticoat, cry, fie!": Creating Spectacle and Agency Through Costuming

Perhaps the most remarkable feature of Jonson's infamous *The Masque of Blackness* was the provocative costuming that was created for its production. The ladies of the court that performed in the masque, including Queen Anne and Lady Mary Wroth, were dressed in garb that exposed their arms, and each wore make-up that blackened their faces. Stephen Orgel suggests that "the real innovation in the costumes for *Blackness*, indeed, was probably the fact that cosmetics were being allowed to do the work of clothing" ("Marginal Jonson" 149). In staging *The Concealed Fancies*, thoughtful use of costuming and cosmetics could allow Jane and Elizabeth to mimic the visual spectacle of Jonson's productions. In particular, the actor portraying Lady Tranquility would probably have worn make-up, as the character highlights cosmetics: "...Now, what say you Toy to the best dress for the face? Do you not think pomatum will do well, and rub it over with scarlet after..." (1.2.39–42). Jane and Elizabeth's writing suggests that they had working knowledge of make-up, and their presumable inclusion of cosmetics in a production of *The Concealed Fancies* demonstrates an awareness of how the actors' appearances could enhance the spectacle of the play. The Cavendish sisters had not yet been born at the time that Jonson's *The Masque of Blackness* was staged; however, the importance of costuming resonates in the dramas that he created for performance at Welbeck and Bolsover, which feature heightened fashions. Therefore, Jane and Elizabeth would have been cognizant of the significant role that costuming played in Jonson's productions. Just as his courtly entertainments foreground visual spectacle and costumes, clothing and appearance are of central importance in the Cavendish sisters' household drama.

The Concealed Fancies highlights the way in which the female manipulates, and is manipulated through, clothing and costuming. The perceived power of clothing in early modern England is evidenced in the sumptuary laws, which dictated the fashions and fabrics that could be worn by people of each social strata in the milieu.[8] Gender, social standing, and, as Peter Stallybrass suggests, aristocratic affiliations, were communicated through clothing and costume (293). Although England's sumptuary laws were abolished in 1604, Jane and Elizabeth's *The Concealed Fancies* underscores the social significance of clothing. As women were unable to own any property, including their clothing, in the early modern period, clothes demonstrated the dependency of women on their husbands (Worsley 71). Women could not own clothing; however, their role in the production of clothes and costumes, particularly for theatrical use, allowed them entry into a potentially authorizing space. Natasha Korda, who has worked extensively on the costume market, emphasizes women's roles in "the production of stage-props, costumes, and scenery for masques and other court entertainments" (214), noting that, "Because women worked in great numbers in the textile and clothing trades, they were particularly actively involved in the manufacture and retail of costumes, props made out of fabric, and other fashion accessories" (212). In *The Concealed Fancies*, Luceny and Tattiney, in their roles as nuns, give the first poor woman a "bow of hope" (4.1.15), or a ribbon, to alleviate her grief. The gift of a ribbon suggests that clothes and accessories are tools that afford women agency, or the hope of agency. The attention paid to accessories and clothing, and the intention to use clothing as a means to gain agency in *The Concealed Fancies,* link female authority to clothing and appearances.

In *The Concealed Fancies*, authority and control are exercised through clothing. Jane and Elizabeth, however, employ clothes as "tools of resistance for Luceny and Tattiney" (Findlay, "She gave you" 268), and I suggest that, in *The Concealed Fancies*, clothing facilitates a balance of power in marital relationships. Presumption plots to manipulate Tattiney when they are married, "[letting] her know that garb, that doth best become her, is ill-favored" (3.3.11–12), and allotting her "once a year ... a gown in fashion" (3.3.31). His intention to control his wife will be executed through control over her attire. However, Presumption's intention to manipulate his wife's behavior by controlling her clothing does not go unnoticed:

> LUCENY: ... Presumption doth throw his cloak as if he intended to govern you.
>
> TATTINEY: Aye, but as I hope to continue my own, I will make him lay his cloak off if his carriage be to slight me...
>
> LUCENY: You're right for I intend to be the same with Courtley [2.3.106–110, 114–115].

Both of the female leads acknowledge the intentions of their suitors to exert patriarchal power, but quickly defend their own abilities to determine their dress and associated behavior. Luceny reveals her plan to undermine her husband's authority. In the Epilogue of the play, Luceny asserts, "...I looked soberly, as if I would strictly observe him, yet dressed myself contrary to his instruction, and my behaviour was according to my dress" (14–17). Thereby, Luceny establishes control over her body. Although it is strongly evident that the sisters will not be submissive housewives, and will use clothing as a means to protest their subordinate position, they remain dutiful wives, holding their "petulant garb," and promising "to love [their husbands] and pray for [them]" (Epilogue 79, 59–60). The development of the female characters and their vocal performance distinguishes *The Concealed Fancies* from the conventional court dramas which had influenced the household drama.

In *The Concealed Fancies*, clothing is discussed, described, and valued; however, the playwrights offer little direction regarding costume design. The reference to Lady Tranquility's "white satin waistcoat" (1.2.56) implies that she may wear such an item, but does not confirm the item as a costume piece. Similarly, there are numerous vague references to cloaks and ribbons. Certainly, it is clear that, in Act 5, scene 2, Tattiney and Luceny wear nuns' habits and Courtley and Presumption are disguised as gods, but the notes regarding the players' costumes are brief and unspecific. The lack of explicit costuming descriptions in the text is indicative of the borrowing, rather than authorial design, of costumes. Although the playwrights avoid providing concrete details for costuming, the power of appearance in the play suggests that, like their lead characters, Jane and Elizabeth are able to employ and refigure clothing. The Cavendish sisters likely used existing costumes not for want of creativity, but, rather, for lack of resources due to their confinement.

The royal entertainments of Jonson that were held at the Cavendish estates may have provided more than inspiration for Jane and Elizabeth's play. As I will argue below, the Cavendish sisters may have appropriated many of the actual costumes from the royal entertainments at Welbeck and Bolsover for a production of *The Concealed Fancies*. Although Findlay does not dismiss the possibility that Jane and Elizabeth could have borrowed costumes from the Jonsonian productions, she deems it more probable that they used their own clothes, and the garments of their father and brothers for their production ("She gave you" 269); indeed, the allegory of the play lends itself to the employment of personal clothing. It is clear that Tattiney and Luceny represent the play's authors, and several critics, including Findlay, highlight this point. The three cousins, Cecily, Sh. and Is., also reflect Jane, Elizabeth, and their younger sister, Frances. In their play, Jane and Elizabeth also create characters that mirror their father and brothers. Had they used the personal items of the people that they allegorized, the allegorical aspect of the play would dominate. However, to focus predominantly on the allegory does a disservice to the text, neglecting the important influence of the masque. I would not entirely discount the possibility that Jane and Elizabeth employed garments from their own wardrobes and those of their relatives; however, I suggest that it is more likely that the sisters appropriated costumes from Jonson's productions, particularly as the court dramas seem to have had a profound influence on their play.

Findlay concludes that the Cavendish sisters would have "had access to the costumes for those previous entertainments" ("She gave you" 264), and I posit that the production of *The Concealed Fancies* would have potentially been constructed to incorporate the costumes and properties from the productions of *King's Entertainment at Welbeck* and *Love's Welcome to Bolsover*. Costumes, in particular, could be expensive and were very valuable to playing companies. Stallybrass emphasizes the value of costumes to the playing companies that owned and re-used them, noting, "Although clothes needed care and alteration, the materials themselves retained much of their value" (295). Because of the cost associated with the creation of costumes and the value that theatrical companies placed on them, I posit that the household, or the court, would retain costumes for subsequent royal entertainments, perhaps altering them to suit new productions. The re-use of costumes within a court or company had been well-established by the time that Jonson's entertainments were staged at the Cavendish estates. Clothing and costumes were commodities, which would sometimes be sold or traded. Korda argues, "costumes and props were often handed down to professional players as payment for court performances when they were no longer deemed 'serviceable' for the latter" (210). As Jonson's masques at the Cavendish estates were staged about ten years prior to *The Concealed Fancies*, the costumes were likely still at the estates, and "serviceable" for Jane and Elizabeth's production.

There are several instances in which Jane and Elizabeth could have recycled costume pieces from the earlier Jonsonian productions. For example, it is possible that the "garlands" (783) that Eros and Anteros don in Jonson's *Love's Welcome to Bolsover* were appropriated by Courtley and Presumption for their 'godly' disguises. However, it is more likely that, having predominantly occupied Welbeck Abbey, the Cavendish sisters would have been more easily able to access the costumes for the production that had been staged at Welbeck. One may only speculate as to the potential uses for the costumes from *The King's Entertainment at Welbeck* for a performance of *The Concealed Fancies*, but there are various noteworthy possibilities. For example, the bride's clothing from *The King's Entertainment at Welbeck,* "with scarfs, and a great wrought handkerchief, with red and blue, and other habiliments" (781), may have been employed in Act 5, scene 5 of *The Concealed Fancies,* where Care discusses bridal linens. Also, both of the female leads require bridal attire in Act 5, scene 6, and perhaps the bride's costume from Jonson's production was worn by Luceny or Tattiney. The "buckram bridelaces begilt, white sleeves, and stammel petticoats" (Jonson, *Welbeck* 781) that Jonson describes the maids as wearing in his production may have been appropriate costumes for the maids and waiting women of *The Concealed Fancies.* The apparel described in *The King's Entertainment at Welbeck* offers an abundance of options for the costuming of the male characters in Jane and Elizabeth's household drama. The stewards, Caution and Discretion, may wear the costumes of the two bride-squires of Jonson's production, who "were in two yellow leather doublets, and russet hose, like two twin clowns" (*Welbeck* 781). I conjecture that the best apparel, the "costly cassock of black buckram" (Jonson, *Welbeck* 779), may have been reserved for the patriarch, Lord Calsindow. Speculative as these costuming choices may be, I suggest that the multitude of possibilities for the employment of garb from Jonson's entertainments is accountable for the lack of specific costuming detail in Jane and Elizabeth's manuscript. The potential recycling of costumes from the earlier productions points to the multiple limitations that were placed on women, even aristocratic women, in seventeenth-century England.

Unable to own property and restricted by the Parliamentary control of their father's estates, the Cavendish sisters commented on their situation by using the "master's tools" in their household play. As Cristine Mari Varholy observes, early modern women generally "received clothing from their fathers, husbands, or masters, men who existed in positions of authority over them" (7). Indeed, the pieces from the Jonsonian productions are inextricably linked with the patriarchy: the playwright, Jonson, is male; the plays were commissioned by the patriarch, William Cavendish; and they were commissioned for England's patriarch, King Charles I. To borrow the clothing and props from the earlier productions would be to be indebted to the patriarch, even in their physical absence. The "scavenging" of patriarchal garments, though, does not diminish the Cavendish sisters' authority in the production of the play. In fact, the way in which they acquire and employ the "master's tools" challenges gender norms; "when [women] circulated or translated clothing ... their behavior was perceived as threatening" (Varholy 7). However, Jane and Elizabeth do not seem to perceive themselves as threatening to patriarchal control. Rather, their temporary appropriation of the clothes, and the masculine power that is therein represented, speaks to their awareness of their altered position in a household without a patriarch.

"Spoken by a woman": Dressing Up Gender

Although I foreground the possibility that Jane and Elizabeth recycled costumes from the stagings of Jonson's courtly dramas, Findlay's argument that the borrowing of the garments of Jane and Elizabeth's "absent male kinfolk" would "raise questions about that [male] authority" (*Playing Spaces* 46) is important. The potential use of the absent patriarch's clothing suggests the occurrence of a fetishization of garments. Findlay conjectures, "If Jane and Elizabeth costumed the actors playing Lord Calsindow and the Stellow Brothers in their father and brothers' clothes, the tantalising possibility of those loved ones returning home might have been brought one 'stage' nearer" ("Playing the 'Scene Self'" 269). How much nearer and more present, then, would the patriarchal figures be if the sisters were the actors donning the garb?

In her exploration of gender performativity in *The Concealed Fancies*, Findlay highlights the way in which the (presumed) casting of Cavendish and Brackley in the roles of Tattiney and Luceny "evokes gender sameness" ("Playing the 'Scene Self'" 169). However, Findlay's emphasis on the real-life sisters and the play-world sisters results in a disproportionately small discussion of the position of the male characters and the real-life men that they represent. As there is, quite inconveniently, no cast list provided in the manuscript, it is impossible to know which role was performed by which actor. Pointing to their family's connection with theatre, Findlay makes it clear that Elizabeth and Jane's play was intended for performance, and that the authors likely took on the lead roles. In "Sisterly Feelings in Cavendish and Brackley's Drama," Findlay, acknowledging that her argument is speculative, specifically casts Elizabeth as Tattiney: "Elizabeth, playing Tattiney, was already married, and therefore well entitled to the confidence of presuming to teach her elder sibling about courtship" (197). However, the role of Tattiney seems to suit the younger Jane, as the character fears that "a younger sister cannot have the confidence to teach an elder" (1.4.5). Although either casting choice is feasible, it is possible that Jane and Elizabeth took on male roles as well as the female leads.

Drag is an important component of early modern theatre. Male actors performed as female characters, and numerous Shakespearean characters, for example, cross-dress. *Twelfth Night's* Viola, *Cymbeline's* Innogen, and *The Merchant of Venice's* Portia, to name a few, are cross-dressers, and all benefit by wearing male disguises. Moreover, those who performed in *The Concealed Fancies* may have been dressed in drag. Jane and Elizabeth's male relatives were absent during the presumed time of production of *The Concealed Fancies*; there are, though, twenty male roles to cast in the play. Cerasano and Wynne-Davies note that, alongside the three Cavendish girls, their two brothers may have been included on a cast list, had one existed (129). However, because of the absence of the Cavendish sisters' father and brothers, it is likely that the male servants of Welbeck Abbey performed as the male characters.[9] However, that the play's authors cast themselves or their sister in male roles is not unthinkable, but, at this point, can neither be substantiated nor refuted. Rather, through allegorizing their brothers and performing as them, perhaps even employing the clothing of William, Charles, and Henry, the Cavendish sisters voice the absent masculine and attempt to retain the masculine presence. Potentially taking on male roles in the production of *The Concealed Fancies* does not mean that Jane and Elizabeth *become* masculine. After all, "The reduction of performativity to performance would be a mistake" (Butler 234). It is not through a dramatic performance that they enact, or potentially challenge, gender norms. Rather, it is through taking on masculine roles, in the play and in the household, that Jane and Elizabeth are able to perform authority and fashion their allegorical selves, and themselves, as authoritative women. Indeed, the Civil War provided opportunities for women to gain agency in the household. Discovering masculine-like agency in their evolving positions in the home, Jane and Elizabeth "renegotiat[e] their position as mistresses rather than housewives" (Findlay, *Playing Spaces* 44). For the Cavendish sisters, the writing and the household performance of *The Concealed Fancies* could have served to express and extend their exploration of their newly-developing agency.

In her important work on gender performativity, Judith Butler points to (in)numerable questions on the establishment of gender identity. For example,

"If gender is constructed, then who is doing the constructing?" (6). As playwrights, Jane and Elizabeth possess agency to construct male and female characters that simultaneously replicate and refigure societal gender identities. In *The Concealed Fancies*, the heroines simultaneously challenge and submit to patriarchal authority. As I have noted, Tattiney and Luceny gain authority, particularly through their use of clothing. However, the heroines submit to the patriarch, Lord Calsindow, and seek his approval at the end of the play. In the Epilogue, Tattiney describes her continuing, though subtle, agency in marriage: "Once he spoke in company according to a discreet husband, then I gave him a modest return of a wife, and yet appeared his mistress" (79–82). Even though she is now a wife, Tattiney suggests that she retains control over her position in her relationship with Presumption. Although the heroines of *The Concealed Fancies* challenge and refashion women's role in marriage, they do not fully subvert their position in the patriarchy. Rather, in becoming wives, albeit manipulative wives, and submitting to the authority of their father, Luceny and Tattiney accept their gender-appropriate station. Moreover, by exploring and refiguring gender roles through private dramatization, the Cavendish sisters tempered the potential for gender subversion.

Constrained by their household situation, Jane and Elizabeth would have performed for a small crowd of friends and family, if *The Concealed Fancies* was performed for an audience at all. Assuming vocal roles in their household drama, the Cavendish sisters challenge performative boundaries. Just as "The part of the presenters [in *The King's Entertainment at Welbeck*] is probably entirely Jonson's" (Baskerville 267), it is more than likely that the two playwrights would have taken on substantial roles in their household play. It was conventional for aristocratic women, such as Queen Anne, to participate in masques; however, their participation was generally voiceless. Orgel asserts that "masquers are not actors; a lady or gentleman participating in a masque remains a lady or gentleman, and is not released from the obligation of observing all the complex rules of behavior at court" (*Illusion of Power* 39). Despite its ties to courtly drama, *The Concealed Fancies* is distinctly a household drama, with a more intimate audience. Indeed, Findlay refers to *The Concealed Fancies* as "primarily a 'family' entertainment" ("She gave you" 260). Therefore, Jane and Elizabeth are implicitly freed from the constrictions of the court and from the conventions of the commercial theatre. The intended audience, which, as I have noted, likely consisted of a small number of family and friends, may have dictated the level of adherence to behavioral prescriptions, in terms of content, costuming, and performance. Situated in the household, *The Concealed Fancies* allowed Jane and Elizabeth to comment on marriage, internment, and family dynamics without destabilizing their social position.

Like their lead characters, the Cavendish sisters fulfilled the roles of wife and mother and were held in high esteem in their community. Elizabeth, in particular, "has been recorded [as a] perfect and pious wife" (Ezell, "To be your daughter" 247). Just as Tattiney and Luceny reconcile their roles as subordinate wives and intelligent women, Elizabeth and Jane were able to negotiate their positions as wives with their authority in writing, and their written contributions and imaginative freedom did not end with their production of *The Concealed Fancies*. Elizabeth's "Loose Papers" and "Meditations" survive, as does Jane's volume of poetry.[10] Emily Smith notes, "[Jane Cavendish's] writing retained popularity among her friends, family, and neighbours" (192), which lends itself to the tradition of manuscript circulation. Existing only in manuscript form until its 1931 publication, *The Concealed Fancies* seems to have been enjoyed by Jane and Elizabeth's companions.[11] As Margaret Ezell notes, there is no proof that the Cavendish sisters' play "was meant to be read by those outside a circle of friends and relatives" (*Patriarch's Wife* 67); however, that they preserved their work in formal, bound copies indicates their potential desire to have their work disseminated. Likewise, although it is unknown whether their family and friends ever witnessed a production of the play, the way in which *The Concealed Fancies* is written, particularly with its implicit references to masque conventions, lends itself to production. Although it is impossible to know whether the Cavendish sisters performed *The Concealed Fancies*, the play enjoyed production.[12]

Like many household plays, there is no concrete evidence that *The Concealed Fancies* was performed in the Cavendish estates. Lisa Hopkins suggests that "it was probably never performed" in Jane and Elizabeth's lifetime; however, she challenges her own assertion, admitting that the play was "almost certainly written for performance [at Welbeck]" (32). Like Hopkins, Findlay acknowledges that there is "no recorded performance history" of *The Concealed Fancies*, but she emphasizes the "strong tradition of Cavendish family theatre that would have provided a supportive family context for a production of Jane and Elizabeth's play" (*Playing Spaces* 45). In concurrence with Hopkins and Findlay's positions, I suggest that, considering the form of the play and the sisters' household environment, it is more likely than not that *The Concealed Fancies* was performed, and that its performance was influenced by the stagings of the royal entertainments at their family estates and by the absence of Jane and Elizabeth's male relatives. Employing the tools and materials, literal and literary, that their father, the Cavendish estates, and Jonsonian productions had afforded them, Jane and Elizabeth created a play that was feasible to produce, even in their circumstances. The Cavendish sisters reproduce the voice of the patriarch in their household drama, and explore nonsubversive potential for female agency in the home. Becoming managers of the family estates, Jane and, to a lesser extent, Elizabeth, gained authority.

Through writing male characters, and potentially adopting male costumes and taking on male roles, both in the play and in real life, Jane and Elizabeth mimic masculinity, filling the gap left by the exile of their father and brothers.

Notes

1. Marta Straznicky's *Privacy, Playreading, and Women's Closet Drama, 1550–1700* (Cambridge: Cambridge UP, 2004) has been a particularly important text.

2. In her monograph, *Playing Spaces in Early Modern Women's Drama*, Alison Findlay explores the ways in which women employed their household spaces for producing plays.

3. Alison Findlay places the writing and performance of *The Concealed Fancies* at Welbeck in late 1644 or early 1645 (*Playing Spaces* 51).

4. Katherine Romack and James Fitzmaurice's *Cavendish and Shakespeare, Interconnections* (Burlington, VT: Ashgate, 2006) includes ten critical pieces on the presence of Shakespeare in Margaret Cavendish's work.

5. Indeed, traces of Shakespearean drama are evident in *The Concealed Fancies*. For example, Presumption's speech in Act 3, scene 3 of *The Concealed Fancies* is reminiscent of Petruccio's speech in Act 2, Scene 1 of *The Taming of the Shrew*, as both men plan to control their future wives. The invocation of Shakespeare's tragic queen, Cleopatra, in Jane and Elizabeth's household play is also noteworthy.

6. Although the entertainments are titled *Love's Welcome; The King's Entertainment at Welbeck, in Nottinghamshire* and *Love's Welcome; The King and Queen's Entertainment at Bolsover*, I refer to them by their more concise, well-known titles, *The King's Entertainment at Welbeck* and *Love's Welcome to Bolsover*. The condensed titles allow the entertainments to be more quickly distinguishable.

7. The Caroline era (1625–1642) is that which followed the Jacobean era and preceded the English Civil War. During the Caroline period, Charles I, whom the Cavendish family had hosted at their estates, was the ruling monarch.

8. Passed in 1363, the first sumptuary law in England was titled "Statute Concerning Diet and Apparel." Queen Elizabeth's sumptuary law was reinforced by her declaration in Greenwich on June 15, 1574.

9. In particular, it is evident that household servants' children participated in the household dramas of Rachel Fane, whose seventeenth-century dramatic writings are currently unpublished. The manuscript of the pastoral masque includes a cast list, although it does not link the actors with specific roles.

10. For the locations of the manuscripts, see Betty Travitsky's piece on Elizabeth Egerton (Brackley, née Cavendish) and Jennett Humphreys and Sean Kelsey's piece on Jane Cheyne (née Cavendish) in the *Oxford Dictionary of National Biography*.

11. In "'To be your daughter in your pen': the social functions of literature in the writings of Lady Elizabeth Brackley and Lady Jane Cavendish," Margaret Ezell suggests that the manuscript of *Poems, Songs, a Pastorall, and a Play* would have likely circulated through the Cavendish and Egerton families.

12. There was a posthumous production of *The Concealed Fancies*, which was directed by Alison Findlay and Jane Milling, and produced by Women and Dramatic Production 1570–1670.

Works Cited

Baskerville, C.R. "The Sources of Jonson's 'Masque of Christmas' and 'Love's Welcome at Welbeck.'" *Modern Philology* (Oct. 1908) 6.2: 257–269. Print.

Brackley, Elizabeth, and Jane Cavendish. *The Concealed Fancies. Renaissance Drama by*

Women: Texts and Documents. Ed. S.P. Cerasano and Marion Wynne-Davies. New York: Routledge, 1997. 127–56. Print.

Butler, Judith. *Bodies that Matter: On the Discursive Limits of "Sex."* New York: Routledge, 1993. Print.

Cavendish, Margaret. *The Life of William Cavendish, Duke of Newcastle, to which is Added the True Relation of my Birth, Breeding and Life*. London: J.C. Nimmo, 1886. Print.

Cerasano, S.P., and Marion Wynne-Davies. *Renaissance Drama by Women: Texts and Documents*. Ed. S.P. Cerasano and Marion Wynne-Davies. New York: Routledge, 1997. Print.

Ezell, Margaret. *The Patriarch's Wife: Literary Evidence and the History of the Family*. Chapel Hill, NC: University of North Carolina Press, 1987. Print.

_____. "'To be your daughter in your pen': The Social Functions of Literature in the Writings of Lady Elizabeth Brackley and Lady Jane Cavendish." *Readings in Renaissance Women's Drama: Criticism, History, and Performance, 1594–1998*. Ed. S.P. Cerasano and Marion Wynne-Davies. New York: Routledge, 1998. 246–258. Print.

Findlay, Alison. *Playing Spaces in Early Women's Drama*. New York: Cambridge University Press, 2006. Print.

_____. "Playing the 'Scene Self' in Jane Cavendish and Elizabeth Brackley's *The Concealed Fancies*." *Enacting Gender on the English Renaissance Stage*. Ed. Anne Russell and Viviana Comensoli. Chicago: U of Chicago P, 1999. 154–76. Print.

_____. "'She gave you the civility of the house': Household Performance in *The Concealed Fancies*." *Readings in Renaissance Women's Drama: Criticism, History, and Performance, 1594–1998*. Ed. S.P. Cerasano and Marion Wynne-Davies. New York: Routledge, 1998. 259–271. Print.

_____. "Sisterly Feelings in Cavendish and Brackley's Drama." *Sibling Relations and Gender in the Early Modern World: Sisters, Brothers and Others*. Ed. Naomi J. Miller and Naomi Yavneh. Burlington, VT: Ashgate, 2006. 195–205. Print.

Jonson, Ben. *Love's Welcome; The King and Queen's Entertainment at Bolsover. The Works of Ben Jonson*. Ed. William Gifford. Boston: Phillips, Sampson, and Company, 1858. 783–4. Print.

_____. *Love's Welcome; The King's Entertainment at Welbeck, in Nottinghamshire. The Works of Ben Jonson*. Ed. William Gifford. Boston: Phillips, Sampson, and Company, 1858. 779–82. Print.

Korda, Natasha. "Women's Theatrical Properties." *Staged Properties in Early Modern English Drama*. Ed. Jonathan G. Harris and Natasha Korda. New York: Cambridge University Press, 2002. 202–229. Print.

Orgel, Stephen. "Marginal Jonson." *The Politics of the Stuart Court Masques*. Ed. David Bevington and Peter Holbrook. Cambridge: Cambridge University Press, 1998. 144–175. Print.

_____. *The Illusion of Power: Political Theater in the English Renaissance*. Berkeley: University of California Press, 1975. Print.

Randall, Dale B.J. *Winter Fruit: English Drama, 1642–1660*. Lexington: University Press of Kentucky, 1995. Print.

Raylor, Timothy. "'Pleasure Reconciled to Virtue': William Cavendish, Ben Jonson, and the Decorative Scheme of Bolsover Castle." *Renaissance Quarterly* 52.2 (Summer 2009): 402–39. Print.

Smith, Emily. "The Local Popularity of *The Concealed Fansyes*." *Notes and Queries* (June 2006): 189–193. Print.

Stallybrass, Peter. "Worn Worlds: Clothes and Identity on the Renaissance Stage." *Subject and Object in Renaissance Culture*. Ed. Margreta De Grazia, Maureen Quilligan, and Peter Stallybrass. Trowbridge, Wiltshire: Cambridge University Press, 1996. 289–320. Print.

Turberville, Arthur Stanley. *A History of Welbeck Abbey and its Owners*. London: Faber and Faber, [1938–1939]. Print.

Varholy, Cristine Mari. "'Rich Like a Lady': Cross-Class Dressing in the Brothels and Theaters of Early Modern London." *Journal for Early Modern Cultural Studies* 8.1 (Spring-Summer 2008): 4–34. Print.

Worsley, Lucy. *Cavalier: A Tale of Chivalry, Passion, and Great Houses*. London: Faber and Faber, 2007. Print.

6

The Wartime Diaries of Dang Thuy Tram: Extolling and Gendering the Heroine's Voice in Postwar Vietnam and Beyond

Hanh N. Nguyen and R. C. Lutz

Lệ Mai[1]	(Tears at Dawn)
Từ trời mưa đổ oan khiên	(From above rain pours, unjust)
Bờ vai bạc mệnh một miền cưu mang	(Luckless in a realm, shoulders to bear)
Trần gian nặng nợ muôn vàn	(A world, boundless in debt)
Mai sau giọt lệ một hàng chẻ đội	(In coming days, row of tears, cleaved in two)
Trịnh Công Sơn[2]	

A wartime doctor loses her diaries, but one volume is picked up and saved from destruction by the enemy. After her death soon thereafter, a second volume is also saved by her opponents. Thirty-five years later, a copy of her surviving diaries makes it back to her homeland. Within two months, it becomes a publishing phenomenon and is translated into many foreign languages. This, in short, is the history behind the diaries of a North Vietnamese female doctor, Dang Thuy Tram.[3] Dang was four years out of medical school when she volunteered to serve as field physician with the North's military forces in South Viet Nam. She fell there on June 22, 1970.[4] The above song by a Vietnamese lyricist captures the mood of Dang's diary rather well. Dang strongly felt the burden of caring for injured and dying comrades, while longing for a peaceful future. Her diaries were translated into English by Andrew X. Pham and published as *Last Night I Dreamed of Peace: The Diary of Dang Thuy Tram* (2007).

There are several reasons contemporary Vietnamese and global audiences have valorized the experience of this fallen doctor. First is the compelling authenticity of Dang's text. Written in one of the hottest battle zones during the conflict in Viet Nam from April 8, 1968 to June 20, 1970, Dang's surviving diaries possess and convey the immediacy of a writer who has lived through momentous experiences. Second, in the Socialist Republic of Viet Nam[5] of today, Dang's diary is welcome as a genuine record of a pure Socialist heroine. Third, in her two surviving diary volumes, Dang shows her human side as well as her official persona as wartime physician and Communist cadre.[6] In particular, Dang's voice is personalized by her longing for love, both in the romantic way that she nevertheless attempts to deny, and in the universal love for her family and comrades and community. Fourth, from an international and in particular American view, her writing is a rare surviving document of the Vietnam War[7] from a North Vietnamese woman's viewpoint. Lastly, in addition to these reasons, another factor is that, according to critic Cam Thi Doan:

> The diary itself has nothing to do with the aura of saintliness that has been recently, and noisily, imposed upon it.... This young woman contained both light and darkness. She was at once noble and down-to-earth, experienced and naïve [215–16].

Given the intense valorization of Dang's text, the issue of its gendering is of key importance when analyzing the success of its reception.

"This life and death struggle"[8]: An Authentic Woman's Voice from a Battlefield

The multifaceted valorization of Dang's text opens up questions of the interrelation of its gendering and the creation of authenticity. Her diaries have been purposefully gendered for marketing, beginning on the essentialist level in which the sex of the author is highlighted and continuing with the adamant promise of a uniquely female perspective on the war situation.[9] This marketing-driven gendering of Dang's wartime diaries has problematical aspects, as it dovetails with the observation of Martine Watson Brownley regarding the situation in patriarchy in which "the [woman's] diary is acknowledged as a legitimate autobiographical text only when ... the times recorded [are] extraordinary" (152). Dang's experience coincides with a momentous event in the history of her country, so that her diary appeals also on that level. This leaves open the question of whether a woman's peacetime journal would have had the same effect.

Beyond this external gendering, there is also an intrinsic, gendered authenticity to Dang's diaries prior to their market entry. Dang is writing about her female self. As Adrienne Shiffman posits:

> Because the female self has been traditionally defined in relation to a dominant other, women's life writing — in the form of the female diary — has been pushed into the literary margins. But ... the ... woman who "writes herself" both deconstructs and reconstructs womanhood [94].

In a similar vein, Marlene Schiwy states that "[j]ournal writing is the most egalitarian of writing modes. What counts is not who the writer is or what she has achieved, but rather the degree of truthfulness, candor, and perceptiveness she has brought to her writing" (25). By availing herself of the accepted format of the diary, but investing her "writing of herself" with an authentic style of her own, Dang created a text that establishes her personalized, autonomous, and participatory perspective on a historical event and some of its consequences.

Reception of her text did not occur without some opposition. Even if atypical, the negative response of Vietnamese critic Tam Nguyen to Dang's text built its rejection on the diary format:

> [T]he genre of the diary is not usually included in the numerous genres [of literature] .... because the diary records everyday happenings, not allowing the diarist to really expand and explore all the characters/persons that the diarist mentions ... the diarist does not have enough space to explore or delve into issues of society at large. [10]

It is from this understanding of literature that preferentializes texts primarily created by male Vietnamese writers that Nguyen downplays the popular appeal and impact of Dang's diary, subtly gendering his dismissal.

The many positive Vietnamese reviewers, such as Phong Le, focus instead on the inherent authenticity of Dang's diary:

> Here is a diary that was written for oneself only ... with such honesty and genuineness with oneself, and was not compromised.... Yet once that diary became a book for the public far and wide, then what was recorded in there suddenly became a mirror of honesty for a time, for a whole generation.[11]

For critics like Le, Dang's writing appeals because it speaks of what are considered simple and meaningful truths about human longing, suffering, and ideals. Le suggests further that Dang's diary adds to the growing body of contemporary Vietnamese literature due to its unmediated nature. In this view, the non-professional woman writer can create a text that holds more veracity and authenticity than finely crafted literary constructs.

Dang's diary is gendered for most Vietnamese readers and critics by its focus on the female perspective on war. As Wendy N. Duong points out, discussing gender in Vietnamese culture and society is difficult because there is not even a local theory or consensus on "feminism" there:

> Discussing feminism... [in] Vietnam ... can be an intellectually dangerous, sensitive, and imprecise task.... Vietnamese researchers of women's studies today define the English word, "feminism," in shorthand as a social movement "aim[ing] to improve the social position of women in concrete ways" [193].

With such a caveat, one should turn to Western critic Joan Alway for an appreciation of the multifaceted nature of the term, who states that "[t]here are many 'types' of feminism, and these types differ in terms of their organizational forms and political strategies" (225). This point is stressed as well by Susan Hanson, who offers a helpful definition:

> Feminism's concern for context is rooted in the feminist view that everyone speaks from somewhere, that there is no such thing as a universal perspective. That which is touted as universal is really ... a view from nowhere [257].

Dang's diary is gendered in Hanson's terms as the writer clearly reveals that she is speaking from somewhere about something and for distinct reasons. She also reveals quite strongly her own views on the issues affecting her life, successfully writing herself into textual existence. For a woman writer to do so is still unusual in contemporary Viet Nam, and particularly in a document from the "American War."

Pamela Stewart comments that the North's leader Ho Chi Minh held these views on female war duties: "During wartime, Ho argued, Vietnamese women bore three responsibilities: caring for children, keeping production going, and fighting ... eliminating any divide between a masculinized battlefront and a feminized home front (503). In Stewart's view, Dang's diary is gendered in its focus on reflecting on status and value of female contributions to the struggle for which Dang volunteered.

With her immediacy and authenticity, Dang's writing represents the kind of often gendered, spatial, and momentary autobiographical recording that is the epitome of the diary and journal. If her writing has to carry the burden of being gendered both externally and internally, then this gendering serves the purpose of creating more immediate, popular, and influential effects on some levels of contemporary Vietnamese reading culture. Vietnamese readers have come to consider Dang's diaries a colorful and honest war account comparable to those provided in school textbooks and male memoirs of the Vietnam War, for example.[12]

On a formal level, Dang's original text[13] is remarkable for its virtual absence of almost any crossed out words or sentences, documenting the concentration with which she committed her thoughts to the page.[14] Because she also kept a professional medical journal, Dang's personal diaries gave her freedom to delve into the private.

Dang's diaries offer remarkable candor as she tells of how often she is burdened with the duties of saving lives and performing as an exemplary cadre. She conveys the picture of a strong person who uses her medical skills to the best of her ability when working in makeshift clinics and literally dodging bombs dropped from American helicopters. She writes of her personal longing for love, both for family and comrades but also a few select men. Pham describes the effect of reading of Dang's life: "Regardless of how the diaries are read or perceived, there are three undeniable truths about the author. First, her heart was noble. Second, her life was guided by ideals. Third, her sacrifice was as tragic as it was heroic" (Dang xx). This view clearly attracted many readers.

As a Vietnamese woman writer, Dang stakes out a position of relative strength for herself, countermanding Confucian sentiments still prevailing in Communist Vietnamese society. In particular, Confucianism stresses female humility and subordination to males. In contrast, Dang's entry for May 9, 1968, opens with a candid claim: "In life, one should be humble, but she should also have self-esteem and an independent spirit. If I am right, I should be proud of myself" (18). At one point the author admonishes herself that she is both subject and object of her text, as in the entry for January 6, 1970: "Thuy [her personal middle name], your life is a book; the lines written there are as beautiful as the lyrics of little songs. Please, write worthy lines" (Dang 176). This is written as the author struggles with what she considers a bourgeois weakness for private happiness, including notions of romance. To indulge in this should never be realized as it could tarnish her status as a selfless Party member.

In general, Dang rejects unselfconscious theatricality. In the same entry for January 6, 1970, she remembers that the long-term object of her unconsummated love, Khuong The Hung,[15] referred to as M. for his pen name Do Moc, once likened the two of them to characters in a popular Communist play. Yet Dang rejects this notion. "M. once asked me, 'Am I Vu Khiem and are you Huong Giang, Thuy?' How can I answer that question now?" (176). The reality of the war situation renders absurd such a self-abrogating subjection to a popular role.

Dang is keenly aware that despite her carefully guarded core of authenticity, she is nevertheless forced to play certain roles. During a surreal trek across an American free-fire zone, Dang likens herself to an actress. On August 5, 1969, she writes: "Now I am also an actor on the stage of life: I am taking the role of a girl in the liberated area, wearing black pajamas, who, night after night, follows the guerrillas to work between our areas and those of the enemy" (Dang 146). On other occasions, she feels she has to act the leading role of cadre at all times in public, writing on February 27, 1970: "I am an actor on stage with many eyes looking at me. I can do it" (Dang 196). This expression of the writer's self-awareness and knowledge of the constructed quality of her public persona allow her to transcend unchallenged, internalized, prescribed (feminine) roles, empowering her female self.

Pursuing another avenue towards empowerment, at least as it increases her self-motivation to endure hardships, Dang aligns herself completely with the Communist ideological doctrine predicting victory for her side. There is also a strong teleological perspective to Dang's writings, such as in the entry for May 20, 1969: "Oh, the perilous days of this last stage!" (121). This refers to the assumed imminence of the last struggles of the war that will lead to the final Communist victory. In history, this would come much later, on April 30, 1975.

Dang clearly valued her diaries as a vital aspect of herself, her personality, and her legacy. After losing her backpack in December 1969, she writes in her new, third volume, which would become her last, on January 15, 1970: "The enemy had robbed me of two diaries. Although I lost those precious pages, I still have the most valuable book — my mind" (Dang 183). Yet for posterity, only what Dang committed to the pages of her last two diaries has remained accessible.

Just as Dang treasured her writing, she makes clear that male comrades also kept such journals. During this period in Viet Nam, writing diaries was not a gendered act per se. Yet the male writer's attitude towards emotional candor was at least in some instances different from Dang's own. About her fellow cadre Thuan, Dang writes on February 24, 1970, "Reading your diary, I know you love me more than anyone else. But why are you hiding things from me? I am so angry with you" (194).[16] About the North Vietnamese soldier who would be killed together with her a few days later, Dang writes on June 16, 1970: "My heart stirs as I read Boi's diary.... His feelings and secrets are the same as mine" (221). Dang appreciates Boi's emotional honesty and perceives a kindred spirit. However, because these and other diaries are apparently lost and so cannot be compared to Dang's text, Dang's surviving diary stands out by giving an unmediated voice from a woman enmeshed in wartime struggle.[17]

There is only one explicit entry, for October 20, 1969, which expresses the diarist's conviction that her work carries weight beyond the personal as a document of importance for the whole nation. Dang writes, "But this diary is not only for my private life. It must also record the lives of my people and their innumerable sufferings, these folks of steel from this Southern land" (158). This is the most candid claim of the woman diarist that her records of her experience matter — and matter on a national, if not international scale. It is a powerful assertion of self-valorization for a classically educated northern Vietnamese woman of her time.

Thus Dang recorded her wartime life, and her writing reveals a woman assured of her own relevance. Her diaries survived her,[18] but only because a South Vietnamese soldier and translator uttered to his fellow American soldier "Don't burn this one, Fred. It has fire in it already" (qtd. in Dang xvi).[19] These famous lines were visualized dramatically in the opening sequence of the sweeping epic Vietnamese film, based on Dang's diaries, entitled *Đừng Đốt (Don't Burn, 2009).*[20]

"We do not regret anything exchanged for freedom and liberty"[21]: A Pure Socialist Heroine

When a copy of Dang's surviving diaries returned to Viet Nam in June 2005, alert Vietnamese government officials immediately sensed a huge scoop. With remarkable alacrity, they were published on July 18, 2005, in Hanoi (Dang xviii). For once, the cultural cadres hit a winner with an increasingly indifferent Vietnamese reading public. For a nation of over eighty million people, the regular print runs of at most 5,000 copies for a first edition of a book are an indication of popular disaffection with national literature (Dang xviii). That the first 20,000 copies of Dang's diaries sold within a month was a sensation (Dang xviii). In Viet Nam and abroad, Dang's diaries have become more than just a mere "girl" thing. Although writing a diary is popularly often still seen as a frivolous and sentimental act of a young and romantic woman, Dang's diaries have escaped this stigma; instead, in Viet Nam they are embraced as a fierce voice from the heroic past.

Dang's diaries are vehemently in favor of the North's war in the South. "I live to fight," Dang writes on July 14, 1969 (134). Dang's diary is not primarily about suffering injustice but fighting to end it. Dang is a warrior with a conscience and compassion who feels sorrow for the human cost of a war that she believes is justified and necessary. When Dang talks of peace, as she does throughout her surviving text, it is peace after Communist victory. Her entry for April 27, 1969, clearly articulates this sentiment: "Last night, a dream of peace came to me.... Oh, the dream is not mine alone, but it's the dream of Peace and Independence burning in the hearts of thirty million Vietnamese" (Dang 111).[22] "Independence" is the code word for Communist rule here. The North's Democratic Republic of Viet Nam did not consider the South's Republic of Viet Nam a truly independent nation, but a puppet regime of the U.S.A. Regardless of a reader's attitude towards the historical veracity of this belief, it indicates that for Dang, peace was possible only on the terms of the Communist side.

In contemporary Vietnamese society, the voice of Dang Thuy Tram serves to invigorate historical memory through a highly personal, authentic, moving, and totally committed text. As Dang writes upon the occasion of the New Year on January 1st, 1970:

> The dreams now are of the American bandits' defeat, and Independence and Freedom for the nation. Only when those dreams are fulfilled will I be able to have my own wishes.... My youth has been soaked with the sweat, tears, blood, and bones of the living and the dead. My youth has been tempered in the perilous trials of the battlefields. Day and night, my youth has burned hot with the fire of hatred [173].

What makes Dang's text so valuable is its authenticity. It was written by a woman who lived, and died, by her words. Dang writes on February 22nd, 1970: "As for myself ... there is nothing to worry about. I have volunteered, I have offered my entire youth to the nation. Even if I must sacrifice my life, there is nothing to regret" (193). Dang stuck to her convictions and lived the life she wrote out for herself.

All these issues beckon many questions. When private diaries and journals are published and publicly read, do these texts serve larger literary, cultural, political, and social causes? In the age of globalization and the wide dissemination of reading materials, Dang's writing becomes a national source of pride, and a transnational subject of debate, criticism, and serious examination. Because these diaries were authored by a young, idealistic woman, Dang's writing has been marketed as gendered. Does her writing, and its publication, move beyond the limits of gendered writing? And what does it mean when a text is deemed gendered as women's writing? As shown above, Dang did consider her diary a public document. But it occupies a double space as it embraces the private as well, as a personal artifact. Does this mean Dang's authorial designs have been realized, albeit with the very help of the despised enemy who took her life but gave her texts to the international public?

Within the limited scope of this essay, we want to give three answers. First, the gendering of Dang's writing voice in the publishing arena and among mainstream readership appears almost unavoidable because of the public interest in her position as a woman physician volunteering for work in a war zone. Second, Dang the diarist, who notices, feels, and comments on things perhaps occluded in the lost pages of her fellow male diarists, is not invisible, but a fiercely committed woman. Third, some of the efficacy and audience appeal result from Dang's writing, which draws its particular narrative and persuasive strength from its very format. Her diary builds on a woman's world of talk and sharing of emotions, and voices concerns about the restrictions a still patriarchal, if self-declared revolutionary society has placed on such subjects. Dang's embracing of her gendered position offers a different perspective into a particularly violent aspect of the Vietnam War. Her diaries capture the immediacy of a struggle.

"A heart is also capable of love and hope"[23]: The Deeply Human Side of Dang

The single most important factor for the successful postwar reception of Dang's surviving diaries was their honesty in acknowledging the personal side of its author. This is often in conflict with the harsh dictates of the Party and the war environment. The two issues troubling the author most are her bourgeois background and her personal longings for love, as a human and also as a woman.

Dang's family[24] was of a Mandarin, aristocratic background. Yet her father, a surgeon, chose for the family to stay in Communist North Viet Nam after partition in 1954, despite knowing he would face political resentment for his bourgeois family background. Dang committed herself to life under Socialism. Yet she reveals that she was occasionally overcome with guilt and blamed herself for having "bourgeois" thoughts, which traditionally were inconsistent with becoming a Communist cadre. On June 2nd, 1968, finding herself reminiscing about her carefree school days, she laments: "Why do these remote, bourgeois, adolescent sentiments return to me today—a cadre struggling in the resistance?" (Dang 25).[25] This line of nostalgia for her former schooldays, including musings on love in the same entry later on, is tender and almost romantic. Here, her words are in stark contrast to the rawness and immediacy of war that she experienced every day.

Even though she wrote under such dire circumstances, Dang's writing was rather lyrical and poignant, expressing her inner self. As a young doctor, Dang felt the need to set an example for others who looked up to her to be a selfless cadre. In a response to Thuan, she records restraining herself on April 6, 1969: "I'm afraid of what they will think of us, afraid that they might misunderstand our noble love, this very innocent but very complex devotion" (Dang 104). This refers to the panopticon-like quality of personal life within the North's forces. There, privacy was at a minimum. Cadres like others were under constant public scrutiny by their comrades so that any display of affection may have been misconstrued, and denounced as "bourgeois activity." There was no room for Dang to express herself fully but in the pages of her diary.

Perhaps most troubling for Dang, and very relevant for her postwar Vietnamese readers who are generally more interested in romance than politics, are her conflicting thoughts on the subject of romantic love. Dang expresses quiet frustration and strong resentment for Khuong (M.), the man she loved since age sixteen. Throughout the diaries she concludes their love is doomed, as on July 5, 1968: "M.—he does not deserve me, either. I have achieved none of the three pillars of life: Ideal, Career, and Love. That's why I cannot avoid being sad" (Dang 32). On April 24, 1969, Dang writes: "I must pare away romantic notions .... Oh, Thuy! Yours is an impossible dream" (110). Because it is impossible for her not to do so, Dang continues to express her longings in her diary, transgressing against strict Socialist norms of utter self-effacement. In doing so, Dang performs the deconstructions and reconstructions of herself as woman cadre and physician that Shiffman has discussed for the woman writer in general. For instance, on July 8, 1968, Dang assesses: "I am bourgeois only in sentiments, not in attitudes as some have claimed" (33). While deconstructing her character as holding publicly denounced sentiments, Dang reconstructs herself by claiming that these are only surface movements, not political beliefs on which (anti–Communist) actions would be based.

While Dang never leaves any doubt about her total commitment to the Party, there is a subtle shading of her devotion that humanizes her voice for the reader. Throughout her diary, and tested by numerous near-death encounters, she expresses acceptance of her eventual death on the battlefield, and admonishes others to do the same. Chillingly, on August 29, 1969, she writes that "I completely understand a mother's love, but ... she must know how to love her son and how to offer him to the nation" (Dang 153). It speaks for Dang's honesty that she does not exclude herself from this, as she writes on June 10, 1970: "Dear Mom, if your daughter has to fall for tomorrow's victory, cry just a little. But be proud because your child has lived a good life. Everyone dies only once" (218). With her complete acceptance of the high probability of her own death, Dang is disgusted by others who lack this acceptance, particularly if they are her superiors. In one of her very rare critiques of the Party, on June 16, 1970, concerning his withdrawal to safety in the face of danger, she exclaims: "It is laughable that the commissioner for the clinic dare not stay with us. He refuses to stay with me .... What else is there to say?" (Dang 221).

Occasionally, Dang's steely resolve is tempered by human frailty that is honestly admitted. On February 19, 1969, she writes cautiously: "And it seems there is a shade of regret in my worries. If the things we fear come to pass, I am ready to die for the final victory. The coming responsibility is so huge I do not want to face reality, for I will only see doubts and impasses" (Dang 93). And in one of the most moving passages of her diary, Dang confesses on August 5, 1969: "Perhaps I will meet the enemy, and perhaps I will fall, but I hold my medical bag firmly regardless, and people will feel sorry for this girl who was sacrificed for the revolution when she was still young and full of verdant dreams" (146). It is here that Dang's humanity overwhelms many readers.

"The other two evaded off the trail"[26]—Mass Appeal Abroad: The Impact of Gender and the Gendering of Dang's Writing

Thirty-five years after Dang's death on a battlefield in South Viet Nam, Dang Thuy Tram's diaries met with wide, positive international acclaim. Particularly in America, home to the "bloodthirsty devils," "bandits," and "imperialists" of her diary, reception was fairly positive (Dang 121, 173, 114). For a deeply committed woman cadre who could never envision that the non–Communist choice of the (Southern) Republic of Viet Nam was a valid option, and who denounced the Southern government as "traitors," this was a remarkable posthumous welcome (Dang 128).

While Dang's diaries were considered "of no military value" by American intelligence in 1970, careful study of them would have revealed much about the mindset of the Communist opponent (Dang xvi). Understanding that the enemy's motivation to fight was as strong as America's resolve, expressed by John F. Kennedy's famous commitment that America would "pay any price, bear any burden" to defend global liberty, Dang's commitment to "Peace and Independence" echoed the American pursuit of "Peace with Honor." In the end, reconciliation between two bitter enemies could come only decades after one side's military victory.

Publication of Dang's diaries also serves to aid historical research, particularly as U.S. scholarship traditionally depended on South Vietnamese sources for Vietnamese perspectives on the war in Vietnam. Viet Thanh Nguyen states: "When it comes to the war in Vietnam and its literary aftermath, what is noticeable is how differently construed these emotions are" in the South and the North (151). Dang's diaries contribute to a fresh view of the emotions and judgments of this war from a North Vietnamese perspective. This is not always a welcome sign to exilic Vietnamese in the diaspora, but this attitude is changing.

Success and popularity of literature is not always about doing something revolutionary or new. There is nothing absolutely new about Dang's diaries except that they survived her and gave her a voice.[27] Because it is what especially Vietnamese audiences can consider feminine writing, the poignancy of the end of her last entry before her death on June 20, 1970, resonates strongly:

> No, I am no longer a child. I have grown up. I have passed trials of peril, but somehow at this moment, I yearn deeply for Mom's caring hand. Even the hand

> of a dear one or that of an acquaintance would be enough. Come to me, squeeze my hand, know my loneliness, and give me the love, the strength to prevail on the perilous road before me [Dang 225].

This kind of agonizing need and extreme yearning for human touch can be read as universal for all humanity. It clearly appealed to Vietnamese and international audiences.

Dang has left behind a powerful legacy of a young, ideologically committed woman who conveyed her sentiments concerning conflicting emotions, responsibilities, and personal human desires and yearnings. As Dang wrote on April 12, 1969, "Why is your heart ruled by sorrow and yearning when it is supposed to be totally devoted to the Party? But...the Party does not say a communist's heart knows only reason and work" (Dang 107). There was ample room in Dang's mind and heart for more than Party discipline. Yet her life was cut too short for her to explore and experience to the fullest this private side of her life.

Notes

1. In Western references, diacritical marks in Vietnamese words are almost always eliminated, and we follow that (unfortunate) decision with the exception of this poem.

2. Trinh Cong Son (1939–2001) was an extraordinary lyricist, writer, musician/composer, and painter. He is often considered the Bob Dylan of Viet Nam.

3. In Vietnamese convention and usage, last/family name (Dang) appears first, followed by personal middle name (Thuy), and first name (Tram). In scholarly and other references, Dang's name appears in this order and we follow suit. The author refers to herself by her personal middle name, as all her three sisters shared her first name.

4. All biographical details are from Dang, Tram Thuy. *Last Night I Dreamed of* Peace.

5. Throughout, when we refer to the country, we will spell it Viet Nam, as is the preferred national version. However, for the war, we use the Western term "Vietnam War," or "American War," as it is known in Viet Nam.

6. Dang was admitted to the Party on September 27, 1968 (Dang 55).

7. For the sake of convenience, we generally use the American/Western term for this conflict.

8. Dang, September 27, 1968 (55).

9. See, for example, the promotional writing on the back flap of the American paperback edition, the choice of a female writer for its introduction, etc.

10. This passage is our translation from the Vietnamese.

11. This passage is our translation from the Vietnamese.

12. I.e., Sơn Khả Vương's Vietnamese memoir entitled *Kỳ Ức Chiến Tranh* (2006) or, in our translation, "memory of war."

13. Scanned version available online at *http://www.archive.vietnam.ttu.edu/resources/tram_diary/*. Accessed on June 25, 2010.

14. Entries are written for each marked day in a handwriting that shows its author's penmanship, trained at Ha Noi's Chu Van An's high school in the late 1950's. For Dang's high school, see Dang vi.

15. Khuong became a captain in the North Vietnamese Army and survived the war to marry another woman. When she fell, Dang carried a picture of Khuong and poems written to him.

16. At this time, Thuan apparently became exasperated with Dang's refusal of romance and became engaged to a fellow medic named Cuc; Thuan was killed by South Vietnamese forces in 1971.

17. Northern male war veteran Bao Ninh's novel *The Sorrows of War* (1996) contains passages which read like a diary, but are fiction. The early novels of Vietnam's pre-eminent woman writer Duong Thu Huong also address the war experience and are in part based on Duong's participation as a woman auxiliary for the North.

18. Duc Pho district of Quang Ngai Province was a hotbed of Communist insurrection and subsequently heavily destroyed by American forces (Dang xii–xiv).

19. The American soldier and intelligence officer is Fred Whitehurst, whose job was to sort out captured documents for U.S. military intelligence. He was about to burn the first diary when his interpreter, Nguyen Trung Hieu, advised him to save it. Whitehurst saved this diary and later a second one in 1970. Against regulations, he took the diaries home with him to the U.S. in 1972. In 2005, Whitehurst and his brother took the diaries to a conference at Texas Tech University. There he made connections and through networking, he was able to locate Dang's family in Vietnam.

20. Directed by Dang Nhat Minh.

21. Dang, 12 May 1968 (19).

22. Dang echoes an ideological assumption that almost all Vietnamese of her time longed for Communist rule, which is not borne out by historical fact.

23. April 12, 1969 (Dang 107).

24. All biographical information in this paragraph is from Dang v–vi.

25. Actually, Dang would only be admitted to the Party nine months later on September 27, 1968. Here, her wishes for this event clouded her writing.

26. After action report of D Company, 4th Battalion, 21st U.S. Infantry, on the engagement of June 22, 1970, that killed Dang and Boi out of a group of four antagonists in Duc Pho district.

27. Compare, for example, Marie Vassiltchikoff, *Berlin Diaries, 1940–1945* (1987), about a White Russian in the service of Germany.

WORKS CITED

Alway, Joan. "The Trouble with Gender: Tales of the Still-Missing Feminist Revolution in Sociological Theory." *Sociological Theory* 13.3 (1995): 209–228. Print.

Brownley, Martine Watson, and Allison B. Kimmich, eds. *Women and Autobiography*. Wilmington, DE: Scholarly Resources, Inc., 1999. Print.

Dang, Tram Thuy. *Last Night I Dreamed of Peace: The Diary of Dang Thuy Tram*. Trans. Andrew X. Pham. New York: Three River Press, 2007. Print.

Doan, Thi Cam. "Dang Thuy Tram, a Variable and an Unknown: Opening *The Diary of Dang Thuy Tram* Forty Years Later." *Journal of Vietnamese Studies* 3.2 (2008): 208–217. Print.

Duong, Wendy N. "Gender Equality and Women's Issues in Vietnam: The Vietnamese Woman-Warrior and Poet." *Pacific Rim Law and Policy Journal* 10.2 (2001): 191–326. Print.

Hanson, Susan. "Geography and Feminism: Worlds in Collision?" *Annals of the Association of American Geographers* 82.4 (1992): 569–586. Print.

Le, Phong. "Tù NhậtKký Đặng Thùy Trâm Sau Khoảng Lặng 30 Năm." *Báo Mới.com*, 26 July 2010. Web. 9 August 2010.

Nguyen, Chung Ba. "The Long Road Home: Exile, Self-Recognition, and Reconstruction." *Manoa* 14.1 (Summer 2002): 34–44. Print.

Nguyen, Tam, and An Nguyen. ""Hiện Tượng" Nhật Ký Đặng Thùy Trâm." *Radio Free Asia.com*. 26 November 2006. Web. 9 August 2010.

Nguyen, Viet Thanh. "Remembering War, Dreaming Peace: On Cosmopolitanism, Compassion, and Literature." *The Japanese Journal of American Studies* 20 (2009): 149–174. Print.

Phan, Aimee. "A Daughter Returns Home — Through Her Diaries," *USATODAY.com*. 12 October 2005. Web. 9 August 2010.

Schiwy, Marlene A. *A Voice of Her Own: Women and the Journey Writing Journey.* New York: Fireside, 1996. Print.

Shiffman, Adrienne. ""Burn What They Should Not See": The Private Journal as Public Text in A. S. Byatt's *Possession.*" *Tulsa Studies in Women's Literature* 20.1 (Spring 2001): 93–106. Print.

Stewart, Pamela. "'Taking One's Part in the Revolution': A Comparison of Women's Labor As Tools of Revolutionary Change in France, Vietnam and Poland." *Working U.S.A.: The Journal of Labor and Society* 11 (2008): 499–522. Print.

7

When Talk Meets Page: The Feminist Aesthetic of Adapted Narration and Language Play

Melissa Ames

In *Space, Time, and Perversion: Essays on the Politics of Bodies,* Elizabeth Grosz addresses the somewhat problematic criteria that often label texts as feminist, feminine, or women-centered. She argues that the four most common determinants of whether a text can be classified as feminist circulate around the sex of the author, the sex of the reader, the content of the text, or the style of the text (Grosz 12). Grosz rejects these criteria in favor of the claim that in order to be feminist a text must "render the patriarchal or phallocentric presumptions governing its contexts and commitments visible," "problematize the standard masculinist ways in which the author occupies the position of enunciation," and "facilitate the production of new and perhaps unknown, unthought discursive spaces — new styles, modes of analysis and argument, new genres and forms — that contest the limits and constraints currently at work in the regulation of textual production and reception" (22–3). Grosz is correct in arguing that the first four mandates are insufficient in titling a piece feminist. The two resting on the biological anatomy of the producer or receiver of the text are problematic, for a male or female can create works of feminist intent just as both can consume them thereafter. Denying the fact that much of women's media is tied to some common themes and/or subject matter would be to turn a blind eye to a very visible truth; to reduce works to their content alone, however, is to miss the bigger picture of how they operate. And here is where this chapter diverges from Grosz's assertion that a feminist text does not have "a distinctively feminine style" (22). Although it is true that not all feminists text share "*a* distinctively feminine style," many tap into common aesthetic stylistic practices to accomplish their goals—the very goals that Grosz claims make texts feminist to begin with (22, emphasis added). While this essay does follow Grosz's call for anti-essentialist readings of texts that might be called "feminist" or "feminine," it does not overlook the fact that a vast majority of them do use similar aesthetic patterns, nor does it rule out the idea that these styles themselves are functioning as feminist. To clarify, it is true that these texts are not feminine due to any anatomical means, but in practice (through their strategic design) they are historically feminist. It is often through adopting, and mutating, noticeably feminine stylistic trademarks that texts are able to draw attention to the androcentric positioning of the role of the author and the text's inevitable tie to the patriarchal world in which it originates. But more importantly, quite often it is the text's ability to capitalize on "distinctively feminine style*(s)*" that allows it to "facilitate the production of new and perhaps unknown, unthought discursive spaces" (Grosz 22, 23). I call these new discursive spaces, which feminist texts comfortably inhabit, the space in-between, and the process through which they are systematically created, *la production feminine.* I coin this term with the French Feminist's concept of "*écriture féminine*" in mind. Whereas their term refers specifically to a type of strategic feminist writing, I alter the terminology to open up the possibility of other types of strategic feminist production—cinematic, televisual, artistic, etc. The notion of "*la production feminine*" would not exclude writing; it simply provides a broader (more functional) conceptual framework.

A key characteristic of such texts is that they are—in the terminology of John Fiske—producerly. Fiske, speaking of television in particular, expanded on Roland Barthes's conceptualization of readerly and writerly texts in order to theorize those that seem to be both simultaneously. Fiske explains that a readerly text is "one which 'reads' easily, does not foreground its own nature as discourse, and appears to promote a singular meaning which is not that of the text, but of the real," while a writerly text "is multiple and full of contradictions, it foregrounds its own nature as discourse and resists coherence or unity" (94). Using these two notions, Fiske argues that a producerly text combines the complex "characteristics of a writerly text with the easy accessibility of the readerly" and that it "relies on the discursive competencies that the (reader) already possesses, but requires that they are used in a self-interested, productive way" (95). The argument presented here is that most feminist texts reside in the space in-between writerly and readerly and are, therefore, producerly; they consist of layered semantic levels, allow for multiple readings and interpretations, and promote active consumption, but they do it under the guise of simplicity with part of their surface goals (which are often the focus of analyses based solely on subject matter alone and not functionality) available at a glance, easily consumed, and understood. Many texts crafted for women (the chick flick, soap, or harlequin, to list just a few) are often reduced to the latter half of this combination (their readerly traits), and it is only when these texts are more properly studied that the former (their writerly attributes) becomes noticeable and one can see that there is much more going on than first meets the eye with these feminine texts.

This chapter analyzes texts that fall on both ends of the spectrum — texts that are often juxtaposed against one another as arch enemies or polar opposites, narratives from across the aesthetic continuum of print literature. For example, Zora Neale Hurston's modernist novel *Their Eyes Were Watching God* will be read against a variety of novels — all of which might be classified as ethnic feminist literature. This part poses the possibility that authors of subordinate status (in relation to gender or race) might strategically utilize this space in-between to create producerly texts that better meet the needs of their particular politics. When one historically does not have (or has not had) access to the official written language, oral communication arises as an alternate strategy. These authors acknowledge this historical fact and enduring communication tactic by highlighting orality and weaving it into their print fictions.

Crossing the literary divide, Margaret Atwood's experimental postmodern novel, *The Handmaid's Tale*, will be analyzed against selected excerpts of *écriture féminine*: works by Hélène Cixous, Luce Irigaray, and Monique Wittig. This grouping showcases the strategic ways that "speech" or "voice" is translated into (or encoded within) print. The subversive qualities of oral communication (even when transported onto the printed page) will continue to be discussed with these examples, as will the possible benefits of gendered communication patterns and/or stylistics.

The literature grouped with Hurston will serve as examples of works that would usually be classified as readerly (although not necessarily correctly so), while the writings of Atwood, Cixous, Irigaray, and Wittig will represent pieces more likely to be classified as writerly. By studying these groups together it will become clear that, though at a glance they appear quite different, they function in many of the same ways, share aesthetic practices, a certain politics, and work through many of the same women-oriented issues. Analyzing these pieces together makes it clear that similar stylistic practices are being used and shared social critiques are being carried through. However, seeking out similarities across the readerly/writerly, oral/print spectrums is not enough. In comparing the aesthetics of these works that could be classified as feminist, I will attend to the ways that the specific format/style of the product affects its utility. The question that surfaces is this: how does the complexity of a work in the same medium (i.e. from traditional storytelling to experimental postmodern narrative) affect the piece's potential for subversive readings and/or oppositional use?

Talking Pages: Strategic Orality and Feminist Literature

That language is not an innocent tool — one operating without intent, without consequence, without covert agenda — is no longer a hidden truth. The task here is to see how language, in the form of storytelling on the written page, is acting as a tool for feminist means. The selected texts loosely termed "feminist literature" all share one hard-to-miss tactic: a stylistic device impossible to overlook that acts as the tie that binds them all together in a flexible union. Each of these texts, though printed and consumed via the typed page, capitalizes on the oral tradition often associated with women's culture. The focus on orality is foregrounded rather clearly in *Their Eyes Were Watching God*, as the novel co-opts the oral nature of storytelling by having the tale (written in dialect) narrated through a conversation between longtime friends. In a quite different way, the idea of orality is translated into print in *The Handmaid's Tale* because Atwood's novel rests on the premise that the narrative itself came into being when cassette tapes housing a recorded version of the story by an anonymous narrator were discovered and the tale was decoded and transcribed. Since these two texts are quite different from one another it probably is not surprising that they have not been read against each other in other scholarly analyses. What is interesting, however, is that although much scholarship exists concerning Hurston's use of dialect and the novel's obvious focus on oral storytelling, Atwood's text does not receive the same attention in this regard. Furthermore, it should be clarified that the majority of the work on orality in *Their Eyes Were Watching God* focuses more on the oral tradition in relation to African American culture and folklore rather than women's culture and/or female storytelling praxis. One scholar who bridges the two concepts is Beverly Yvonne Lumumba. She reads *Their Eyes* alongside of other texts that she calls "listenerly" and demonstrates how they portray "the storytelling experience of the African American oral tradition and black feminist theory" (Lumumba 217). Despite the vast amount of research already done on orality in *Their Eyes*, what seems to be lacking are comparative readings that discuss the utility of this aesthetic and the probable reason that authors outside of dominant culture might find this stylistic device empowering.

Their Eyes Were Watching God is the story of Janie Crawford, her journey of independent self-discovery and the pain, love, and loss that accompany it along the way. Like much of life and storytelling, her tale and travels are that of one circle: "Ah done been tuh de horizon and back" (Hurston 191). Written almost entirely in dialect, this text, as previously mentioned, foregrounds not only women's oral tradition but also that of African American culture and folklore. Importantly, the entire text is told; it unfolds as an extended flashback narrative — in one single nighttime, catch-up porch conversation (just out of sight and earshot of the gossiping community in the backdrop) between Janie and her best friend, Pheoby. Janie's choice to break her silence and tell her tale sparks the beginning of this novel and a plethora of scholarly debates surrounding whether or not this act is self-empowering.

Scholarly analyses of *Their Eyes* differ as to whether Janie's story actually has any power once she does break her silence. Many of the arguments focus on Hurston's choice of point-of-view and its benefit (or lack thereof) for Janie as a character, as well as its effect on the reader/listener (imagined or real) of her fictional tale. Anne McCart Drolet praises the work, claiming "Hurston's third-person omniscient narrator creates a 'womanist' voice of an African American woman who 'talks back' to both the white culture's racist expectation of subservience and lack of 'civilization,' and her own African-American community's sexism and colorist attitudes" (3027). Likewise, Christine Marie Parke-Sutherland commends Hurston's use of this experimental point of view to create what she calls a "relational 'we,'" claiming that this practice increases the novel's overall effect on the reader (3599). Parke-Sutherland defines this strategically used point-of-view as one that highlights the power/knowledge relationship and the relational subjectivity "constructed between the verbal-ideological worlds of authors, narrators, characters, and readers" (3599). However, not all academics have praised Hurston in this regard. Ryan Simmons summarizes the many criticisms of *Their Eyes*, analyzing at length Hurston's curious choice of point-of-view. Many scholars have argued that in having the tale told by an omniscient third-person narrator, rather than a first-person one, Hurston implies that Janie has not in fact won her voice and self—a crucial point of this work according to most feminist readings (Simmons 182). Simmons questions whether "Hurston is intentionally illustrating 'women's exclusion from power, particularly from the power of oral speech'" (182). This latter read would be quite different from this one, which sees Hurston's use of the oral tradition—third-person narration aside—as highlighting women's success within that communication milieu. *Their Eyes* illustrates women's exclusion from the power of *written* communication and their subsequent success in oral culture as a result. Hence, Hurston's blending of oral speech and written word, to an extent that the former overpowers the latter in its own genre—the print novel—can be seen as a purposeful acknowledgement of (and rebellion against) this patriarchal communication mandate.

Although women may not have been given much of a choice concerning their banishment from the realm of written word into that of the oral, Hurston's novel demonstrates the accidental (and sometimes detrimental) power women gained through this placement. This novel opens with a scene that highlights the power of women's talk, in particular the gossip culture into which they have been indoctrinated.

> Seeing the woman as she was made them remember the envy they had stored up from other times. So they chewed up the back parts of their minds and swallowed with relish. They made burning statements with questions, and killing tools out of laughs. It was mass cruelty. A mood come alive. Words walking without masters; walking altogether like harmony in a song.
>
> 'What she doin' coming back here in dem overhalls? Can't she find no dress to put on?—Where's dat blue satin dress she left here in?—Where all dat money her husband took and died and left her?—What dat ole forty year ole 'oman doin' wid her hair swingin' down her back lak some young gal...' [Hurston 2].

This novel uses the actual spoken words of the characters to showcase a negative side of women's culture where the dialogue between the female characters broadcasts the ways women have been socialized to judge one another and utilize their words as weapons in the task.

This text, although full of complicated nuances and important messages, would seem to (at a glance) fall into the aforementioned classification of readerly. After all, the author does not strive to lose her reader, the storyline once worked through is rather straightforward, and all narrative play (whether it concerns the language of the narrative tale or the temporal disruption present in the plot) can be overlooked if one focuses more heavily on storyline rather than style. Although this classification makes sense, it could also be argued that Hurston's text is actually producerly—it is portraying itself as readerly to undercut its writerly qualities.

Just as some literary works have their writerly characteristics overlooked, so do some (seemingly writerly) pieces have their readerly traits ignored. This is often the case with more experimental literature. The next pieces discussed do not necessarily read with the same ease as a novel like *Their Eyes*; they often remind readers of their status as text and highlight the use and abuse of language. These more writerly texts come in the form of postmodern novels like Atwood's *The Handmaid's Tale* and more experimental, overtly feminist, writings by women such as Wittig, Cixous, and Irigaray.

The Handmaid's Tale shares some characteristics with Hurston's text; it too is an oral story although this fact is only fully explained in its closing appendix with the fictionalized part entitled "Historical Notes." It is the story of a nameless narrator, allowed only the servitudal name of "Offred" (depicting her status as the property "of Fred," her master), and it begins *in media res*. Readers meet Offred in the midst of the early years of the Gilead regime's restructuring, and through her meandering story only learn bits and pieces of the world she knew before and how her current reality came into existence. It is the historical notes that aim to fill in the blanks. The appendix offers readers "a partial transcript of the proceedings of the Twelfth Symposium on Gileadean Studies, held as part of the International Historical Association

Convention held at the University of Denay, Nunavit, on June 25, 2195" (Atwood 299). The keynote speaker, Professor James Darcy Pieixoto, delivers his talk entitled "Problems of Authentication in Reference to *The Handmaid's Tale*" (Atwood 300). Through Pieixoto's monologue readers learn that the story they have just read is supposed to have been a constructed manuscript, one created by the piecing together and re-ordering of thirty decoded cassette tapes (re-ordered and translated, ironically, by two *male* scholars), so the story, indeed, is an oral one. In less than ten pages, Atwood allows her fictionalized academic persona to give the historical overview of the pre–Gilead period (which would be the time period of the novel's actual creation, the late twentieth century), the rise of the Gilead regime, and vague allusions to the remapped, re-ordered world present in its aftermath. Humorously, this added part, which does provide many answers but also prevents full closure with the myriad of questions it then begs, ends with the speaker's logical closing line: "Are there any questions?" (Atwood 311). Atwood's piece draws attention to its status as text — the postmodern play of text-within-text-and demonstrates one way in which a novel like this could be more readily classified as writerly.

Subversive Stylistics: *Écriture Féminine* and Beyond

It is interesting to look at the works of the French Feminists in conjunction with this more traditionally narrative-based text in order to see that all of these diverse selections are actually aligned in many ways. A solid starting point lies in the explanations that each writer gives for her own writing or the practice of crafting *écriture féminine*. Like Grosz, Cixous cautions: "[g]reat care must be taken in working on feminine writing not to get trapped by names: to be signed with a woman's name doesn't necessarily make a piece of writing feminine" — it is not an act tied to biology by any means ("Castration" 52). She also argues that it is not a new language being created but "[a] virgin way of listening and making the always newold language speak" (Cixous, *Reader* xxi). According to her, a feminine text is unpredictable, sometimes disturbing, it "starts on all sides at once, starts twenty times, thirty times, over," is always endless, without closure, it "goes on and on and at a certain moment the volume comes to an end but the writing continues and for the reader this means being thrust into the void" (Cixous, "Castration" 53). Irigaray discusses *écriture féminine*'s ability to draw attention to the fragmented identity of women, to reject masculinist valuings, and attack different senses (primarily that of touch). Irigaray argues that such texts manage to accomplish these tasks while simultaneously crafting a seamless fluid end product.

The question surfaces: *what does writing itself do*? Is writing itself active enough; can it promote political change? On the benefits of writing, Cixous claims: "[w]hen I write, language remembers without my knowing or indeed with my knowing" (*Reader* xxi). It is a practice of "un-forgetting, of un-silencing, of unearthing, of unblinding oneself, and of un-deafening oneself" (Cixous, *Reader* 83). The follow-up question then might be: why struggle for a *female* writing? In fact, is such really possible? Teresa de Lauretis argues it is possible and beneficial: "[w]riting ... presupposes possession of the phallus — symbolically speaking; and for a woman to write is to usurp a place, a discursive position, she does not have by nature or by culture" (80). On the contrary, Wittig would argue *not* to embark on a quest for a specifically female form of writing, that such a thing does not exist, that the term *écriture féminine* is merely an academic invention, a term spawned in part from women's domination and political backlash. She writes:

> That there is no "feminine writing" must be said at the outset, and one makes a mistake in using and giving currency to this expression. What is this "feminine" in "feminine writing?" It stands for Woman, thus merging a practice with a myth, the myth of Woman. "Woman" cannot be associated with writing because "Woman" is an imaginary formation and not a concrete reality... "Feminine writing" is the naturalizing metaphor of the brutal political fact of the domination of women, and as such it enlarges the apparatus under which "femininity" presents itself [Wittig 59].

But as her statement implies, she is against the terminology and the conceptualization more so than the actual practice of women writing — or even in writing in a particular purposeful way. Wittig would not argue against the power of writing, but against the notion of a writing linked to the myth of Woman, one that would perhaps exaggerate culturally indoctrinated traits of said universal Woman. However, the practice (terminology aside) does not necessarily need to be seen as linked to the mark of gender. *Écriture féminine* is a political tactic; it adopts stylistic devices that may fly under the banner of feminine to some extent, but it does so for an ultimate goal. The aesthetic itself is *functional*, even if it does, indeed, have some underlying tie to stereotypes concerning the constructed genders. Also, despite her dislike of the term, arguably it is a practice that she actually carries through, for not many would find a problem with characterizing her novel *The Lesbian Body* as an instance of *écriture féminine* with its shared aesthetic trademarks and feminist motifs.

Écriture féminine allows for the expression of multiplicity, the sex which is not simply *one* or singular, as one of the many interpretations of Irigaray's infamous title implies. Cixous writes: "[i]t is not a question of making the subject disappear, but of giving it back its divisibility" (*Reader* 29). *Écriture féminine* allows the writer to step outside of the male logic, and it acts as a tool to allow "woman to negotiate a place for herself within a symbolic order designed to protect the masculine" (Cixous, *Reader* 71). It does this often by purposely sidestepping the linear narrative style of masculine authorship; it critiques the pronouns enforced by patriarchal culture; and it crosses subject matter thresholds crucial to feminist means. But *écriture féminine* is not alone in any of these goals — the end products of *écriture féminine* just broadcast their intent more vocally. All of the texts referenced here can be seen doing many of the same things.[1]

Where Spoken Speech and Written Word Align: Giving Voice to Feminist Themes

One common goal of all of these texts is to give voice to their female protagonist(s). By making these women speaking subjects, their identities are developed, and their stories are shared and hopefully remembered. Returning to the example of *Their Eyes Were Watching God*, although the experiences Janie has in Hurston's novel are important, they have no power to affect anyone besides herself while she remains silent. In having Janie re-live her experiences through the oral recap to Pheoby, Hurston, like many feminist writers, develops the idea of speaking to share, speaking to be understood, speaking to pass on wisdom, and speaking in order to remember (and have others remember). Another excellent literary example of a text that tackles this goal is Gayl Jones's novel *Corregidora*. This work (notably another text, created by an African American writer, that might be classified as "feminist") attacks female orality from a different angle — through that of the blues song. Jones tells the tale of the protagonist's, Ursa's, struggle to come to terms with her own emotional and sexual trauma, the psychological repercussions of her abusive slave heritage (both on her and her maternal ancestors before her), and the daily fight to survive in the racist, sexist world that suffocates her ability to stand and speak on her own terms. To clarify, her story is not simply told — it is sung. Jones's text is one of inner monologue juxtaposed with flashback and blues lyrics, repeating, circling back in the call and response refrain ways of blues music itself and, not unimportantly, feminist storytelling in general. Specifically, in *Corregidora* four generations of women share their stories through the lips of Ursa who has been trained to tell the tale over and over so as to "never forget" (Jones 9).[2] The women whose pain and hardships are captured in Ursa's tale are nameless throughout the text; they themselves remain for the most part voiceless, but her songs allows them and their story to exist, to matter, to live on. Both of these examples demonstrate the power of oral communication to translate experience and feeling from speaker to listener (fictional or real). While these two selections show storytelling between women taking the form of personal conversation and stylized performance, these are obviously not the only avenues for such moments of oral sharing to occur. Quite often (in fiction and reality) such moments of spoken "show-and-tell" are often more blunt and even didactic — as is the case in most spoken speech that takes the form of advice giving.

In *The Handmaid's* Tale, the narrator remembers the years before the political upheaval and the family moments she used to share with her husband and feminist mother:

> Her hair was gray by that time, of course. She wouldn't dye it. Why pretend, she'd say. Anyway, what do I need it for, I don't want a man around, what use are they except for ten seconds' worth of half babies. A man is just a woman's strategy for making other women (...) They aren't a patch on a woman except they're better at fixing cars and playing football, just what we need for the improvement of the human race, right? That was the way she talked, even in front of Luke. He didn't mind, he teased her by pretending to be macho, he'd tell her women were incapable of abstract thought and she'd have another drink and grin at him. Chauvinist pig, she'd say. Isn't she quaint, Luke would say to me, and my mother would look sly, furtive almost. I'm entitled, she'd say. I'm old enough, I've paid my dues, it's time for me to be quaint. You're still wet behind the ears. Piglet, I should have said. As for you, she'd say to me, you're just a backlash. Flash in the pan. History will absolve me [Atwood 120–121].

Although this passage crosses the line between advice giving and preaching, the foundation still is the speaker's experience. As in all advice, the narrator's mother's life experiences (her "story") motivate the words she passes on to her daughter. And, as is true to some extent with all literary works, these words also stem from the social experiences (and resultant cultural commentary) of the author herself— for which the novel is often both praised and criticized.[3]

Regardless of the form of the speech (conversation, song, or diatribe), on some level the goal seems the same: to foster woman-to-woman bonds. Quite often these texts drenched in orality focus specifically on female storytelling as a device to create intergenerational bonds. While many feminist texts tackle this theme, it should not go unnoted that a vast majority of literary works that do so could be classified minority/ethnic texts. For example, Louise Erdrich's *Love Medicine,* Amy Tan's *The Kitchen God's Wife,* and Alice Walker's *The Color Purple,* to list just a few, all touch on the function of storytelling within family structures. *Love Medicine* incorporates the orality of women's storytelling through the intergenerational story of two intricately linked Native American families, the Kashpaws and the Lamartines. It is a story of lying and truth telling, of secret keeping and secret sharing, of the power of words both said and unsaid. Similarly, although progressing in a slightly less complicated fashion, *The Kitchen God's Wife* also foregrounds women's oral culture through the story of Pearl Louie and her mother, Winnie. Like Erdrich's story, this is one of two interwoven culturally hybrid families — the Chinese American Louies and the Kwongs. One final example of this nature is *The Color Purple*, which offers up a different type of orality, a type of talk/communication that relies on paper for enunciation. Walker's novel is comprised completely of letters — letters written by the main character, Celie, to God (in the vein of diary-esque entries) and her estranged sister, Nettie, and those of Nettie in return to Celie. All of these novels focus on oral storytelling's potential to bridge intergenerational gaps and foster close interpersonal bonds between women.

Beyond the focus on orality, these examples of feminist literature also share something else quite important: a non-traditional narrative pattern that connects them to writings of the French Feminists and the postmodern praxis of writers like Atwood. Although, like Hurston's novel, each of these works could easily (although problematically) be classified as "readerly," much is going on beneath their easily "read" storylines. For example, Erdrich's text has a fragmented nonlinear narrative style and incorporates several first-person speakers, constantly shifting points of view, both temporally and perspectively. Unlike Erdrich though, Tan tells her story exclusively through the alternating first-person narrative accounts of the mother-daughter pairing and capitalizes on the device of flashback to intersect the storylines. Walker's novel differs from the two examples in that it progresses primarily in chronological order. However, like Hurston, Walker uses vocabulary reminiscent of slave narrative and folk vernacular full of figures of speech and rhythmic patterns of African American women's culture and frames her novel in a very postmodern text-within-a-text fashion as the narrative unfolds through a series of "letters" by different characters. These examples again show the producerly status of texts written by authors outside of dominant culture. These novels — with their merging of oral and print culture — allow (and even covertly encourage) their straightforward narratives to overshadow their complex, strategic aesthetic design and (purposely) mask many of their underlying goals.

One of these goals is to entertain a theme that, at first, might seem to contradict their heavy focus on women's speech. All of these novels pose the question of when to speak and when to keep silent. In these moments, the focus is not on the affectually-charged nature of women's speech (and the bonds that such speech creates) but the political and/or personal implications of speaking up in general. In recent years, the practice of having female characters speak up when they normally would not has shifted from the private/personal realm into the more public/political realm. Many postmodern literary works aim to speak that which societal codes forbid, to break them down — hence, the emphasis on subject matter considered taboo and the call for using forbidden or unacceptable languages. This arguably is the battle cry of the French Feminists as well; it is the practice implemented in their *écriture féminine*; it is the practice carried through in more subtle ways in the feminist literature, walking a fine line between the oral and the written, the readerly and the writerly.

Until this point the analysis of these texts has focused on how they work, but it is also important to analyze *why* they work as they do. Their narrative structures are purposeful and often tied to the material they deal with. These pieces all offer up moments of social critique, many centered on patriarchal society and the constructed nature of gender created by it. Sometimes these motifs are the driving force behind the work, sometimes just a line tucked away to be teased out. At other times it is a recurrent tackling of important social issues. For example, Hurston addresses the double oppression (sexism coupled with racism) which women of color experience through this part of character dialogue:

> "Honey, de white man is de ruler of everything as fur as Ah been able tuh find out. Maybe it's some place way off in de ocean where de black man is in power, but we don't know nothin' but what we see. So de white man throw down de load and tell de nigger man tuh pick it up. He pick it up because he have to, but he don't tote it. He hand it to his womenfolks. De nigger woman is de mule uh de world so fur as Ah can see..." [14].

She also addresses the stereotypes often associated with women and the inevitable shutdown that many women experience having to live out their existence in such rigid roles. Take for example this first spoken comment by Janie's husband Joe and her resulting internal thoughts "'Somebody got to think for women and chillun and chickens and cows. I god, they sho don't think none theirselves'"; "So gradually, she pressed her teeth together and learned to hush. The spirit of the marriage left the bedroom and took to living in the parlor. It was there to shake hands whenever company came to visit, but it never went back inside the bedroom again" (Hurston 71, 72). Although the various societal concerns these works attend to are important, the way these works operate is more so. These works enable feminist concerns to live on past the pages, the front and back covers that keep them bound, because the stories themselves do not end — like the problems they tackle, these pieces refuse to reach closure and, hence, refuse to conform to the standard of storytelling.

Walter Benjamin argues that "the art of storytelling is *coming to an end*," but ironically, the texts discussed here, very much in the vein of the oral storytelling tradition, reject this practice (83, emphasis added). Another crucial characteristic of storytelling for him is the practice of repetition: "[f]or storytelling is always the art of *repeating* stories" (Benjamin 91, emphasis added).

This, of course, is seen in feminine writing. Benjamin credited the written novel as the beginning of the end of storytelling — the death of this oral tradition — yet with *écriture féminine* and various forms of feminist fiction, the practice of storytelling is alive and well in print media. Concerning the repetitive endless nature of *écriture féminine* in particular, Cixous writes: women's "writing also can go on and on without ever inscribing or distinguishing contours," that "[a] feminine textual body is recognized by the fact that it is always endless, without ending: there's no closure, it doesn't stop, and it's this that very often makes the feminine text difficult to read: For we've learned to read books that basically pose the word 'end'" (*Reader*, 44, "Castration" 53).

The non-normative, oral narrative pattern of feminist work is not the only characteristic worthy of attention.[4] Like the written pieces, those resting in the visual arts realm also offer up hidden substance. Although this essay cannot do this discussion justice, other "feminist" texts can be analyzed to prove that the readerly and writerly blend — the producerly quality that is feminist art — is not tied to the written word (or the narrative tale) alone.

Conclusion

Returning to Grosz's key assertions concerning what makes a text feminist, it should now be clear that much of women's media actually fits her definition. The texts analyzed here, by addressing feminist concerns and foregrounding the constructed nature of gender, expose the phallocentric way in which texts do *not* have to operate. These women-oriented products raise questions concerning the authority, the fixity, of authorship and text — ironically (or not) very postmodern goals in general. And, most importantly, the pieces highlighted here prove that women's media — with their new genres, forms, and mutated stylistic practices — offer up innovative discursive spaces and modes of reception. These pieces from across the spectrum show that although all feminist texts do not share "*a* distinctively feminine style," they do operate in similar ways and do benefit by adopting shared feminine *styles* (Grosz 22, emphasis added).

It should also be clear from looking at these texts that the double stigma allotted to women's culture, its lowered status acquired by its association with the less dominant gender, has helped the producerly nature of feminist texts to go unnoticed. All too often texts such as these are only seen for their readerly qualities — the ease at which they can be digested, the surface level, the stereotypically feminine traits they broadcast. This readerly side often overshadows the complicated underbelly of the individual texts where the writerly aspects are alive and thriving out of the limelight (or patriarchal searchlight). Of course, it is true that many texts operate in this producerly fashion. After all, when John Fiske coined the term he was talking about televisual texts in general, and the majority of said texts are aimed at a mainstream (masculine) audience. But feminist texts do seem to systematically *use* this producerly space to their own advantage. These texts appear as a patchwork of meanings, interweaving levels that allow for diverse analyses and (active) use.

That many of these texts operate in this manner but are often only seen for their readerly side is not necessarily a detriment, nor is it necessarily an accident either. The readerly trumping the writerly (at a glance at least) in feminist texts can be seen as a defense tactic, a covert strategy of *la production feminine* that allows much of their purpose to go unnoticed, unchallenged, and, hence, unfeared by the police dogs in charge of securing the patriarchal status quo. So while many have been offended by the titling on women's media as throw away culture desperately hanging onto the bottom rung of the lowbrow ladder, the eye rolling and balking that these texts receive could be seen as a hidden positive — for as long as these texts are considered of minimal importance, glanced at and discarded with a blink of an eye, they remain a powerful tool to continue developing feminist work like the cultural secret agents that they are.

Notes

1. To clarify, I am not the first to suggest that these texts in particular could be considered variations of *écriture féminine*. Elaine Neil Orr suggests that Hurston is a practicioner of *écriture féminine* in *Their Eyes*. Likewise, in *The Cambridge Companion to Margaret Atwood*, the argument is made that many of Atwood's texts showcase her continuing engagement with the concept of *écriture féminine*.

2. Jones emphasizes this theme of speaking to remember to the point of spelling it out quite literally: "'My great-grandmamma told my grandmamma the part she lived through that my grandmamma didn't live through and my grandmamma told my mama what they both lived through and my mama told me what they all lived through and we were suppose to pass it down like that from generation to generation so we'd never forget'" (9).

3. Shirley Neuman argues that this dystopian "novel hypothesizes the logical extension not only of Puritan government but also of the agenda articulated during the 1980s by America's fundamentalist Christian Right" (857). Neuman views Offred, "a fictional product of 1970s," as a clever representative of the backlash against women's rights that Atwood would have witnessed in the early 1980s (856). However, Atwood's text is not always praised in academic circles. Kim Loudermilk condemns Atwood's response to (and corresponding narrative creation of) the feminist trends of the 1970s, 80s, and 90s. Loudermilk argues that Atwood creates a detrimental "fictional feminism" in *The Handmaid's Tale* (4469). She defines this "mythologized version" of feminism as being "uniformly antimale, antisex and politically ineffective" (as can be seen in part by the mother's tirade above) (4469). Loudermilk utilizes the term fictional feminism because she sees it as being "indeed, made-up" growing "out of fictional narratives, the stories we tell and are told about feminism" (4469). Far from being subversive and stimulating social change, Loudermilk reads novels such as *Handmaid* as working "to contain the potential of feminism to create any profound and lasting social change" with its perpetuated myths (4469).

4. Other scholars have noted this marriage of orality and print literature. In her study of Nora Zeale Hurston and Alice Walker, Africa Ragland Fine discusses the fact that "the relationship between oral and written communication is not a dichotomy, but a continuum when elements of both can coexist" (999). Her theorization of this phenomenon, which she terms "second orality," is much like my conceptualization of "producerly" texts. My reading of *Their Eyes* aligns with Fines's argument that Hurston draws attention to "communication that encompasses both oral and literate elements" and through this process helps "shape the theme and purpose of" the novel (999).

WORKS CITED

Benjamin, Walter. *Illuminations: Essays and Reflections.* Ed. Hanna Arendt. Trans. Harry Zohn. New York: Schocken Books, 1969. Print.

Cixous, Hélène. "Castration or Decapitation?" *Signs: Journal of Women in Culture and Society* 7.1. (Autumn 1981): 41–55. Print.

_____. *Hélène Cixous Reader.* 1979. Ed. Susan Sellers. New York: Routledge, 1994. Print.

de Lauretis, Teresa. *Technologies of Gender: Essays on Theory, Film, and Fiction.* Bloomington, IN: Indiana University Press, 1987. Print.

Erdrich, Louise. *Love Medicine.* 1984. New York: Perennial, 1993. Print.

Fine, Africa Ragland. "Second Orality in *Their Eyes Were Watching God* and *The Color Purple.*" Florida Atlantic University, 2001. *MAI* (2001): 999A.

Fiske, John. *Television Culture.* New York: Routledge, 1987. Print.

Grosz, Elizabeth. *Space, Time, and Perversion: Essays on the Politics of the Body.* New York: Routledge, 1995. Print.

Howells, Corall Ann, ed. *The Cambridge Companion to Margaret Atwood.* Cambridge: Cambridge University Press, 2006.

Hurston, Zora Neale. *Their Eyes Were Watching God.* 1937. New York: Harper and Row, 1990. Print.

Irigaray, Luce. *This Sex Which is Not One.* 1967. Trans. Catherine Porter and Carol Burke. Ithaca, New York: Cornell University Press, 1985. Print.

Jones, Gayl. *Corregidora.* 1975. Boston: Beacon Press, 1986. Print.

Lumumba, Beverly Yvonne. "Words without Masters: Harriet Jacobs' and Zora Neale Hurston's Listenerly Text." University of Colorado at Boulder, 1995. *DAI* 57 (1996): 217A.

Neuman, Shirley. "'Just a Backlash': Margaret Atwood, Feminism, and *The Handmaid's Tale.*" *University of Toronto Quarterly* 75.3 (Summer 2006): 857–868. Print.

Orr, Elaine Neil. *Subject to Negotiation: Reading Feminist Criticism and American Women's Fictions.* Charlottesville, University of Virginia Press, 1997. Print.

Parke-Sutherland, Christine Marie. "Imagining Relation: Otherness in American Women's Experimental Fiction." University of Michigan, 1991. *DAI* 52 (1992): 3599A.

Simmons, Ryan. "'The Hierarchy Itself': Hurston's *Their Eyes Were Watching God* and the Sacrafice of Narrative Authority." *African American Review* 36.2 (Summer 2002): 181–193. Print.

Tan, Amy. *The Kitchen God's Wife.* 1991. New York: Ivy Books, 1999. Print.

Walker, Alice. *The Color Purple.* 1982. New York: Harcourt Brace Jovanovich, 1992. Print.

Wittig, Monique. *The Straight Mind and Other Essays.* Boston: Beacon Press, 1992. Print.

8

Blurred Boundaries and Re-Told Histories: Julia Alvarez's *How the García Girls Lost Their Accents*

Sarah Himsel Burcon

Trinh T. Minh-Ha reflects on exiled people's "dehumanization" due to "relocation-reeducation-redefinition, the humiliation of having to falsify [their] own reality," maintaining that if exiled people do not speak upon relocating, they risk "being said" (246). "Being said" is a prevalent theme in Julia Alvarez's 1992 novel, *How the García Girls Lost Their Accents*. Alvarez resists being said by attempting to fill in some of the blanks of history. She accomplishes this, in part, through the storytelling strategies of narrative voice shifts and reverse chronology, both of which challenge ideas about the "normal" plot and structure of a novel. In addition to using these narrative devices to offer a fresh look at history, Alvarez tells a story that crosses social, historical, and ethnic divides, creating a space for inquiry into the intersection of story and history, as well as past, present, and future. By blurring the boundaries between genres and time periods, Alvarez invents new methods of remembering the past. Equally important, she draws attention to issues of gender oppression by re-telling a portion of history that has historically been viewed from a patriarchal viewpoint. Through her revision, or re-remembering, Alvarez demonstrates that history, like gender, is a social construct.

The notion of "memory" is not homogenous across time or across cultures. Frances Yates in her seminal text, *The Art of Memory,* traces the course of memory as it evolved as an art developed by the ancients through the end of the Renaissance. Yates explains how the art of memory began as a system in which rhetors would establish *loci* (literal places such as a room or a building) to house images of objects that would enable the rhetor to recall a speech at a later time (374). Memory, in that particular time and place, served a specific function: to facilitate speech recall. During the Middle Ages memory was employed to promote the spread of Christianity. Religious rituals like Communion, for example, worked to ensure that people became, or stayed, connected with their religious past and therefore became, or remained, good Christians (Yates 155). Alvarez employs memory for yet another function, and this is to problematize feminist concerns. Writing from two points of view simultaneously — Dominican and American — Alvarez utilizes memory, along with storytelling, to emphasize themes surrounding gender and identity. In her novel Alvarez both records and revises history to connect the past with the present, thus ensuring that her stories endure.

The García Girls is a semi-autobiographical story about exile. Alvarez tells of four sisters — Carla, Sandi, Sofía, and Yolanda — who, along with their parents, move from the Dominican Republic to New York. The Garcías are compelled to move due to the role the father, Carlos, played in a plot to overthrow Rafael Trujillo, dictator from 1930–1961.[1] Like the García sisters, Alvarez lived in the Dominican Republic during the Trujillo regime, and also like the Garcías, Alvarez experienced the pull of two different worlds and two different worldviews. Alvarez has commented that she considers herself a "hyphenated person" in that her narratives result from her living in two worlds that "sometimes clash and sometimes combine" (qtd. in Suárez 120). This observation speaks to her, and the García girls', dual identity as both American and Dominican women. In her novel Alvarez tells of the implications of a fractured identity, especially as it relates to gender given her interrogation of the experiences of Latina women moving back and forth between two cultures.[2] However, "identity" in *The García Girls* is much more complex than negotiating between two cultures. As David Mitchell points out, one of the goals of the postcolonial writer is to "destabilize the binary of the postcolonial writer's 'absence' from, or 'presence' in, a geographical homeland" (166). The novel is not merely a reflective narrative about dislocated people who present themselves differently depending upon their geographical location; rather, it is a narrative that complicates Western notions of identity and multiculturalism,[3] especially in regard to gender.

In addition to being semi-autobiographical, *The García Girls* is also based in part on historical fact. Peter Middleton and Tim Woods point out that "the sense of the past itself has changed and most readers no longer trust official histories to be reliable, since they recognize the degree to which all knowledge of the past is a construction" (65). Alvarez shows that history is indeed constructed, of myths about gender and identity for example. Just as important, though, she also shows that memories, recounted by way of her fictionalized family, are just as likely to be constructed. Through her use of a multi-narrational style, Alvarez highlights how memories of the past are adapted to fit the needs of the person recalling the event in the present. For example, when readers are exposed to Yolanda's version of the day they were forced to move from their home, they understand—after reading of other events told from different perspectives—that the story would be different if Fifi were telling the same story. These issues centering on identity and memory extend beyond the scope of the protagonist in this novel. Indeed, they have implications for any "hyphenated person" who has felt the pull of two distinct cultures that often collide at the same time that they combine.

Discussions of perspective and historicity point to the importance of memory in the novel. History books tell of Trujillo's despotic reign, but Alvarez presents a more personal account. Middleton and Woods maintain that the past is a "rewritable text according to the authority and power of those doing the rewriting" and continue that the success of historical novels "depends on the way in which they address this widespread interest in history-making by offering themselves as models for an understanding of the past" (10). Alvarez, through the examination of the lives and changes in identity of these four young girls, offers a new understanding of the past, an understanding that is fully aware of the "historical complexity" of the past while at the same time "training the reader in a cultural anamnesis as a prelude to becoming a better historian" (Middleton and Woods 10). Not only is memory complex in *The García Girls*; it is active as well. Alvarez, in illuminating recollections about past events, creates a new history rather than relying on a history that has already been told.

Non-linearity and Varying Points of View

Questioning history has become a common practice in the present era and is also a preoccupation with postmodern literature, to which Alvarez's text belongs. Themes and concepts such as fragmentation, multiplicity, opposition to "universal experience," questioning of identity, and clashes between traditional and non-traditional values are all concerns that are linked with the postmodern period, just as non-linearity and experimental writing are some features that critics perceive as emblematic of postmodern style. Authors writing during this period have often explored these concepts and issues as they related to race, class, gender, and ethnicity. Through her multi-narrational approach as well as reverse chronology in *The García Girls,* Alvarez, too, highlights and wrestles with gender and identity issues. The novel, divided as it is in chapters told from varying points of view, represents the fragmentation of identity. This fragmentation, I argue, translates into an ambivalence toward history. Thus, the novel underscores that what one has been told or what one has read in history books is not an objective truth. Instead, there exist multiple truths.

One particular feature of postmodern writing that is significant to this argument is the sense of non-ending that critics associate with postmodern fiction, a feature that is also sometimes associated with feminist writing. In Victorian novels one often finds closed, or "death or marriage" endings, while in modern novels, authors frequently leave the reader with open endings. Brian McHale puts forward the question: What happens when narratives do neither of these things, narratives that are "poised between the two because they are either multiple or circular endings?" (109). Alvarez, who begins her novel at the end (that is, in the present), considers this question. She also takes into account several perspectives, all of which emphasize multiple endings, as well as middles and beginnings, hence allowing the reader to determine the "truth" of these events. In the first chapter, for example, Yolanda is in the Dominican Republic, but the reader is not offered any background about her — why is she there? Why did she leave?— until later in the novel. This happens throughout the novel: the reader must continue reading — going backward in time — to make sense of the present. As Gayle Greene argues in "Feminist Fiction and the Uses of Memory," "though the linear sequence of language commits us to reading forward, understanding requires re-readings and depends on knowledge of the end" (307). Through the use of the circular ending, Alvarez does not interpret the multiple realities for the reader. On the contrary, she involves the reader in this process of locating truths, the most important of which is the truth Yolanda discovers: it is impossible to recover the past completely — or her home, language, or culture — in the Dominican Republic. While living in the United States is certainly not without its difficulties, returning to the Dominican Republic also offers its own set of problems, one of which involves being a woman in a culture defined by patriarchal, "macho" structures.

Just as multiple realities and identities are critical to a discussion of Alvarez's text, so too are the themes, and the methods she uses to convey these themes. Alvarez recounts the family's memories in reverse chronology rather than narrating in a linear fashion. She begins her story in 1989 in New York and ends in 1956, when the girls are still living in the Dominican Republic. The use of this particular narrative device provides the readers with the opportunity to participate in the events along with the storytellers. Certainly, the relationship between storyteller and reader is important insofar as an author can create empathy when she engages her reader in this journey of discovery. Further, Yolanda—discovering *as she remembers*—points once again to the notion of memory as active rather than passive. Through her narrative journey, Alvarez stresses ruptures in time and memory.

Remembering backward also encourages the reader to anticipate the beginning (of the girls' lives, which is where a novel traditionally begins) and work through issues—such as sexuality, Americanization, and invention/language—along with the storytellers. In addition to reverse chronology, Alvarez uses varying points of view in her story, and specifically, female points of view: in each chapter one of the sisters (or, infrequently, the mother or maid) speaks, sometimes in first person, but more often in third person. I argue that both of these structural elements allow for a complication of accounts of memory and history, as well as an examination into cultural myths about women's roles in American and Latin society. Alvarez intertwines memory with storytelling to resist traditional, patriarchal narratives of history, gender, and identity and thus works to raise consciousness about feminist discourses prominent during what has been termed the third wave of feminism, a period which called attention to the lack of voices from women of color and postcolonial subjects.

As many critics have pointed out, "becoming American" is a predominant theme in *The García Girls.* Certainly this is a theme that addresses identity in general, and gender in particular as it relates to this novel. In the Dominican Republic, each of the girls has had an idea about what it means to "be American." For example, when their grandparents bring them presents from New York City, they view America as an exciting place full of remarkable things. But once they are actually confronted with the "real" America after their move, "becoming American" means something entirely different. "Losing their accents," as is evidenced by the title, is an important factor in their Americanization and also in the altering of their identities. For example, the girls have stones thrown at them in school by their peers because of their accents, which prompts their mother to ask them what they had done "to provoke them" (Alvarez 135). The mother's comment can be read as an attempt to avert confrontation, either with her daughters or with the children throwing the stones, who might cause more problems for them in this new country. Yolanda answers by calling her "Mom," which the girls never do, "except when they wanted her to feel how much she had failed them in this country" (Alvarez 135–136). From their perspective, American moms do not fuss at their daughters, and furthermore, they protect their daughters from such situations. Losing their accents is meant both literally as well as metaphorically in that this loss of an accent indicates that they have become more American. But this new-found Americanization comes at the expense of possibly losing part of their Spanish identity: the accent is a large part of what ties them with their language, their family, and their culture. Certainly, this ironic title critiques the notion that one can be one thing or another; rather, both the title and the novel highlight the fact that people possess multiple subject positions simultaneously. Alvarez, writing about Latina women who move back and forth between cultures, underscores that this notion of "Americanization" is ambiguous at best and certainly not some seamless process.

Alvarez divides her novel into three parts, each of which contains five chapters. Part one extends from 1989–1972; part two from 1970–1960; and part three from 1960–1956. The first chapter is titled "*Antojos*" and is told from the third person point of view. Yolanda has returned to the island after being away for five years, and her extended family have planned a party for her, complete with an "Island cake"—a cake shaped as the Dominican Republic. They do not know that Yolanda is entertaining the idea of returning to live. An *antojo*, according to Yolanda's Tía Carmen, is "like a craving for something you have to eat" (Alvarez 8). This craving, in actuality, represents the craving that pervades the novel: it is the craving to belong.

Adulthood: Language, Sexuality, and Color-Coded Identity

The reader discovers in chapter one of *García Girls* that Yolanda has an *antojo* for guavas. She goes into the mountains to look for some, although her aunts and cousins have warned her that it is dangerous to venture out alone. Her family alludes to trouble in the country, and the reader later finds out that this trouble in the country is precisely what prompted the García family's move to the U.S. years ago. Yolanda says she can take the bus, at which point her cousins and aunts all laugh. Her cousin Lucinda jokes: "Can't you see it!? Yoyo climbing into an old *camioneta* with all the *campesinos* and their fighting cocks and their goats and their pigs!" (Alvarez 9). Lucinda alludes here to the fact that Yolanda has been away for a long while and is therefore not used to such situations, especially given her difficulty in communication. It is noteworthy that her cousin refers to her as Yoyo in that this name choice predicts the rest of the story, which is Yolanda's sense of going back and forth, like a yoyo, between two cultures, two countries, and two languages.

As she goes up into the mountains, driving her cousin's Datsun, Yolanda wonders to herself how she would call for help if she were to have an accident: "In English or Spanish?" (Alvarez 13). This is a question that creeps in throughout the novel: how does one negotiate one's life, in one's native language or the second language? Or is either language adequate? After finding guavas with the help of some island boys, Yolanda starts to head back but gets a flat tire. Two men approach her, which reminds her of her family's warning not to go alone: "You will get lost, you will get kidnapped, you will get raped, you will get killed" (Alvarez 17). She is unable to speak at first, causing the men to mistake her for an *Americana*. Yolanda does not dispel this belief. She speaks in English, while at the same time indicating that she has family in the area. Yolanda's actions reflect two ideas simultaneously: she dissociates herself from the men — and by extension, from the island — by not speaking their (her) language; but at the same time she integrates herself into the island by pointing out the familial connection. In this first chapter, then, readers recognize Yolanda's desire to belong, conflicted as it is. The men change her tire and Yolanda returns to her aunt's house, unharmed. Silvio Sirias notes that English "comes to represent safety, her way out of the predicament" (33). Indeed, speaking English does offer her protection. Additionally, this encounter foreshadows the novel as a whole in its reference to language. Although English offers her protection in this particular instance, English does not offer a haven later in the novel given that two of the daughters are institutionalized because of a breakdown in language, as will be discussed later in this chapter.

The chapter "The Four Girls" concentrates on the underpinnings of the girls' identity issues, issues which have in part taken root due to their growing up in a culture which privileges male children. Avarez tells the reader how the girls were "color coded" in the Dominican Republic: each girl received the same item — clothes, bedspread, and so forth — but each girl got these items in one particular color to distinguish her item from another sister in order to, according to their mother "save time" (Alvarez 41). Carla (the oldest, and a child psychologist) comments on this color-coded identity in an essay, saying "the color system had weakened the four girls' identity differentiation abilities and made them forever unclear about personality boundaries" (Alvarez 41).Carla's comment offers insight into the women's identity formation. Alvarez writes that, despite their ages, they are still referred to as "the four girls." The girls recall that when their mother is asked, "No sons?" she replies "apologetically," "Just the four girls" (Alvarez 41). The language used, added to the grouping of the sisters into a single unit, "the four girls," highlight the fact that the girls'/women's identities have been shaped by this system.[4]

The chapter "The Four Girls" concentrates on sexuality and identity as they relate to all of the sisters. However, in chapter four of part one, Alvarez focuses on these two issues as they relate to Yolanda. It is titled "Joe" and begins:

> Yolanda, nicknamed *Yo* in Spanish, misunderstood *Joe* in English, doubled and pronounced like the toy, *Yoyo*— or when forced to select from a rack of personalized key chains, *Joey*— stands at the third-story window watching a man walk across the lawn with a tennis racket [Alvarez 68].

In one sentence the reader learns that Yolanda has at least five different names. *Yo* in Spanish means "I." Ironically, her name indicates a single identity, although it is obvious from the beginning that Yolanda possesses at the very least dual identities: Latina and American, and now, in fact, five more identities within the two ethnic ones. The subject of this chapter is Yolanda's first marriage. Yolanda is married to an American, a "monolingual" man, which is one source of their problems. Yolanda, a writer, enjoyed playing rhyming games with her husband, John. The game consisted of making up poems using words that rhymed with their names. Yolanda, for example, says "John's a hon, lying by the pond, having lots of fun," and John responds, "And you're a little squirrel! You know that?" Yolanda counters: "Squirrel doesn't rhyme" (Alvarez 71). However, John replies that nothing rhymes with "Joe-lan-dah" (Alvarez 71).The inability to play the rhyming game indicates John does not see the necessity of recognizing Yolanda's multiple names,which in effect, represent her multiple identities. At the end of this game, Yolanda remarks, "*Yo* rhymes with *cielo* in Spanish" (Alvarez 72). Alvarez writes, "And Yo was running, like the mad, into the safety of her first tongue, where the proudly monolingual John could not catch her, even if he tried" (72). In pointing out that John is "proudly monolingual,"— that is, that he does not even make the attempt to understand her in the language into which she was born — Alvarez stresses Yolanda's need to be understood. Yolanda offers a rhyme in both English and Spanish: "I" rhymes with "sky" and "*Yo*" rhymes with "*cielo.*" In both rhymes, Yolanda cleverly uses the first person singular "I" and produces a rhyming word, "sky," in each language, which demonstrates the thought she has put into the game. However, John cannot participate in the game in even one language, which is problematic since language is important to Yolanda in terms of her identity as a person as well as her identity as a writer. Through his failure to play the game, John also fails to recognize the importance of either scenario.

In playing the rhyming game, Yolanda literally tries to make sense of language, to establish and confirm her identity. However, this game has not served its purpose because she soon begins to hear only "babble" rather than words in a conversation. Clearly, language and identity are closely linked in this story. It is true that the García girls are bilingual. However, this chapter reveals that being bilingual does not help them to truly understand — or be understood by — another person or culture. Yolanda goes to her parents after her breakup with John and then eventually into a private facility where she fantasizes about her psychiatrist: he would "[make] her one whole Yolanda" (Alvarez 80). Certainly, this notion of "unity" is precisely what Alvarez critiques throughout the novel: the multi-narrational style, the reverse chronology, and the content of the novel all highlight the reality that unity is something that cannot be achieved.

As readers move forward into the story — but backward in time — they learn of Yolanda's first adult sexual encounter, an issue strongly linked with how she resists being categorized by a single identity. "The Rudy Elmenhurst Story," one of the few chapters told in first person point of view by Yolanda, takes place during the sexually permissive 1960s, when "everyone was sleeping around as a matter of principle" (Alvarez 87). Yolanda is in college, but despite the era, she is not promiscuous. She meets Rudy in class and they begin dating, but she does not sleep with him. This makes him angry and prompts him to say he thought she would be "hot-blooded" since she was "Spanish and all" (Alvarez 99), thus underscoring the stereotype of the overly amorous Spanish female. After they break up because of this refusal, Alvarez brings the reader forward in time five years. Yolanda meets him when she is in graduate school, but by this time she has had other lovers. The two meet, and after they have spoken for awhile, Rudy (whom she refers to as the guy "who had haunted my sexual awakening with a nightmare of self-doubt"), explodes, "Hey, Jesus Christ, I've waited five years, and you look like you've gotten past all your hang-ups. Let's just fuck" (Alvarez 103). Alvarez emphasizes several issues here. First, Rudy's comment about Yolanda not fitting the "hot-blooded Spanish" girl stereotype speaks to how Latina women (and Latino men) have been viewed by Americans. Second, in using first person in this chapter, as opposed to third person, Alvarez wishes to examine how Yolanda viewed her world during college. College is a critical period in her life due to her developing views about sexuality, both as an American and a Latina woman. First person point of view allows for a more personal reflection by Yolanda, who is — and has always been — struggling with understanding her identity. She does not fit the stereotypical role of the "hot-blooded" Latina girl, whom Rudy envisions; nor does she belong in the same category as her female Island cousins, who are compliant to their boyfriends' and husbands' wishes. Yolanda certainly does not fit the 1960s stereotype of the sexually permissive American girl. She does not, in fact, feel she belongs anywhere, despite her strong desire to do so.

Adolescence and Ambivalence: Escaping/Claiming a Past

Using varying points of view along with reverse chronology, Alvarez challenges traditional ideas about the "normal" plot and structure of a novel. Indeed, as Jennifer Bess points out, "The linear journey that characterizes traditional Western literature must be shattered for the purposes of attacking the Western hegemony, revealing the truth of what has been lost and creating a new vehicle of communication" (82). Alvarez creates a new vehicle of communication by way of the structure of this novel. Parts two and three, like part one, use varying points of view and are told in reverse order: part one presents the García girls as young women; part two centers on their adolescence; and part three focuses on their childhood years in the Dominican Republic.

Part two depicts adolescent girls trying to understand themselves not only as young women, but as young women living in a culture very different from the one into which they were born. They return to the Dominican Republic often to visit, but with each visit, they feel more alienated from their former country and their island family. In the first chapter of this part, "A Regular Revolution," the reader learns of their initial years in the U.S. Alvarez writes of how the girls suffered taunts at school, with names like "spic" and "greaseballs" (Alvarez 107) being hurled at them. In this chapter, the girls speak of their experiences as one unit:

> We learned to forge Mami's signature and went just about everywhere, to dance weekends and football weekends and snow sculpture weekends. We could kiss and not get pregnant. We could smoke and no great aunt would smell us and croak. We began to develop a taste for the American teenage good life, and soon, Island was old hat, man. Island was the hair-and-nails crowd, chaperones, and icky boys with all their macho strutting and unbuttoned shirts and hairy chests with gold chains and teensy gold crucifixes. By the end of a couple of years away from home we had *more* than adjusted [Alvarez 108–109].

It is ostensibly odd that they speak in the first person plural "we," especially given their negative comments about the "color-coding system." It appears from this excerpt that they are now more accepting of this unified identity, but only when it represents the positives that Americanization affords them.

The girls evidently begin to enjoy American life, in large part because of the freedoms they are permitted, or the liberties that they take in America that they could not take in the Dominican Republic. Their parents, however, are not oblivious to these new freedoms and what they threaten. Therefore they send them to the Island every summer to prevent them from taking this new-found freedom as a given. It is during one of these visits (a year long visit for Fifi, whose visit is prolonged after being caught in possession with marijuana) that Fifi meets a young man on the island. When her other three sisters arrive for the summer, they observe how Fifi's new boyfriend, Manuel, treats her. They also note that Fifi accepts this treatment. She has become one of the "hair-and-nails cousins":

> Fifi can't wear pants in public. Fifi can't talk to another man. Fifi can't leave the house without permission. And what's most disturbing is that Fifi, feisty, lively Fifi, is letting this man tell her what she can and cannot do [Alvarez 120].

One must consider the term "machismo" and how it relates to Dominican society in order to get a better insight into this passage. Machismo is defined as an exaggerated sense of manliness or power. The qualities associated with machismo — such as bravery, strength, and importance — are characteristics that the "ideal man possesses within a patriarchal society ... in such a society, machismo becomes institutionalized" (Sirias 44). The reader notes how machismo is institutionalized in that, even though Fifi has been living in America for a number of years, she changes when she travels back to the island. Hence, the reader discovers in this chapter — and in this part as a whole — how easy it is (at least outwardly) for a person to adapt to a culture and become part of it. But just as important, and seemingly contradictorily, the person may revert back to the earlier cultural prescriptions. Suarez refers to this ambivalent attitude as "anxiety of representation," given their "desire to escape the haunting, mysterious past" while at the same time that they wish to "claim that past" (138). Certainly, the García girls are caught up in an anxiety of representation, as the episode with Fifi reveals. For Fifi, part of Manuel's appeal is that he represents a past that she did not have, a past that she would (perhaps) like to claim. This is made apparent in Fifi's reaction to Manuel's treatment of her:

> Fifi sees him [Manuel] and her face lights up. She is about to put aside her book, when Manuel Gustavo reaches down and lifts it out of her hands. "This," Manuel Gustavo says, holding the book up like a dirty diaper, "is junk in your head. You have better things to do" [Alvarez 120].

Fifi responds that he "[has] no right to tell me what I can and can't do" (Alvarez 120). However, after Manuel roars off in his pickup truck, Fifi later begs him to forgive her, which underscores her ambivalence, or "anxiety of representation." Fifi wishes to escape this past about which she is ignorant at the same time that she wants to be a part of it.

Childhood: Invented Histories and Story Ghosts

In the third and final part of *The García Girls* Alvarez emphasizes the need to revise history in order to move forward. At the same time, she points out that the revised history is not a simplistic version of history. Rather, it is complex and ambiguous. Alvarez focuses strongly on the intersection of memory, storytelling, and identity in this part, filling the reader in about the girls' lives in the Dominican Republic and what brought them to the United States in the first place. The first chapter, titled "The Blood of the Conquistadores," tells of Papi hiding from Trujillo's men. The very title indicates conflict in that the conquistadores were 16th century Spanish conquerors who instituted Spanish rule in the New World by overthrowing Native American populations. Prior to the beginning of the novel proper, Alvarez provides the reader with a family tree in which the maternal line dates back to the conquistadores. As Jennifer Bess points out, drawing this link between the maternal side of the family and the conquistadores indicates complicity in the losses of the past. That is, including a family tree that shows the Garcías as heirs of the conquistadores highlights that their position as exiles in the United States is much more complex than the victim/oppressor binary would have one believe. As exiles in the United States, the Garcías are not only victims. They themselves have a history of being oppressors as well. Bess argues that Alvarez "[digs] deeper not to recover an irrecoverable past, but to acknowledge that it *is* irrecoverable and demand her characters' ownership of their complicity in that loss" (81). As I have argued, it is the form of the novel, complete with gaps and silences, that "is fundamental to its ability to memorialize the permanence of loss and silence ... its structure illuminates the Garcías own complicity in the suffering rooted in colonial history" (Bess 81). Through the use of this title, the family tree, and the form of the novel, Alvarez emphasizes the complexity of revising history.

The maid, a black Haitian woman named Chucha, plays a large role in this chapter in terms of revision. Chucha turned up on the girls' grandfather's doorstep the night of "the massacre when Trujillo had decreed that all black Haitians on [their] side of the island would be executed by dawn" (Alvarez 218). Within this particular chapter, Alvarez unexpectedly switches from 3rd person to Chucha's first person voice, telling about the family's last day on the Island: "they are gone, left in cars that came for them, driven by pale Americans ... the color of zombies, a nation of zombies" (221). Chucha continues:

> All in black, I saw the *loa* of Don Carlos putting his finger to his lip in mockery of the last gesture I had seen him make to me that morning. I answered with a sign and fell to my knees and watched him leave through the back door out through the guava orchard.... And then the deep and empty silence of the deserted house [Alvarez 222].

The fact that Chucha is the storyteller works to subvert generalizations about the homogeneity of culture and emphasizes the need for those who are marginalized to tell their own stories. Chucha, a Haitian servant, is an outsider in the García family, yet she tells this story in first person point of view. Alvarez's choice of switching point of view is significant. Readers might conclude that since the girls are too young to clearly remember the day of their departure, they get to hear from someone who would have a clearer recollection. Furthermore, in giving Chucha a voice, Alvarez highlights that even as the girls go into exile, they still have privileges that Chucha does not. In this part, then, the reader recognizes the collusion of patriarchy with colonialism. Chucha has not had a voice up until this point, and therefore Alvarez stresses this collusion by allowing Chucha to speak in first person. In this chapter Chucha recalls this life changing event, as opposed to other sections in which the girls narrate in third person point of view. The latter point of view prompts the reader to speculate on how much is actual memory and how much the girls — and the reader — have "filled in the blanks" of the past. The form of the novel makes apparent these blanks in the girls' history and memory. Although a single story is configured in each chapter, there are gaps between the chapters that the reader must fill in. Alvarez uses the gaps to underscore the notion that the girls' memories of the past are not seamless. Indeed, Chucha later relates: "They will be haunted by what they do and don't remember. But they have spirit in them. They will invent what they need to survive" (Alvarez 223). They must revise history, then, in order to move forward and survive.

Alvarez moves still farther back in time in the chapter titled "The Human Body," a portion that offers a glimpse into the teachings reserved for Latina girls. Alvarez writes:

> On her latest trip to New York City, my grandmother had taken her unmarried daughter, Mimi, along. Mimi was known as "the genius in the family" because she read books and knew Latin and had attended an American college for two years before my grandparents pulled her out because too much education might spoil her for marriage [228].

While the grandparents hold education in high regard, at the same time they feel that too much education — especially an American education complete with more liberal views — might cause a young woman to become dissatisfied with marriage. Mimi, returning from a trip to New York, gives Yolanda a "book of stories in English [she] could barely read but with interesting pictures of a girl in a bra and long slip with a little cap on her head that had a tassel dangling down" (Alvarez 229). The book to which she refers is, in fact, the story of Scheherazade, the girl from *The Arabian Nights* who tricks a sultan — by means of storytelling — into letting her live. Yolanda recalls: "The story was not half bad: Once upon a time a sultan was killing all the girls in his kingdom.... But then, the girl pictured in bra and slip ... this girl and her sister were captured by the sultan. They figured out a way to trick him" (Alvarez 232).

The story is significant because it highlights the power of art, and storytelling in particular. *The Arabian Nights* begins at the end and uses nested stories to emphasize the power of storytelling, much like Alvarez's narrative. Yolanda, like Scheherazade, survives in a foreign world by telling about her experiences. Alvarez tells of one such experience:

> Back in the Dominican Republic growing up, Yoyo had been a terrible student.... But in New York, she needed to settle somewhere, and since the natives were unfriendly, and the country inhospitable, she took root in the language. By high school, the nuns were reading her stories and compositions out loud in English class [141].

The reader gleans from this passage that Yolanda has an almost physical need for storytelling. She writes in order to fit in and to make sense of her surroundings.

In the final chapter of the novel, "The Drum," which takes place chronologically at the beginning of the young girls' lives, Yolanda speaks in first person. Yoyo finds a kitten and wants to keep it, although she is told that it will die if she takes if from its mother. When Yoyo sees the mother cat, she hides the kitten inside a drum her grandmother bought for her on her last trip to New York. Later, however, she throws the kitten out the window when she becomes frightened upon seeing the mother cat outside looking for it. Yolanda recalls how she "detested the accusing sound of meow. I wanted to dunk it into the sink and make its meowing stop" (Alvarez 288). After the wounded kitten disappears, Yolanda's nightmares about the mother cat begin: "the cat came back, on and off, for years" (Alvarez 289). The cat represents the homeland they lost; the kitten symbolizes the sisters, who are torn from their home. The nightmares, then, are Yolanda's way of expressing this loss. Just as Yolanda took the kitten from its mother, she and her sisters feel they have been taken from their homeland. She and her sisters, too, go back, on and off for years but do not feel they truly belong in the Dominican Republic, just as they do not belong in America.

Yolanda condenses the rest of the story in the last paragraph of the novel: they moved to the U.S.; the "cat disappeared"; her grandmother grows old; Yoyo went to school and read books; she grew up, "a curious woman, a woman of story ghosts and story devils" (Alvarez 290). The collapsing of the story is significant for a few reasons. Alvarez/Yolanda writes: "You understand I am collapsing all time now so that it fits in what's left in the hollow of my story?" (289). In collapsing time, she demonstrates how the past and present merge rather than remain separate. In this chapter, and in the novel as a whole, Alvarez invents new methods of remembering the past, a past that has historically been viewed from a patriarchal viewpoint. Alvarez, through the use of storytelling and memory as narrative techniques, emphasizes the need to resist "being said."

NOTES

1. Trujillo seized power in 1930, brutally murdering thousands of Haitians, the number of which is still unknown.

2. Indeed, several other writers fit into this category of a "hyphenated person": Amy

Tan, Maxine Hong Kingston, Leslie Marmon Silko, Sandra Cisneros, Theresa Hak Jyung Cha, and Jamaica Kincaid to mention only a few.

3. Ellen McCracken speaks to this notion as well, arguing that Alvarez "uses formal and thematic transgression to reveal identity to be an unstable category, undergirded by gender, ethnic, and class 'trouble,' to adapt Judith Butler's term" (6).

4. Later in the chapter, Yolanda is knitting a blanket for Fifi's baby. We read: "Yolanda is addicted to love stories with happy endings, as if there were a stitch she missed, ... and if only she could find it, maybe she could undo it, unravel John, Brad, Steven, Rudy, and start over" (Alvarez 63). Roberta Rubenstein provides an interesting insight here, arguing that "[Yolanda's] observation serves as a vivid metaphor for the narrative as a whole as Alvarez, through Yolanda, moves backward to unravel-and to 'fix' or reknit in a more deliberate and coherent design-the interrelated meanings of language, identity, and loss" (Rubenstein 70).

Works Cited

Alvarez, Julia. *How the García Girls Lost Their Accents.* New York: Plume, 1992. Print.

Bess, Jennifer. "Imploding the Miranda Complex in Julia Alvarez's *How the Garcia Girls Lost Their Accents.*" *College Literature* 34.1 (2007): 78–105. Print.

Greene, Gayle. "Feminist Fiction and the Uses of Memory." *Signs* 16.2 (1991): 290–321.

McCracken, Ellen. *New Latina Narrative: The Feminine Space of Postmodern Ethnicity.* Tucson: University of Arizona Press, 1999. Print.

McHale, Brian. *Postmodernist Fiction.* New York: Methuen, 1987. Print.

Middleton, Peter and Tim Woods. *Literatures of Memory: History, Time and Space in Postwar Writing.* Manchester, UK: Manchester University Press, 2000. Print.

Minh-Ha, Trinh T. "Writing Postcoloniality and Feminism." *The Post-Colonial Studies Reader.* Eds. Bill Ashcroft, Gareth Griffiths, Helen Tiffin. New York: Routledge, 1995. 264–268. Print.

Mitchell, David T. "The Accent of 'Loss': Cultural Crossings as Context in Julia Alvarez's *How the García Girls Lost Their Accents.*" *Beyond the Binary: Reconstructing Cultural Identity in a Multicultural Context.* Ed. Timothy B. Powell. New Brunswick, NJ: Rutgers University Press, 1997. 165–184. Print.

Rubenstein, Roberta. *Home Matters: Longing and Belonging, Nostalgia and Mourning in Women's Fiction.* New York: Palgrave, 2001. Print.

Sirias, Silvio. *Julia Alvarez: A Critical Companion.* Westport, Connecticut: Greenwood Press, 2001. Print.

Suárez, Lucia M. "Julia Alvarez and the Anxiety of Latina Representation." *Meridians* 5.1 (2004): 117–145. Print.

Part III

Performative Spaces: Constructing and Instructing Gendered Behavior

9

Bodies in Dialogue: Performing Gender and Sexuality in Salsa Dance

Aleysia Whitmore

Dance holds a special place in the realm of expressive communication as a form of performance that constructs, reinterprets, and reflects ideas about bodily experience, the self, and society. Anthropologist Ted Polhemus explains, "the deepest and most fundamental foundations of being a member of a particular society are inevitably corporeal," as "an individual's first and most rudimentary experience of his or her society is via bodily manipulation and physical education in its broadest sense" (6). Dance allows its participants to enact "socially constituted and historically specific attitudes toward the body" (Desmond, "Embodying" 37).[1] In salsa, a music and dance genre with roots in Cuban *son* and Afro-Caribbean music, dancers take part in a dialogue about the body and gender.

As a social dance, salsa encourages wide participation, and as an expressive performance, it offers dancers a privileged arena for the enactment of various identities. Of these, sexual and gender identities are especially visible, as dancers, recognizing the links between the body, movement, and sexuality, manipulate the signifiers of gender and sexuality on the dance floor. This chapter examines the dancing body and its relationship to gender in salsa dance. Specifically, it addresses participants' varying perceptions and performances of body, movement, gender, sexuality, and dance. As these performances are intimately connected to their contextualization in a space in which Latin Americans of diverse backgrounds and non–Latin Americans meet and interact, a variety of gender ideologies are constantly in play on the dance floor. Thus, it is essential to study how dancers' diverse perceptions and performances intersect with larger cultural and societal discourses concerning gender.

I begin with a general discussion of dance as a medium of expressive communication, drawing on dance and gender theory. Subsequently I address the salsa scene in Providence, Rhode Island, U.S.A., where I carried out fieldwork in 2008–2010. Interviews with dancers and accounts of my own experience on the dance floor show how the Providence salsa dancers interpret specific movements as expressions of gender and sexuality.

Dance as Expressive Communication

Dance is part of a non-verbal realm of expression that "is marked as one of interior expressivity and thus often popularly regarded as revelatory of deeper emotions, feelings and desires" (Desmond, "Introduction" 6). Many see dance as more authentically expressive than speech because it is a form of expression more directly connected to the body and the self. As a result of its branding as authentic and pre-verbal expression, dance is often seen as the symbolic practice that most directly and effectively communicates important notions of identity and society without the intermediary of verbal language.

Because it is seen as a medium of communication, dance is often referred to and studied as a type of language. Maria Pini explains that "bodies develop choreographies of signs through which they discourse" (112). Similarly, Polhemus argues that "movement and other physical styles in any society are imbued with symbolic meaning with the result that how we use and move our bodies is inevitably the occasion for the transmission of ... socio-cultural information" (6). Both of these writers imply that, just as in language, in body movement there are grammatical rules as well as a common vocabulary whose meanings are culturally specific and learned.

Although it is helpful to examine dance as a type of non-verbal language, problems arise as dancers, observers, and academics translate this corporeal language into a verbal language. Asserting the primacy of verbal language in human thought processes and perceptions, Polhemus explains that because much of corporeal language cannot be or is not translated into verbal language, many of its meanings are never recognized (6). However, it is clear by looking at dance scholarship that dancers and academics put a lot of energy into expressing in verbal and written language the elements of dance that do seem to exist outside verbal communication. For instance, Tomie Hahn takes on this problem in her ethnography of Japanese traditional dance transmission; she narrates and conveys what she calls "sensational knowledge" to the reader in creative ways so that the reader might vicariously "know the body" in a sense comparable to her own knowledge (8).

Thus, in considering corporeal language and its relation to verbal language, these two systems of communication must be recognized as interconnecting systems to be translated with care and creativity—although some aspects of corporeal knowledge will inevitably be lost in translation. As a result of these limitations in understanding and writing about what bodies are communicating, dance scholars have much to gain from adopting a methodology that pays attention to diverse perceptions of corporeal language and knowledge on the dance floor; the more people involved in translation, the greater the vocabulary for communicating the sensory and corporeal.

It is important to also recognize that dancers' translations of corporeal language are dependent upon their cultural backgrounds and their understandings of the meanings of various movements. As Alexandra Carter explains, "the interpretation of dance is ... contingent upon the recognition of common cultural meanings ascribed to signs, symbols, patterns, structures, etc." (250). Thus, just as one must learn a language to communicate effectively, one must also learn a corporeal system of communication when learning to dance. These systems of communication can be seen as coming from communities of practice that develop their own dialects. However, meanings of dance do not only come from communities of practice. They also originate from individuals. Unlike verbal language, which requires an understanding of the community of practice before an individual is able to participate, any person can immediately take part in dance, moving, and interpreting these movements for themselves. Thus, beginner dancers may not find meaning in dance based on the norms of a specific community of practice. It is possible that some dancers will never become fluent in the language, but will instead develop their own idiolects.

Gender and sexuality are especially apposite to the study of dance partly because dance, sexuality, and gender are all viewed as closely tied with the pre-verbal and the physical. In a study with dancers of varying abilities, Helen Thomas observed, "women would link the dancer's grace or strength to ideas about masculinity and femininity" (*An-Other* 70). Thomas writes that as women commented on the elegance of female dancers, "underneath the surface of this talk there lay an idea of an 'ideal' female body, which dancers, ... appeared more likely to reach" (*An-Other* 70). Like Thomas, Desmond has observed that dancers are quite aware of the association that dance and its movements have with gender and sexuality "because of the historically specific links drawn between body, movement, and sex, and the performers' manipulation of those signifiers" ("Introduction" 6). Desmond explains that these manipulations interact with a larger societal discourse, as dancers' "motions gain their meanings in relation to dominant discourses about 'male' and 'female,' about 'masculine' and 'feminine'" ("Introduction" 4).

Judith Butler argues that gender is materialized through performance, and that the ability of the performance of gender to have any meaning for the performers or observers is based on the concept of "citation." Similar to corporal language, performative acts repeat a "coded utterance" that is identifiable within an accepted model, or language (qtd. in Butler 13). Thus, when a dancer moves in a certain way, he or she cites certain ideas or aspects of societal discourses that others sharing the dancer's background recognize. Butler argues that gender needs to be constantly reiterated through performance and that this need for reiteration is "a sign that materialization is never quite complete, that bodies never quite comply with the norms by which their materialization is impelled" (2). Because it needs to be constantly performed and redefined, gender will always remain slightly unstable and prone to change. Thus, dancers, as they perform, are constantly materializing, rematerializing, and destabilizing notions of gender. In salsa, gender is further destabilized as people of various backgrounds converge on the dance floor with different corporeal languages. One person's interpretation of the meaning of his or her own movement could be very different from his or her partner's interpretation.

An Introduction to Salsa

A genre with Afro-diasporic roots, salsa was developed by Puerto Rican and Cuban immigrants in New York in the 1960s. Salsa became a genre that expressed these communities' cultural identities and their experiences with violence and poverty in the *barrios* in which they lived. As it spread to urban centers in Puerto Rico, Cuba, the Dominican Republic, Colombia, and Venezuela, the music became a translocal expression of marginalized *barrio* experiences. Thus, at first salsa was the music of local and transnational communities of *entendidos* (people in the know, connoisseurs) who could understand and relate to the exclusively Spanish lyrics and urban experiences (Santos Febres 184). As the music spread throughout the Americas and Latinos from different parts of Latin America migrated to New York and began to take part in the scene, salsa developed into an expression of pan–Latin identity, and performing salsa became a way for diverse communities to join in "performative constructions of *Latinidad*" (Washburne 7).

Salsa has since been taken up all over the world, both by Latinos and non–Latinos. For example, the Japanese salsa band Orquesta de la Luz has gained worldwide recognition for its stylistic mastery of the American tradition.[2] In

Dakar, musicians have incorporated Senegalese musical elements into the music.[3] In major international centers like New York and London, non–Latinos have expanded the genre, popularizing salsa dance lessons, and incorporating salsa into the ballroom dance scene.[4]

Salsa in Providence

In Providence and the surrounding area several clubs and restaurants offer a "Latin" or salsa-themed night once a week which, along with special events such as the Providence Salsa Ball, make up the Providence salsa scene. Although the clubs are small by big-city standards, they generally attract a sizable and loyal following that returns every week. Most of the clubs and restaurants hire DJs to provide the music. As of this writing, the only club that was offering live music on a regular basis (the Black Repertory Theater) has recently closed. The majority of this research was conducted in two clubs in Providence: the Latin Jazz and Salsa Night at the Black Repertory Theater, and Salsa on Sundays at Platforms.

The Dancers

Salsa clubs in Providence attract a diverse group of dancers, including students and professionals, both of Latin American descent and non–Latin Americans, and ranging in age from 20 to about 70. Many of the Latin Americans claim Dominican heritage, reflecting the large population in the Providence area from the Dominican Republic; others come from regions all over Central America, South America, and Mexico. In addition, people from various regions in Africa and Asia as well as Americans of diverse heritage also attend the salsa clubs.

Dancing Gender in Salsa Clubs

Salsa dancers are very aware of the ways that their dance is a performance in which they "strut their stuff" for onlookers (Mary). One dancer likened dancing to the performance that male animals engage in to attract partners.

> The lion has this mane and you know he trying to impress and show off ... and like peacock is the same thing like [a] male bird with like 25 different colors on the feathers. I think salsa is kind of like that for males [Paul].

What this performance communicates is affected by the associations that dancers have with salsa, their cultural backgrounds, and their views on gender.

Race and the Sexualized Body

An important, but not always recognized presence in salsa clubs is race, a concept that both overtly and subtly intersects with perceptions and performances of gender. Despite the fact that numerous people of Latin American heritage identify as white, in the United States, many conflate being "Latin" with a non-white racial identity. As a result, salsa is often associated with a non-white "other," and images advertising the dance commonly feature people of African heritage or of mixed-race. Desmond points out that race, like gender, is "closely tied to the body and physicality," and thus one's materialization through physical movement ("Introduction" 6). Race often determines the type of woman or man a person is thought to be. Frances Aparicio explains that, while the white female body is constituted by Victorian ideals, the black female body is not (42). Instead, the black female is seen as a being that embodies rhythm, movement, and exotic pleasure (Aparicio 44, 143). Desmond writes that North American white culture has linked "blacks with sexuality, sensuality, and an alternately celebrated or denigrated presumedly 'natural' propensity for physical ability, expressivity, or bodily excess" ("Embodying" 43).

Because salsa is associated with people of African descent and non-white "others," the exoticism and sexuality commonly attached to black women has been projected onto salsa. Today, many argue that North Americans and Europeans find salsa dance clubs to be an exciting escape from the mundane. Writing about this phenomenon, Desmond explains that Caribbean dances allow white people "to perform, in a sense, a measure of 'blackness' [and thus exotic sexuality] without paying the social penalty of 'being' black. An analogue might be "slumming"—a temporary excursion across lines dividing social classes in the search for pleasure" (Desmond "Embodying" 43). This is reinforced as club promoters use sexual portrayals of non-white bodies as marketing strategies for salsa clubs. These images advertise the salsa club as a tourist destination where foreign music and bodies congregate in a place removed from clubbers' everyday lives.

Salsa's association with a racialized "other" thus complicates dancers' performances and perceptions of gender and sexuality. It aids in attaching sexual connotations to the dance, affecting the ways in which women perform and the ways these performances are viewed. For instance, white women often feel that it is more permissible to dance in sexually suggestive ways and openly express their sexuality at salsa clubs than it is in other places they frequent. In addition, people often assume that female dancers who are mixed-race or black are better at this kind of expression. Less experienced white male dancers are sometimes reticent to ask Latin American women to dance out of a fear that they will not be able to perform well enough.

Encountering Gender in Salsa Dance

Salsa dance is a partner dance in which dancers generally adhere to a few basic rules of interaction. Almost exclusively male-female couples occupy the dance floor and the man is expected to find a female partner and extend an invitation to dance. He is then supposed to lead the dance, as his partner follows his cues as to when to begin moving to the music, what moves to execute, and when to stop dancing.

Dancers have varying views on salsa's association with performances of the sexual. Many dancers of European American background recognize the sexual in salsa dance as a striking part of their experience. One dancer explained that salsa, as a couples dance in which people move together in a close embrace, naturally evokes the sexual in people. Another dancer asserted, when a man and a woman are dancing together, "it's really primal" (Marc). This dancer remarked that the sexual and flirtatious undertones of salsa were part of what makes the dance fun, explaining that he sees the Afro-Cuban style of dancing as more flirtatious than other styles because of its emphasis on hip movements (Marc).[5]

Some dancers, especially those of Latin American background, have a more nonchalant take on the sexual aspects of dancing. One dancer commented that the dance was "like having sex." Another dancer recommended that I observe how a female dancer moved her buttocks so that I could replicate this sensual move. These dancers did not seem to think they were expressing something novel or inappropriate. For them, being comfortable with and showing off the sexual nature of one's body is just a part of dancing salsa. Another dancer who is of Latin American descent told me, "I've been to Mexico several times and that stuff [sexy dancing] is the norm ... it doesn't seem as odd to me I guess" (Mary).

Dancers who are not of Latin American descent recognize this attitude and at times exaggerate and capitalize on it. One dancer asserted that sexualized performance is just more acceptable in the salsa dance setting:

> I think it's more of the Latin culture though because I think ... over there showing an object of desire is normal. Show this beautiful girl dancing in skimpy clothes might be just a normal way of doing it [Paul].

Thus, the exotic sexuality attached to salsa because of its associations with the non-white "other" is combined with the sexual discourse surrounding Latin culture and couples dancing to create and reinforce perceptions of salsa dance as sexual.

Salsa advertising also often explicitly promotes the more "sensual" nature of the dance. A website advertising a series of local salsa workshops explains,

> We will be blending sensual Rumba moves into your bachata steps, tantalizing your salsa turn patterns with intense embraces like in the Paso Doble, and incorporating cozy Tango body contact.... We will define the missing elements in most social dances — body contact and sensuality through musicality ["Addicted"].

Although salsa is marketed as a sexy, sensual dance, dancers view and perform these elements differently. Some see salsa as free from sexual pressures because of the clear rules of interaction in the dance, and others see the dance as inherently sexy and steeped in a culture in which this is normal. At the same time, these views are not mutually exclusive, as a dancer could view the dance as inherently sexy, but also not feel that people are "hitting on" him or her. These varying perspectives on the sexual nature of salsa dance deeply affect the ways in which dancers perform and perceive gender and sexuality in the salsa club.

Gendered Movement

In salsa, through performances that play with the sexual and sensual in the dance, women and men both materialize and interpret gender performance in various ways. Although there is a community of practice that generally agrees on what movements are masculine and which ones are feminine, there are also many different interpretations of the meanings of these gendered moves. This ambiguity of meaning is a result of the many different ways in which people of varying cultural backgrounds interpret the dance "language" (as explained by Carter above), and the ways in which individuals continue to, as Butler puts it, materialize, rematerialize, and thus destabilize gender.

Some scholars have looked at specific salsa movements as materializing the feminine and masculine in dance. Jonathan Bollen writes that "girly" movements are "up and over the top arm gestures," and male movements are more grounded and "down and dirty" (304, 306). These movements and the ways in which they render gender visible illustrate how corporeal language works on the dance floor. The symbolic meanings of specific gestures, however, are difficult to ascertain and are in most cases ambiguous because of the many ways people of different cultural backgrounds interpret meaning. Therefore, in this examination of the materialization of gender in dance the focus is not only on isolated movements and their symbolism, but also on how various aspects of dancers' performances interact to construct a gendered dancing body.

Similar to Thomas' findings that women perceived female dancers as embodying an "ideal" body, in Providence, perceptions of women's beauty is a factor less of their actual physical attributes, and more of the ways in which they move on the dance floor. Dancers like discussing what movements they find attractive, and some have remarked on grace and subtlety as giving dancers beauty. One dancer explained,

> a graceful, gracefully moving body is more fun to watch than like a crazy spin or crazy moves.... They [dancers] don't have to be moving to every beat. They can pause and wait and those kinds of things add a lot of accent to the dance and I think that's because it connected very well with the music and that's beautiful [Paul].

In addition to determining beauty through grace and subtlety, dancers also find certain moves such as hand gestures and hip movements to be especially attractive when executed by women and others to be more appropriate for men. It is through the gendered meanings that dance movements have acquired that men and women construct gendered identities in salsa. As one dancer explained, men "do not move and turn too much. You [men] are like more of the leading figure so you just play cool and if you can just stand there and spin the girl all around you that's the most masculine like form" (Paul). As a result of this separation of roles in movement, this dancer saw the way men and women are viewed through movement to be unfair. "She does all these moves and the credit goes to the guy" because he is the one that led the movement and decided what she would do (Paul). This dancer sees the man as treating his partner at times like "an object that he is manipulating" (Paul). As a result of the very different gendered roles in salsa, the amount of individuality and agency that men and women have in dance is often a topic of discussion and disagreement.

As seen in the above quote, some men do not see women as having much agency in their movements or in creating an individual style. One male dancer asserted, "women's styling, they all look the same ... as you get better you will look like someone else. I don't think that as you get better you will really develop your own style" (Marc). Because women go into every dance with a more generic style that they will to adapt to the style of their partner, some men see women as lacking room for individual expression in salsa. Although this dancer speaks of this lack of individual style in a negative way, many dancers see the ability for a woman to be able to change her style to fit with the style of her partner as an important skill in and of itself.

Many dancers also assert the presence of individuality and agency among female dancers. Even though dancers repeatedly assert, "you are only as good as the [male] dancer you dance with," dancers still recognize that women's movements are not completely defined by their partners. Men often discuss how intimidated they are by good female dancers, and women have been known to walk off the dance floor in the middle of a dance because they are unsatisfied with the quality of their partners. Men also comment that they are concerned with ensuring that they entertain their dance partners with enough spins and more intricate moves. One dancer even discussed the existence of the "rebel move" in which "the guy is trying to lead her [the female dancer] into a move but then she can break away from it and do her own thing and...[the move] surprises the guy ... forcing him to do something else to recover" (Paul). Salsa dance movement is thus not as one-sided as it initially seems. Through disrupting the accepted roles and norms of movement, as well as asserting their own standards of dance, and their own interpretations of what constitutes skill, women are not only asserting individual agency, but they are also constantly destabilizing gender and rematerializing it.

This can also be seen in the ways the ways women use specific movements to both attract dance partners and to construct their gendered identities. "Tight and taught" hand and arm gestures in which women separate their fingers, throw their arms in the air, comb their hair, and flick their wrists are considered quintessentially feminine (Marc). In considering the lower body, dancers have claimed, "women's movements are all about the hip rotation ... it looks really good" (Marc). In her research with salsa dancers in the midwestern U.S., Joanna Bosse found that new salsa dancers often see hip movement to be the most important and attractive aspect of the dance. She writes, "outsiders to the genre ... singled out only the movement of the hips as the root of salsa's energy and perceived sexual appeal. Many fixated on the hip movement and worked exclusively on its performance" (52). This approach to salsa can also be seen in Providence, as dancers new to salsa often pay special attention to their hip movement, often awkwardly moving them in exaggerated ways.

Some see these hip and arm movements as purely sexually suggestive in meaning and thus performed by women to attract men and cater to men's expectations and definitions of what is beautiful. One male dancer explained that people expect women's dancing to be sexy. "If the woman doesn't look sexy enough or she's not you know styling a certain way I think people will look down on that" (Marc). However, a female dancer did not see these movements as having purely sexually suggestive meanings meant for a male audience, explaining that moving one's hips is "kind of like really embracing like the crux of your womanly body.... It's pretty sexy you know and it's fun to be sexy" (Mary). Women often embrace the femininity of their movement and its sensuality, at times obviously performing for their partners, but at times performing only for themselves without concern for the male gaze. In salsa, confidently asserting gender difference by accenting stereotypically feminine physical attributes, such as wide hips and large buttocks, materializes gender in a way that many women see as assertive and feminine. Being able to dance sensually is considered a good dancing skill, especially for women, as not only is salsa associated with an exotic sexuality, but this is one way in which women are able to improvise, add embellishments, and express individuality as they follow their partners, as men cannot lead their partners in these movements. Although some may read these performances more simply as sexy, others see the confidence portrayed in displaying and moving these isolated body parts as beautiful and powerful (some men are too intimidated to dance with women with very good control and creativity in these movements).

Quoting Audre Lorde, Christy Adair writes, "for women, a source of power, which can provide energy for change, is the erotic...[it is] 'an assertion of the life-force of women; of that creative energy empowered'" (80). For Lorde, this stands in contrast to the objectification of the woman's body, which she considers pornographic. Through their physical demonstration of their sexual selves, women assert their sexuality and their desires, thus reclaiming their full sexual voices and constructing a positive female sexuality in which they find individual pleasure (Hutton 20). Not only is this agency powerful but it is also destabilizing to gender norms, because, although women are defined by their sexual organs, they are not normally considered to have sexual feelings or desire. Open desire is normally reserved exclusively for men (consider, for example, who makes "cat calls" on the street) (Thomas, *Body* 40). Thus, women, in their performance of their female sexuality, take on a traditionally male role as they assert themselves and take control of the corporeal discourse of desire. By asserting sexual desires, women also establish their ability to "judge bodies as sites of attraction" and define beauty ideals for men (Lewis 248).

Male salsa dancers often admit that they are jealous that women's movements are traditionally more sensual and sexually suggestive than men's movements. One dancer explained, "guys only do footwork and steps and stuff but they don't do anything that's like really that sexual. They don't do anything that makes the dance fun.... Footwork looks cool but dances are fun when there's a flirtation" (Marc). Even though men lead the dance, women are in control of the flirtation and the sensuality. At times men take up feminine hip and hand movements because they see the moves as attractive and sexy. These movements do not lose their association with femininity and men who take them up are at times seen as being "gay" (Paul). One male dancer said, however, that being called gay does not matter so much, as this kind of movement is "fun to do and it is actually attractive" (Marc). Although most times women execute moves in front of a more static male partner, at times, really accomplished male dancers will appropriate this style and dance in front of their female partner, executing twirls and throwing their hands in the air. Even though most dancers clearly understand which movements are more feminine and which ones are masculine, they have very different views on the meanings of these movements. Women's movements can show agency as well as powerlessness. They can be sexy and demonstrate control. When men appropriate them, they remain feminine, but the ways in which this appropriation is seen are dependent on previously held views of both the importance of flirtation in salsa and views on homosexuality.

Conclusion

Dance offers a privileged arena for the enactment of various identities, especially sexual and gender identities. In such a symbolic practice, it is important to examine gestures, moving bodies, and the corporeal language they express, along with the ways in which these movements interact with the larger societal and cultural discourses on race, gender, sexuality, and the body. Gender and sexuality are materialized on the dance floor as dancers manipulate the corporeal language and its built-in signifiers of sex and gender. Dancers find power and joy in playing with these signifiers and subverting gender norms, and their resulting conceptions of their own and others' bodies offer insight into gender discourses in and outside of the dance club.

Even though these signifiers and experiences are difficult to translate into verbal language, and their meanings are often ambiguous or contradictory, paying attention to the ways in which people experience the music allows scholars to more deeply explore and interpret the various meanings salsa dance may have. As Tomie Hahn explains, dance performance "encourages priorities of sensation that subtly affect the nature of perception itself. Dance finely tunes sensibilities, helping shape the practices, behaviors, beliefs, and ideas of people's lives" (3).

The next step for salsa researchers is to explore and compare bodily experience and "sensational knowledge" in salsa scenes all over the world. Because of salsa's widespread popularity — not only in the Americas and in Latin American diaspora communities, but also in places like Jordan, Ghana, India, and Singapore — this exploration of the body, dance, and gender, and its relationship to larger societal discourses could be vastly enlarged, as scholars look at how these practices and discourses come together in these diverse locations and examine the ways in which the corporeal discourse in salsa dance, and the cultural gender norms associated with it, are adopted in different cultural contexts.

Acknowledgments

I would like to thank Professor Kiri Miller at Brown University for her guidance during my research and her feedback on earlier drafts of this chapter, the dancers who generously gave their time to talk with me, and Sarah Burcon and Melissa Ames for their helpful comments.

NOTES

1. For similar views, see also Delgado pg. 4 and Hanna pg. 17.

2. See Shuhei Hosokawa, "Salsa No Tiene Fronteras: Orquesta De La Luz and the Globalization of Popular Music," *Situating Salsa*, Ed. Lise Waxer (New York: Routledge, 2002): 289–311.

3. See Shain 2002, 2009.

4. See Norman Urquia, ""Doin' It Right": Contested Authenticity in London's Salsa Scene," *Music Scenes: Local, Translocal, and Virtual,* Ed. Andy Bennett and Richard A. Peterson (Nashville: Vanderbilt University Press, 2004): 96–112; Patria Roman-Velazquez, *The Making of Latin London: Salsa Music, Place and Identity* (Brookfield, Vermont: Ashgate Publishing Company, 1999).

5. Although people openly discuss sexual performance in salsa, some recognize its existence but speak disdainfully about that aspect of going to salsa clubs. One dancer who is not of Latin American background described overtly sexual movement at the salsa club as "disgusting." He described some people at the clubs as "going for the kill," or going to pick up women when they enter the dance floor (Paul).

WORKS CITED

Adair, Christy. *Women and Dance.* New York: New York University Press, 1992. Print.

"Addicted.2.Dance." Sydonee Dance Productions. n.d. Web. 3 April 2010. Online.

Anne. Personal Interview. 17 October 2009.

Aparicio, Frances R. *Listening to Salsa.* Hanover, New Hampshire: Wesleyan University Press, 1998. Print.

Bollen, Jonathan. "Queer Kinesthesia: Performativity on the Dance Floor." *Dancing Desires: Choreographing Sexualities on and Off the Stage.* Ed. Jane C. Desmond. Madison, Wisconsin: University of Madison Press, 2001. 385–14. Print.

Bosse, Joanna. "Salsa Dance and the Transformation of Style: An Ethnographic Study of Movement and Meaning in a Cross-Cultural Context." *Dance Research Journal* 40.1 (2008): 45–64. Print.

Butler, Judith. *Bodies That Matter.* New York: Routledge, 1993. Print.

Carter, Alexandra. "Feminist Strategies for the Study of Dance." *The Routledge Reader in Gender and Performance.* Ed. Lizbeth Goodman with Jane de Gay. New York: Routledge, 1998. 247–50. Print.

Delgado, Celeste Fraser. "Preface." *Everynight Life: Culture and Dance in Latin/o America.* Ed. Jose Esteban Munoz Celeste Fraser Delgado. Durham: Duke University Press, 1997. 3–8. Print.

Desmond, Jane C. "Embodying Difference: Issues in Dance and Cultural Studies." *Cultural Critique* 26 (1993–1994): 33–63. Print.

_____. "Introduction. Making the Invisible Visible: Staging Sexualities through Dance." *Dancing Desires: Choreographing Sexualities on and Off the Stage.* Ed. Jane C. Desmond. Madison, Wisconsin: The University of Wisconsin Press, 2001. 3–34. Print.

Hahn, Tomie. *Sensational Knowledge: Embodying Culture through Japanese Dance.* Middletown: Wesleyan University Press, 2007. Print.

Hanna, Judith Lynne. *Dance, Sex and Gender.* Chicago: University of Chicago Press, 1988. Print.

Hosokawa, Shuhei. "Salsa No Tiene Fronteras: Orquesta De La Luz and the Globalization of Popular Music." *Situating Salsa.* Ed. Lise Waxer. New York: Routledge, 2002. 289–311. Print.

Hutton, Fiona. *Risky Pleasures?: Club Cultures and Feminine Identities.* Abingdon, Oxon: Ashgate Publishing, Limited, 2006. Print.

Lewis, Linden. "Masculinity, the Political Economy of the Body, and Patriarchal Power in the Caribbean." *Gender in the 21st Century: Caribbean Perspectives, Visions and Possibilities.* Ed. Barbara Bailey and Elsa Leo-Rhynie. Kingston, Jamaica: Ian Randle Publishers, 2004. 236–61. Print.

Marc. Personal Interview. 16 October 2009.

Mary. Personal Interview. 14 November 2009.

Paul. Personal Interview. 11 October 2009.

Pini, Maria. "Cyborgs, Nomad and the Raving Feminine." *Dance in the City.* Ed. Helen Thomas. New York: St. Martin's Press, 1997. 111–29. Print.

Polhemus, Ted. "Dance, Gender and Culture." *Dance, Gender and Culture.* Ed. Helen Thomas. New York: St. Martin's Press, 1993. 3–15. Print.

Roman-Velazquez, Patria. *The Making of Latin London: Salsa Music, Place and Identity.* Brookfield, Vermont: Ashgate Publishing Company, 1999. Print.

Santos Febres, Maya. "Salsa as Translocation." *Everynight Life.* Ed. Celeste and Jose Esteban Munoz Fraser Delgado. London: Duke University Press, 1997. 175–88. Print.

Shain, Richard M. "The Re(public) of Salsa: Afro-Cuban Music in Fin-De-Siècle Dakar." *Africa: The Journal of the International African Institute* 79.2 (2009): 186–206. Print.

_____. "*Roots in Reverse: Cubanismo in Twentieth-Century Senegalese Music.*" *International Journal of African Historical Studies* 35.1 (2002): 83–101. Print.

Thomas, Helen. "An-Other Voice: Young Women Dancing and Talking." *Dance, Gender and Culture.* Ed. Helen Thomas. New York: St. Martin's Press, 1993. 69–93. Print.

_____. *Body, Dance and Cultural Theory.* New York: Palgrave Macmillan, 2003. Print.

Urquia, Norman. ""Doin' It Right": Contested Authenticity in London's Salsa Scene." *Music Scenes: Local, Translocal, and Virtual.* Ed. Andy Bennett and Richard A. Peterson. Nashville: Vanderbilt University Press, 2004. 96–112. Print.

Washburne, Christopher. *Sounding Salsa: Performing Latin Music in New York City.* Philadelphia: Temple University Press, 2008. Print.

10

"Tell me, does she talk during sex?" The Gendering of Permissible Speech on *Dr. Phil*

Diana York Blaine

Dr. Phil McGraw is by no means the first clinical psychologist to perform a kind of televised therapy,[1] but with the impressive imprimatur of Oprah Winfrey behind him, he swiftly became the most famous. After beginning as a frequent guest on her talk show, he was ultimately given his own, under Winfrey's corporate structure, which remains one of the most highly-watched daytime television programs to date.[2] Because of the enormous weight that McGraw has ended up wielding over daytime viewers and consumers of popular culture at large, it is important to look critically at what ideologies he propagates, particularly in reference to women, the audience for whom talk shows were invented and for whom these programs ostensibly ameliorate difficulties.

Yet while the *Dr. Phil* juggernaut definitely bears scrutiny as to its ideological content, very little research has been published on the program.[3] Lori Henson and Rhadika Parameswaran broadly examine the ways in which McGraw both propagates and constructs hegemonic masculinity through self-presentation and control of audience participation.[4] However, no study exists that closely examines ways in which this conservative representation of masculinity affects the ability of female guests to define their own lives in a format ostensibly designed to advance the interests of women. Therefore, this chapter seeks to further knowledge of the ways McGraw's show codifies conventional sex roles, particularly by controlling the speech of female guests. I will demonstrate that far from promoting the construction of the female as an active agent of her own destiny, McGraw imposes a conventional paradigm of male dominance, idealizing the silent female and reinforcing a hierarchy predicated upon the heterosexual nuclear family in which the woman plays the role of supporter to the aggressive husband. And although he frequently touts himself as an empirically-trained scientist, McGraw continually asserts this agenda regardless of the evidence presented before him: no matter what the individual guests divulge as the particulars of their situation, he insists that men are sexually and physically aggressive and women are not. In doing so, he makes clear that the problems being posed are consistently those of the failure of the female to live up to patriarchal expectations for women, particularly subservience and silence. To effect this diagnosis, Dr. Phil routinely pathologizes female sexual agency when it outstrips that of the male partner.

While my interpretation draws on a number of episodes of *Dr. Phil* that have run over the last seven years, this essay focuses most specifically upon a close reading of a 2002 episode of *The Oprah Winfrey Show* that features McGraw as an expert on marital sexual relations. Titled "When Sexual Appetites Don't Match," the program centers on three couples who are experiencing major tension in their relationships due to dissimilar sexual desire. Throughout the narrative McGraw operates upon clearly established codes of compulsory heterosexuality and normative masculinity and femininity. According to this code, men are hypersexual and deserve to be serviced. Women, conversely, do not desire sex and must be pressured to participate in it for the health of the relationship — meaning, specifically, that failure to keep the man happy sexually equates with failure of the marriage. Paradoxically, if the women exhibit independent sexual desire, it is marked as unnatural and a danger to the success of the union. Marital failure, according to McGraw's script, must be avoided at all costs, at least on the part of the women involved, who carry the sole burden of keeping the union emotionally and sexually healthy.

The main problem with McGraw's conservative construction of male-female marriage and sexuality lies in the fact that in two of the three cases presented on the program, it is the *man* who has been the unwilling sexual partner. Yet instead of adjusting his men-are-dogs/women-are-frigid paradigm, Dr. Phil insists upon imposing his worldview on the couples, badgering the women and bucking up the men until they reach a kind of coerced agreement that the wives need to be more willing sexual partners and the men just need to sit back and rest on their hyper-heterosexual masculine laurels. Thus by the end of each segment, McGraw proves that the females are at fault, either unwilling to perform with an eager sexual partner or having an unhealthy addiction to sex that he suggests the sexually masterful husband will be able to quell by getting her "caught up." As I will show, these conclusions that he draws are utterly bizarre in light of the actual testimony of the people involved, revealing that McGraw silences women by imposing a patriarchal worldview. I will also demonstrate how each woman attempts to voice her own sense of a feminist identity and right to self-determination only to be shamed and muted by McGraw for her unwomanly striving for satisfaction. In each case, as he moves to control the wife, McGraw appeals to the husband to side with him. In this way the program exemplifies how hegemonic masculinity is won "not only through coercion, but through consent, even though there is never a complete consensus" (qtd. in Henson and Parameswaran 290).

Imposing Hegemonic Masculinity: Three Case Studies

Amy and Jeremy

In this first of the segments, a young married couple seeks Dr. Phil's help because the wife has lost all sexual desire for her husband. Following the conventional format, the show first presents a video excerpt of the couple discussing their problem. In this clip both state that the arrival of children changed the dynamic between them. Wife Amy gives three reasons for her declining libido. She itemizes her busy schedule, including work, school, and domestic duties, as we see her enter her house at the end of her day, saying "Looks like a tornado went through. I'm exhausted, and Jeremy wants attention from me. This is not the '70s. I mean, I work too" ("When" 2). She also discusses her postpartum body loathing, saying she cannot imagine ever feeling sexy again, her body a "roadmap with stretch marks and purple varicose veins" ("When" 3). And she says that she finds it difficult alternating between the roles of "mom" and "sexy wife" ("When" 3).

Each of these complaints reveals her struggle to find a sense of integrated identity while working and going to school and serving the interests of others, especially her children and her husband. Wife Amy's issues clearly all relate to the institutionalized structure of heteronormative marriage under capitalism and the conflicting demands of modern constructions of femininity. Significantly, her comment "This is not the '70s" shows her expectations of marriage have been informed by the second wave of feminism, in which women sought civil rights identical to those of men. According to this post-feminist paradigm, she will be treated as an equal partner in her marriage, not as the servile spouse expected in more traditional family structures. And yet, as she notes, while she and Jeremy both work, when they come home, the sharing of the duties ceases. She finds herself pulling what sociologist Arlie Hochschild has termed "the second shift," another full-time job for women of household chores and parenting duties (Hochschild 4). Note that the couple agrees they had a wonderful and active sex life until the advent of their children. Suddenly, Amy's desires for her husband cooled as she found herself relegated to a role she assumed had died with her grandmother's generation. But unlike the rhetoric, the reality of equality only stretches so far in conventional marriage.

This expectation on the part of young women like Amy does not take into account a lack of feminist socialization on the part of males. In fact, in many ways, the mass media script for hegemonic heterosexuality has gotten even more conservative in the last several decades, intensifying even more after 9/11.[5] Hence Jeremy believes he *is* participating in the household duties sufficient to satisfy his role as considerate spouse: "She says I need to do more around the house as far as helping with the kids, doing the laundry, doing the dishes, and I feel I do a lot around the house, but she says I need to do more. And — and — that's...." Here Amy cuts him off and asserts, "It's not equal. I feel we both go to school, we both work full-time, we're both parents. It should be split down the middle" ("When" 5). Dr. Phil's response to this clear assessment of the political problem in their home? "OK. But here — here's my question. Why are you not interested in having sex?" ("When" 5).

At this point McGraw begins to replace her feminist desire for equality with the desire to be a cheerful and submissive wife by urging her to indoctrinate herself into having positive feelings about marital intercourse. Because Amy has mentioned several problems she is experiencing with her own sexuality, including negative body image, the conflict with mothering and being a "sexy wife," and — most compellingly — her clear dissatisfaction with the sexist delegation of domestic duties, McGraw informs her that she has a counter productive "internal dialogue" taking place throughout the day ("When" 10). He chastises her for what he terms this negative programming. Thus the problem has ceased to be one of structural inequity and institutionalized patriarchy and becomes the failure of one individual to propagandize herself all day long about how much she wants to please her man. This ideology recalls that of Marabel Morgan, conservative Christian author of *Total Woman*, who urged wives to greet their husbands at the door wearing nothing but Saran Wrap in order to keep the male's attention.

The construction of masculinity deployed here reflects similarly retrograde characteristics. The segment focuses entirely on Amy and her failure to perform effectively as a sex partner. McGraw, the established authority figure and self-appointed representative of rational thinking, treats husband Jeremy as a sympathetic figure, driven mad with desire by his recalcitrant spouse. When asked by the doctor earlier in the episode if she likes her husband, Amy replies that he is often grouchy "...because I am not giving in" ("When" 4). "[Y]eah," McGraw concurs, "that'll make a guy grouchy" ("When" 4). Male aggression receives approbation from the psychologist, justified by a lack of sufficient intercourse. And later Jeremy complains that any time he tries to be romantic, she shuts him down because she does not want him to try and coerce her into having sex. In a conspiratorial tone, McGraw attempts to get Jeremy to admit that indeed intercourse — not romance — is all he really wants. The host naturalizes what he represents as animalistic: "Well, she's pretty much right, isn't she? Because aren't you pretty much like a crazed dog at this point?" ("When" 6). And later McGraw says "...when you are absolutely sex-starved and crazed, that's pretty right" ("When" 7). McGraw pressures Jeremy to say that his libidinous urges render him incapable of anything but the desire to mate. The young man acquiesces, adding "That is correct. I mean, she can walk by and just give me that look and I'm just ready right now, you know" ("When" 7). McGraw cuts him off and, turning to Amy, asks "And that's not flattering to you at all?" ("When" 7). Again, McGraw trivializes her problem and turns it into a failure on her part to appreciate this valuable male attention.

The doctor repeatedly frames the issue as Amy's inability to be a servile sex partner to the male. Ignoring the wife's depiction of her situation, McGraw legitimizes the husband's complaints and threatens her with deserved desertion if she fails to submit: "You are sending a message that is going to say, you know, you can either — we can either have an active intimate life, or we can't. And when you send that message, you choose the consequence that goes with it. Are you trying to tell him to leave?" ("When" 9). "No," replies Amy. "Absolutely not" ("When" 9). "Do you expect him to stay under the current conditions?" he continues severely ("When" 9). Amy, again the focus of the doctor's relentless gaze, reformulates her own desire that they be equal as the desire to meet her husband's sexual expectations. "I'd like him to [stay]" she says,

> but I don't know. I — we've sat up many nights and talked about it, and I told him, I was like, if there was something I could take to make me get aroused or feel something, I would. But I just don't. And I don't know what's causing it. I don't know if it's the stress or something else ["When" 9].

Her transformation from independent individual to failed wife nears completion at this point as she has forgotten her own overt assertion at the beginning of the episode that she wants an equal partnership and is not in one. McGraw has become her epistemological authority,[6] as his way of knowing totally usurps hers. Now that she has fallen in line with the program, retreating to confusion and self-doubt, he changes his approach, softening his aggressive stance towards her: "It's not like you — you — you've done something wrong here and you need to be punished or ridiculed in some way. [Which is exactly what he has been doing.] And I also hear you say you have a willing spirit" ("When" 10). After diagnosing her as frigid, he provides the solution: "And so what you have to do is you have to say 'I want to look at Jeremy's needs as legitimate, and I want to ask myself is there something I can do to meet those?'" ("When" 10). McGraw reinforces the male's right to sexual access to the female, suggesting this central cultural privilege has become vulnerable and needs defending.

Amy's needs, on the other hand, do not get the same validation from McGraw. Now that he has told her what to think, and say, and do, he directs his attention to the husband. The obvious advice for Jeremy would be to contribute more to the burdens of running the household. Indeed it appears the doctor is going to prescribe just that when he says, "And, Jeremy, you have to look at Amy's needs and say, 'I'm going to consider these to be legitimate. What can I do to help her with *these thoughts and these feelings*?" ("When" 10, emphasis added). By not asking Jeremy how he can help her with the dishes and the laundry, McGraw casts Amy's needs entirely as emotional ones thus eliding her earlier pleas for her husband to participate fully in the running of the home. Thus Jeremy's role is not to change the diapers of his own children but to help his wife condition herself to want to have intercourse with someone she resents. Amy's "needs" have been transformed from the need for an equal partnership, as she stated earlier by saying "I mean this isn't the 70s," to the need to want to have sex with her husband even though she does not. He does give Jeremy one more piece of advice now that the doctor has validated the husband's demands for intercourse: "you can't just dog-pile her in the foyer" ("When" 11). McGraw again naturalizes heterosexual masculinity as animalistic as he leeringly suggests the husband hold off attacking the wife until they are in the bedroom. This minor concession to the feelings of the wife only further emphasizes that the power structure favors the male.

Indeed, McGraw returns one last time to Amy in order to reinforce the overall message of patriarchal privilege. As he does so, the tone shifts from the friendly and conspiratorial one he has just shared with Jeremy, becoming again severe and disapproving. Reminding her of the negative things she has said and believed and felt about her marriage, McGraw twice admonishes her that she is "running [her] husband off" ("When" 10–11). No mention is made of Amy's deep dissatisfaction with the conventional and unequal structure of their marriage nor — in spite of McGraw's earlier assertion that "in terms of differential diagnosis" he seeks "the simplest explanation first" — does he proffer the most obvious solution, that Jeremy participate equally in the running of their home, thus validating Amy as a person. But the doctor cannot simultaneously prescribe this *and* propagate patriarchal heterosexuality: "McGraw's recuperation of traditional masculinity in the service of his "get real" therapy does not speak to the unequal division of domestic labor, the greater burdens of parenting borne by women, or the transformation of gender relations"

(Henson and Parameswaran 301). Hence his construction of husband as a needy animal serves to keep intact a power structure that excludes women from fully exercising their humanity within the grounds of traditional heterosexuality and also excuses men from important central tasks considered trivial, like child care and cleaning. Oprah chimes in to reinforce this patriarchal worldview, noting that Jeremy has ended up at the bottom of the "pecking order." But clearly, in the "pecking order" of this household, as on this program, Amy comes last.

Robert and Alyssa

This first couple exactly matched the normative narrative of male/female relations in which the frigid woman denies the deserving spouse sex and he rightly starts sniffing around elsewhere for what he should be getting at home. Acting as sex therapist in spite of a lack of training in this field, McGraw framed the issue as the failure of female compliance. Within these parameters the political is adamantly personal rather than the other way around, and Dr. Phil maneuvered comfortably through this territory. The next couple, however, presents a completely different dilemma. In this case, the mild mannered, soft-spoken conventional wife has endured years of a sexless marriage, starting with the wedding night and the honeymoon. Unlike the first couple, they have gone for over a year at a time without sex. Now, she says, after listening to programs like *Oprah* and reading several unnamed books, she understands that she is responsible for her own happiness and has decided to divorce. Under this threat the husband has agreed to intercourse, and she finds herself confused at his sudden willingness. She says she wrote the *Oprah Winfrey* show for a solution.

In this case the husband's failure to conform to the expected hyper-sexual code of masculinity established in the earlier segment immediately arouses McGraw's skepticism and he swiftly seeks to re-establish the norms of male desire. The husband says perhaps he has been putting other things ahead of sex in the relationship, "family and work and everything that I provide for the family, I always thought came first before that part, you know" ("When" 12). Phil needles him, unwilling to accept this unacceptable explanation. "But — but — but these are not mutually exclusive things," he stutters. "I mean, you say you put emphasis on family and work and money and all that, but you do go to bed at night, right?" ("When" 12). "Absolutely," replies Robert ("When" 12). McGraw continues, "And you don't work while you're in bed." "Right," says the man ("When" 12). Dr. Phil: "And so you're there. The two of you are alone. Door shut. You're there. And it's just not natural that you're just laying there thinking about work or — or something. What is it you don't like about it? What is it that's unappealing to you?" ("When" 12–13). Note here that he again appeals to nature to explain the inevitability of masculine sexuality. Male sex just happens. All it takes is to be in bed with a female. And so he is flummoxed by this man's lack of desire. Yet in the earlier segment he never asked Amy if she enjoyed having sex nor did he tell her that her lack of desire was unnatural. Indeed he reified her lack as natural, dismissing her very real objections to the situation in her marriage that made her view her spouse with disdain.

Because McGraw insists upon this sexist code of male/female relations, he literally cannot speak outside of it. A man who does not want sex? Impossible. Men want sex, so words literally fail McGraw when confronted with a case that does not fit his paradigm. "No, I'm serious," he says, lest the presence of a non-sexual male be taken as a trivial issue:

> You say you got to be in the right frame of mind. I — I'm just — I — I just — I don't get — I — I — and I'm not trying to be hard on you. I'm trying to understand what you're telling yourself for six years about this. What — what — what — what do *you* say about this? ["What" 13; emphasis added].

At this point the stuttering and nearly speechless McGraw turns to the wife, refusing to speak to the man who does not have an acceptably masculine sex drive. She does her best to tell her story, that she has tried to understand for a long time, that at first he said she was special and so they should wait until marriage, but then,

> the wedding night came and went, and the honeymoon came and went, and I was just — you know, sometimes I wish I could have said, "OK, there's a problem here and I need to move on," because I — but I didn't realize, I guess at that time, nor did I express to him right after we were married that that was really important to me, because I wanted to make this marriage work ["When" 13].

Notice her conventional expectation that keeping the marriage intact was her job, and that her silence was also a required part of this normative femininity. "I wish I could have said..." she tells Phil, only now having the nerve to speak up after reading self-help books and watching *Oprah*.

But instead of continuing with this narrative of female empowerment, encouraging the very self-determination *Oprah* purports to offer, the structure of the discourse again turns towards the wife as the source of disruption in the marriage. Alyssa explains that once she said she was leaving, Robert "kind of turned around and said, 'Oh, well, OK, let's do it'" ("When" 13). She wonders why now he is willing after turning a deaf ear to her concerns over the last six years. McGraw wonders too, and forced to readdress the man, again loses his ability to speak coherently: "Well, really, Robert, I — what's — what — what — what's up with all of this?.... It is — I mean, what's missing here?"

("When" 13). Improbably, Robert replies "a willing partner," referring to his wife ("When" 14). At this point in the episode, Robert suddenly transforms into a sexually frustrated husband, another Jeremy craving sex from his frigid spouse. McGraw, finding the opportunity to reinterpret the floundering session through his conservative paradigm, falls into line with this version of events and sternly portrays the wife as an unwilling sexual partner denying the husband his marital rights. Suddenly forced to account for her own lack of sexual interest in spite of the fact that it was her husband's lack of sexual interest that alienated her affections, Alyssa admits that "In the last year, he has tried to initiate a couple of times, but, as I said, in my letter, I don't want it anymore. So now I've — now I guess it's my problem" ("When" 14). Upon hearing this apparent admission of guilt, McGraw, having won the battle, suddenly reverts to his folksy southern persona.[7] He relays an anecdote about a couple he met who had been married 52 years. McGraw says that when he asked how they stayed married, the wife replied "We just never fell out of love at the same time.... And I thought that was really a — a great observation," McGraw says, "because you do have ups and downs. You — you do yin and yang within a relationship" ("When, 14).

Re-established now in his role as paternal admonisher of wayward wives, he defines the problem as one of balance, invoking Eastern philosophy in order to do so. And so Alyssa transforms into another Amy, even being asked the same question now that they have the same problem: "Do you love your husband?" ("When" 14). She says she does, so he tells her that since Robert is now a willing partner, she needs to work on staying in the marriage:

> Go to counselors. Go to your pastor. Read books. Come here. Do whatever you can do to try to put it on, because I don't want you to be looking at your daughter 10 years from now and her say "How come I had to grow up without my daddy?" and you have to say, "Well I don't know. We just couldn't get it together at the same time, and I got tired of it." That's not much of an answer to a child that has to deal with that ["When" 15].

McGraw is correct, of course, that prematurely ending a marriage out of boredom and impatience would be inadvisable, even repugnant, but to characterize that as what is happening in this situation can only be done by ignoring the facts and imposing a patriarchal worldview that deems wives as powerless appendages to husbands. McGraw uses the symbol of the child as an aggressive tactic to invoke sentiment against Alyssa's desire to free herself from this dysfunctional relationship, instead shaming her as a heartless mother damaging an innocent victim. As to his advice that she read books, Alyssa has read books, and those very books were what showed her that she needed to act on her own behalf given that her years of sexless marriage were accompanied by a spouse who refused to deal with the situation or take her complaints seriously. Remember earlier wife Amy tells McGraw that she has spent many agonizing hours trying to figure out what is wrong with her so that she can be a willing sexual partner to her husband. Viewers have no evidence that Robert has done the same soul-searching. He now points the finger at his wife and McGraw heartily concurs.

As to what the husband's lack of libido signifies, McGraw, although acting in the role of sex therapist, remains clueless. Nonetheless he works to naturalize Robert's mysterious condition before shaming Alyssa for having desired an active sex life in her marriage:

> Whatever's going on with you, you haven't told me, Robert. I mean, I don't know what it is, and maybe you don't know what it is, so you don't know how to put words to it.....I mean, whatever keeps you from being motivated sexually to be with your wife, whether you call it a problem, or just a characteristic or whatever, just a threat's not going to change that ["When" 15].

Robert's unwillingness to engage sexually, unlike Amy's unwillingness, is explained away as a "characteristic." McGraw never tells Robert he is "running off" his wife. In fact, McGraw does the opposite, policing the boundaries of Alyssa's freedom and running her back into the marital corral:

> [Y]ou have come to a point that you have a willing partner here, and I would really, really encourage both of you to give this thing a shot where both of you are on the same page at the same time, because I believe, particularly when you have children involved, if you're going to get out of a marriage, you have to earn your way out ["When" 15].

In the previous segment, husband Jeremy was given no such admonition, that he needed to earn his way out of a marriage with children, in spite of the fact that he was still having sex regularly with his wife and was also threatening to get sexual satisfaction elsewhere, an idea McGraw explicitly endorsed. Male privilege champions the desires of the man on this episode of *Oprah*, undermining the possibility of the feminist marriage Amy believed she was entering into and needed to be in to remain a desiring subject. Alyssa, on the other hand, has gone over a year without any sex, has spent years longing for sexual interactions with her spouse, beginning with their sexless honeymoon, and yet is still told she is to blame for not being a willing bed partner to her husband and that her role as mother supercedes her own sexual agency. Thus the couple becomes resituated in the conventional heterosexual paradigm wherein the lustful male finds rejection at the hands of a nagging and uncaring spouse.

DAVID AND BARBARA

The third segment presents another couple with sexual dysfunction, again a case in which the wife desires more sex than she gets from her mate. But unlike the woman in the previous case, ebullient honeymooner Barbara is unwilling to wait six years to address this issue. In their introductory video, she and her husband, both in their forties, spar about how much sex they have. He says a lot, she says a little. However, there can be no real dispute, for wife Barbara documents the days they had intercourse. "He'll say to me, 'Barb, it hasn't been that long.' And I'll say, 'Oh yes it has been that long, because I mark it on the calendar. And I do mark it on the calendar with a little heart. And that's my little symbol, so that I know that's the night we did it," she says ("When" 16). To this David replies that he fears showing Barbara affection because she will immediately assume he wants to have sex with her. "I may just be wanting [to] have her close to me, to touch her, feel her, or kiss her just to let her know I love her," he explains ("When" 16). This complaint mirrors that of husband Jeremy in the first segment who says that his wife, too, misreads his attempts at affection. In the earlier case, however, Amy fears that he *is* coming on to her. In this case, Barbara *hopes* that he is.

Yet McGraw does not suggest that Barbara's sexual desires are natural, which starkly opposes the way he handled the parallel situation with the younger couple. In fact in the earlier segment when Jeremy said that sometimes he *is* just trying to show affection, McGraw talked him out of this claim by taking Amy's side. Thus McGraw could represent the husband as an animal single-mindedly intent upon intercourse. "Well, she's pretty much right, isn't she?" says McGraw ("When" 6). "Because aren't you pretty much like a crazed dog at that point?" ("When" 6). While this had not been the point that Jeremy was trying to illustrate — he was voicing frustration over his inability to be romantic, not sexual — McGraw uses the force of his authority, phrasing his response in a series of questions designed to compel agreement on the part of the man in order to adhere to the code of normative masculinity established on the program. In this code, men do not ever want to show affection. Affection is the territory of the female. Men only have a desire for heterosexual intercourse. And women only have the desire to avoid it. Therefore McGraw does not — cannot — address David, the husband in this segment, with the same assertion, that he is really only showing Barb affection to get sex, because his wife is complaining that she is not getting it. So McGraw returns to his normative script and begins to reformulate the evidence at hand to fit. The paradigm dictates that men are hypersexual, and the absence of sexual desire in women is natural. From this perspective any sexual desire women do exhibit that does not match the husband's needs is unnatural, threatening to the stability of the male-centered hetero-nuclear family, and in need of containment.

Because this view frames female desire as dangerous and in need of controlling, McGraw strives to humiliate Barbara for relating her truth. Expressing her frustration at the infrequent intercourse in her new marriage, Barbara says

"I'm in my 40's. I think I'm speaking for a lot of American women here. This is the prime of my life. I want to enjoy my sexual life. He's just tired all the time, Dr. Phil, and I'm so tired of him being tired" ("When" 17). Instead of validating her concern, one that she links to a larger institutional problem with the structure of compulsory monogamy and heterosexual marriage, McGraw attempts to deflate her by reacting as if she has been intemperate in her speech: "OK. Now, say what you mean. Don't..." ("When" 17). This expression conventionally mocks someone who has been too assertive. But instead of taking the hint that she has stepped outside of the parameters of acceptable female speech, Barbara cuts him off and says "All right. I will. I feel really strongly about this" ("When" 17). Since McGraw failed to intimidate her with his first joking admonishment to silence herself, he then turns to her husband and says, "...David, does she talk during sex?" ("When" 17). "No," he replies, "actually, she doesn't" ("When" 17). "Well," says McGraw, "I — I'd think that would be a motivator of its own" ("When" 17). In other words, her speech about self-empowerment so offends McGraw that he suggests the one reason her husband might consider having sex with her is simply — and sadistically — to silence her.

Here the person in the supreme position of authority clearly flags female speech as unnatural and in need of control. There can be no mistaking his attempt to shame Barbara for having the nerve to express herself as a desiring subject. She and McGraw may both be individuals, but his program strives to deploy a conservative patriarchal worldview and thus there can be no space for assertive females. Semiotically everything on the program works to emphasize McGraw's wisdom and insights, from the prominent use of the term "Doctor" to the exclusion of audience participation to the enormously high chairs that suit his tall frame and make most of his guests look like big babies. Therefore we cannot underestimate the power wielded by this man, watched by millions of viewers, nor should we minimize the damage that such cruel comments have the potential to inflict. While he claims to be a scientist, lapsing into medical jargon when he wants to remind this guests that he is in charge, in this case he completely abandons any sense of professionalism and instead resorts to a crude sexist attack in order to utterly disempower and shame this female who has sought his guidance and yet had the nerve to assert her own will.

The wife's voicing of sexual desire not only breaks the code of femininity that the conservative program propagates but it also exposes the artifice of the construction of masculinity deployed as well. She can only be dissatisfied sexually if she is in a union with a man who does not have the power to sexually satisfy her. Bram Dijkstra notes that concerns over the sexually voracious wife grew under early capitalism and its increasing demands on the male in the public sphere, one destabilized by the loss of ancient support networks for men. Performance on the job in this new industrial economy was seen as draining of men's vital forces; having to perform in the home as well became a potential source of debilitation. While social critics began noting this issue in the nineteenth-century, McGraw's handling of this couple's sexual issues reflects these older fears of the desiring female. So he moves decisively to silence her as well as to reinvigorate the flagging construct of masculinity that her complaining voice illuminates.

In order to do so, he must make her desire unnatural and the husband's behavior, or lack of behavior, natural. This first attempt to coerce her into silence meets with her disapproval. After his crack about having sex with her only to silence her nagging tongue, she says "Dr. Phil, come on." He says he was teasing, which he was. But the fact that it was a joke in no way means that it did not carry real and important ideological messages clearly meant to undermine her. She next attempts to stand up for herself by explaining that "I'm being my authentic self here" ("When" 17). Her use of the term "authentic self" refers specifically to a best-selling book McGraw had published the previous year. Called *Self Matters*, it calls for readers to find their "authentic selves." Barbara, clearly having read this book, operates on its thesis that she deserves to be true to herself. Yet, ironically, when she does so in the presence of its author, and her "authentic self" does not parallel his prescription for acceptable femininity, he moves swiftly to silence that self in order to maintain the illusion that real women do not want to have sex, and, therefore, that real men are motivated sexually under all circumstances.

Therefore he next moves to directly pathologize her sexual agency. If she wants to have sex more than the husband wants to have sex, then she must be sick. As usual he invites the husband to join him in this endeavor, using male bonding as a tool against the lone female trying to establish her needs as legitimate. Acknowledging one more time that he was just teasing, and disingenuously dismissing the idea that teasing can be serious, he says, "But now seriously, though, there's something that — that I picked up out of this tape, David, that I want to ask you about. You have said that you think that she is like addicted to this and over — overfocused on it and that it — her energy for it is not healthy, is that correct?" ("When" 18). David sees his lead — the "doctor" has diagnosed "addiction" — and so he runs with it, claiming that if "we make love three times a week, she wants it five times a week. If we want — if— if we make love five times a month, she wants it more" ("When" 18). The problem with this creative accounting lies in the fact that the wife has material proof of the number of times they have intercourse, and it is nowhere near five times a month, let alone five times a week. One assumes that were near-daily intercourse her reality she would not be on national television seeking a solution to its absence. Of course neither McGraw nor the husband feels compelled to clarify this, because both of them get to maneuver comfortably back into safe waters, those of the normative virile male and his unstable dysfunctional wife.

Whatever the actual number of incidents of marital sex, McGraw's narrative requires that the female be the problem. So he suggests to the husband that two pertinent issues need addressing. Surprisingly, given the nature of the dysfunction, one is David's purported sexual mastery, which McGraw suggests has gotten her really "highly motivated" ("When" 18). "You've got to own that part of it," he says ("When" 18). Suddenly the man who is always "too tired" to have sex has been reformulated into such a remarkable bed partner that his wife seeks sex from him simply because he is so powerful. Once again as dictated by the script of hegemonic masculinity, men have voracious sexual appetites and are masters at the game of love, awakening women to the pleasures of sensuality. Of course David will want to "own" the notion that his sexual mastery has caused a grown woman to transform into a desperate teenager.

Not content to leave the problem at the feet of the male's fictive sexual prowess, McGraw overtly pathologizes Barbara's desire. Suggesting that her request for more sex reflects a sickness on her part, Dr. Phil says to the husband, "Maybe after she kind of got caught up, that maybe would relax a little bit, and you would have — you would have more of a natural flow" ("When" 18). In the previous sentence, "that," as in "that maybe would relax a little bit," refers to Barbara's sex drive, something overheated and unnatural that needs to be defused, even at the dire cost of having sex with her. Absolutely nothing is said about her having a legitimate need for intercourse. Recall the first wife, Amy, on the other hand, who was explicitly told to look at Jeremy's sexual needs as "legitimate." The only difference here? The sex of the people involved. In McGraw's patriarchy, men's desires are legitimized — even championed — and women's are derided and pathologized as unnatural.

Immediately after he has identified Barbara as a sex addict who should be silenced, there is a commercial break during which someone on the crew apparently reads him the riot act because he returns to the stage and gives the following speech to the husband that strives to neutralize the repellant misogyny of the entire segment:

> What I'm concerned about is if you've labeled her in your mind, if you've put a label on her in your mind as being wrong in what she wants, then basically you dismiss this as her problem instead of something that the two of you negotiate a plan that you can both be excited about. And so if you — if you put a label on it — you're wrong, you're overmotivated, you're in some way inappropriate there — then you divorce yourself of it and you don't have any involvement in coming up with a solution. It's her problem. She needs to fix it ["When" 19].

This all sounds logical but the only problem with his temperate soliloquy is that *McGraw* is the one who has just spent the whole segment labeling her as wrong and overmotivated and inappropriate. This is the same man who told the husband that if she stops talking during sex, he is surprised the man does not give in to her requests for intercourse just to silence her. This is the same man who said that her desire was unnatural and her behavior addictive. Perhaps one of Oprah's producers found his egregious sexism egregious, sending him back out to give an impotent coda about not pathologizing female sexual desire.

But because the concept of legitimate female sexual agency does not fit into McGraw's paradigm, he next rejects the notion that the husband be held accountable for his behavior in spite of the egalitarian speech that he has just given. To do this, McGraw draws attention to men's supposed inability to function emotionally in relationships. He deploys this appeal to strategic ignorance on the part of husband only when it reinforces male privilege, since this part of the script of normative masculinity requires that nurturing be done exclusively by women. Men cannot be caregivers, either physically through domestic chores, or emotionally, through relationship maintenance. They get to be along for the ride while women do the work. McGraw introduces this concept after Oprah comments that partners need to be able to ask for what they want. He adds, "And be specific. I mean, because I've said men don't get it, but we are trainable" ("When" 20). The invocation of the word "trainable," another appeal to nature, suggests that men are non-human animals — begging the question of why a man is in charge of the marital therapy being proffered — and thus cannot nurture relationships. They merely want sex and thus women need to do the sexual, and emotional, servicing. He continues, "We just need — you just put the dots close together and connect them with a bright line and we can figure things out" ("When" 20). Anti-feminists often charge the feminist movement with being anti-male. But it is actually this type of conservative discourse that insists upon such a limiting definition of masculinity. Here the doctor portrays men as infantilized mental defectives, needing bright lines and close-together dots in order to help them succeed. Yet this accusation of simplemindedness only pertains when the servile burdens of the private sphere are being allocated. When it comes to running the world — here represented by the household — men are clearly and rightly in charge, and women who object must be silenced.

Notes

1. Dr. Joyce Brothers, Dr. Ruth, etc. come to mind. See Shattuc's chapter "Freud vs. Women: The Popularization of Therapy on Daytime Talk Shows" (111–136).

2. While the show's ratings have slipped somewhat, in 2010 it remains second only to *Oprah* in daytime talk popularity, attracting 4.5 million viewers per day, the majority female.

3. The three major articles on the show are Henson and Parameswaran, Jones, and Egan and Papson.

4. In *Masculinities*, Connell defines hegemonic masculinity as "'the culturally idealized form of masculine character' at a particular historic moment" (qtd. in Henson and Parameswaran 290).

5. See Henson and Parameswaran, 304–6, for a full consideration of how this conservative turn manifests itself on the *Dr. Phil* show.

6. See Egan and Papson for a discussion of the ways in which McGraw establishes himself as the source of moral authority, using religious structure in secular form in order to do so.

7. Southern regionalisms are part of his propagation of a hegemonic masculinity in which "the rural 'country' mythology of the south has become the raw material for an increasingly 'conservative national consciousness'" (Henson and Parameswaran 299).

WORKS CITED

Dykstra, Bram. *Idols of Perversity: Fantasies of Feminine Evil In Fin-De-Siecle Culture.* Oxford: Oxford University Press, 1986. Print.

Egan, R. Danielle, and Stephen Papson. "'You Either Get It or You Don't': Conversion Experiences and *The Dr. Phil Show.*" *Journal of Religion and Popular Culture* 10 (2005): n. pag. Web. 28 Feb. 2008.

Jones, Eric. "A Communitarian Critique of Dr. Phil: The Individualistic Ethos of Self-Help Rhetoric." *Ohio Communication Journal* 46 (2008): 73–93. Print.

Henson, Lori, and Radhika Parameswaran. "Getting Real With 'Tell It Like It Is' Talk Therapy: Hegemonic Masculinity and the *Dr. Phil Show.*" *Communication, Culture & Critique* 1 (2008): 287–310. Print.

Hochschild, Arlie. *The Second Shift: Working Parents and the Revolution at Home.* New York: Penguin, 2003. Print.

Shattuc, Jane. *The Talking Cure.* New York: Routledge, 1997. Print.

"When Sexual Appetites Don't Match." *The Oprah Winfrey Show.* KABC Los Angeles. 5 Feb. 2002. Transcript. Print.

11

Read My Profile: Internet Profile Culture, Young Women, and the Communication of Power

Ashley M. Donnelly

New Technologies and Established Ideologies

As Internet usage becomes more and more integrated into the lives of a large portion of the world's population, it is inevitable that the way we think about communication will change. How, with whom, and when we choose to communicate with friends, colleagues, and even strangers, have altered dramatically in the last 20 years. As telephones, computers, PDAs, and traditional print mediums become more and more integrated, the immediacy and accessibility of information and methods of communication seem to develop almost daily, and the discourse surrounding such advancements is lively. As David Buckingham explains in his collection *Youth, Identity, and Digital Media*,

> popular discussions of the Internet, for example, veer between celebration and paranoia; on the one hand, the technology is seen to create new forms of community and civic life and to offer immense resources for personal liberation and empowerment, while on the other it is believed to pose dangers to privacy, to create new forms of inequality and commercial exploitation, as well as leaving the individual prey to addiction and pornography [11].

Such discourse, argues Buckingham, is typical of attitudes of "technological determinism,"[1] in which technology is seen as having the capability to bring about dramatic change independent of how or why it is used (11).

To assume that technology will alter humanity simply because of its existence or, conversely, to assume that technology is *incapable* of altering social or psychological systems in and of itself ignores "the complex and sometimes quite contradictory relationships between media change and social power" (Buckingham 12). Despite the endless possibilities that new technological advances offer, the fundamental ideologies of social systems are not, necessarily, destined to change as well. Established ideological systems can and do help shape new technologies. This is clearly evident in the new "profile culture" of the Internet.

Internet profile culture encourages users of any site that shares information to create an informative "sketch" of themselves before they interact with other users. This began with gaming, social networking, and dating websites, but is now commonplace from news websites to greeting card sites. When users set up a profile, they are prompted to post a main photograph and detailed information about themselves. The information requests begin with basic demographic prompts (like age, name, location, etc.) typically followed by requests for information about "interests" and sometimes "beliefs."

While many scholars believe that online communication allows users to present their "real" selves, as will be discussed in detail, below, I argue that the architecture of profiles is actually restrictive, forcing users to rely on pre-established cultural signs to construct their online identities. These signs are rooted in mainstream, Western culture which is predominantly patriarchal and heteronormative.[2] For women, young women in particular (who are most likely to communicate using these sites and more traditionally vulnerable to the pressure of social norms), this means that before they can enter into actual discourse with others on social networking sites (SNS), dating, or other profile-based sites, they are already in a submissive position (by having been identified as "women" in a patriarchal system) that limits their ability to articulate their individual power.[3]

What follows is a theoretical[4] exploration of the restrictive nature of profile culture and its impact on young women. I will specifically focus on how these restrictions affect young women's[5] awareness of and ability to communicate a sense of personal empowerment.

Online Identities

Using computer-mediated communication (CMC) to initiate and maintain relationships is more popular than ever before, and participation in online communication is now commonplace for certain segments of U.S. mainstream culture. For example, in a 2007 survey by Ellison, Steinfielde, and Lampe, 94 percent of undergraduates surveyed were members of the SNS Facebook

(Ellison, Steinfielde, and Lampe 1153). As of January 2008, popular SNS MySpace had over 110 million active worldwide users and Facebook had over 60 million active users.[6] Even online dating, which had previously been stigmatized in popular culture, has evolved from a marginal to a mainstream social practice. According to a study by Ellison, Heino, and Gibbs that featured CBS News surveys, in 2003 at least 29 million Americans (2 out of 5 singles) used an online dating service and in 2004, on average, there were 40 million unique visitors to online dating sites each month in the U.S." (416). A social demography study of Internet dating identified it as a $1 billion industry (as of 2008) with projections that it will grow 10 percent annually through 2013 (Sautter 556). It is no wonder that the discussion of online identity issues is so vibrant in both the scholarly community and popular media.

The most prevalent concerns about CMC and identity center on issues such as identity theft, safety (particularly in relation to children), stalking, and the representation/misrepresentation of the self. The discourse surrounding the presentation of the self online is of particular interest for this investigation of profile culture. While news headlines, investigative journalists, and even popular television shows highlight the dangers of purposeful misrepresentation on dating sites or in chat rooms, implying that such distortion is commonplace, much contemporary scholarship focusing on issues of self-presentation online argues that people use CMC to present their "true" selves.

Many investigations into online communication and self presentation have based their work on noted sociologist Erving Goffman's *The Presentation of Self in Everyday Life* (1959). Most focus, in particular, on his discussion of the art of impression management and his distinction between "expressions given" and "expressions given off"—the difference between signals and cues one consciously manipulates to form impressions and those unconscious acts that help the audience form impressions independent of the subjects' intended performance (Goffman, *Presentation* 4–7). For example, in Hope Jensen Schau and Mary C. Gilly's 2003 article "We are What We Post? Self Presentation in Personal Web Space," the authors base much of their research on Goffman's discussion of the manipulation of signs and self presentation, yet argue that though Goffman "asserts that the presentation of self is contextual, based on a specific setting and facing a definable and anticipated audience" on personal Web sites, users are able to "self-present 24/7 beyond a regional setting to the virtual world" (387). Schau and Gilly's work proposes that through personal Web pages, people are able to associate themselves with artifacts through links and other forms of digital association that offer "greater freedom to express their identities ... rather than through [just] ownership or proximity. Thus, consumers' ideal values may be revealed more clearly in personal Web space than in [real life]" (Schau and Gilly 387). Their study suggests that personal Web pages allow greater control of expressions given and reduce the impact of expressions given off. While this may certainly be valid for those pages that are constructed completely by individual users, profile-based sites, by their fundamental construction, undermine such individual control. Although the creation of a personal website has progressively gotten easier, many users prefer preconfigured social media as a more user-friendly means of developing an online presence. Adolescents, for example, arguably seem to find preconfigured social media easier to maneuver than the media needed to create full websites. Teenagers are a key demographic frequently studied for their use of preconfigured social media.

In "Online Communication and Adolescent Relationships," Kaveri Subrahmanyam and Patricia Greenfield show

> that adolescents are using [online communication sites] primarily to reinforce existing relationships, both with friends and romantic partners. More and more they are integrating these tools into their "offline" worlds, using, for example, social networking sites to get more information about new entrants into their offline worlds [119].

Research consistently supports the notion that adolescent and young adult users of SNS utilize the sites to strengthen their already existent social networks rather than engage in entirely new networks online (Lampe, Ellison, and Steinfeld 35–443). These findings suggest that users of SNS will be more honest in their presentations of self because this presentation is easy to verify in "offline" space by their peers. Teenagers, however, are not the only CMC users to concern themselves with the links between their online and offline presence.

In their 2006 study of self-presentation and online dating, Ellison, Heino, and Gibbs found that "if participants aspire to an intimate relationship, their desire to feel understood by their interaction partners will motivate self-disclosures that are open and honest as opposed to deceptive" (417), undermining popular assumptions of the overwhelming threat of misrepresentation on dating sites. Though their findings suggest that participants are more willing to present their "true selves" in their mediated relationships, the authors argue that

> due to the asynchronous nature of CMC, and the fact that CMC emphasizes verbal and linguistic cues over less controllable nonverbal communication cues, online self-presentation is more malleable and subject to self-censorship than face-to-face presentation. In Goffman's (1959) terms, more expressions of self are "given" rather than "given off" [418].[7]

Though to some extent the control of presentation is more malleable in certain kinds of discourse, such as in "statements of self" on dating profiles and in email communication between potential dates, there is a tremendous amount of information given off on structured profiles that influences relationships before any direct interaction takes place.

The research above (and similar studies) focus on the *intent* of the user in CMC situations. Scholars have focused on the controllable presentation of the self and on expressions given rather than given off. Yet regardless of user intent and regardless of the type of site on which users are communicating, when working within the boundaries of a pre-configured profile, the "selves" presented are subject to the ideological confines behind the architecture of the profile itself.

Cultural Signs

Goffman's *Presentation of Self*, though over 40-years-old, has been, as discussed above, undoubtedly influential in the ongoing discourse of online representation. His 1979 work *Gender Advertisements* has similarly been seminal in the study of gender and visual culture. In 2009, Sut Jhally produced the video *The Codes of Gender*, an exploration of the gendered language of advertising photography, based on Goffman's original work. In *Gender Advertisements*, Goffman calls ads "hyper-ritualization" (84). Ads are such small glimpses of "life" that they exaggerate the mundane, thus magnifying certain ideological issues. Goffman argues that patriarchal culture of Western society is magnified in advertising. Jhally expands upon this thesis in his original work on the subject, *The Codes of Advertising* (1987), and then again in *The Codes of Gender*, applying the same theoretical approach to contemporary visual culture as Goffman did to the culture of the late 1970s. *The Codes of Gender* explores Goffman's central claim that gender ideals are the result of ritualized cultural performance, uncovering a remarkable pattern of masculine and feminine displays and poses. It looks beyond advertising as a medium that simply sells products, and beyond analyses of gender that focus on biological difference or issues of objectification and beauty, to provide a clear-eyed view of the two-tiered terrain of identity and power relations. It offers sustained focus on how our perceptions of what it means to be a man or a woman get reproduced and reinforced on the level of culture in our everyday lives ("Codes of Gender").

What I propose is that Goffman and Jhally's argument of ads as hyper-ritualization can be applied to online profile construction as well. As ads operate with intent to sell items, profiles in essence attempt to "sell" the self, or one's idea of oneself, and thus fit in with the marketing strategies of advertisements. This theory is best exemplified through a study of the main photographs on profiles; but before looking at such photographs I will discuss how the text component of profile construction is limiting and constrictive to heteronormative and patriarchal ideals.

The majority of profile-based sites lead new users through a series of prompts with drop-down menus to begin profile construction. The first information requests ask for demographic information such as location, age, relationship status, and gender.[8] On social networking sites and many dating sites, the next series of prompts ask users questions like "what are you here for" followed by a drop-down menu with responses such as "friendship," "dating," or "networking." After basic prompts, both SNS and dating websites ask questions about employment, education, and even income. MySpace and dating sites also ask questions about appearance, including height, weight, body type, and hair and eye colors. Further prompts engage with "interests" such as music, movies, books, and sports. Many ask questions such as "do you smoke," "do you drink," and "do you have tattoos" followed by questions about religious beliefs and political affiliations. The majority of profile-based sites use drop-down menus for responses, and therefore responses are limited to those available in the menu. Facebook formerly allowed users to offer open-ended responses to many of their prompts, but in May of 2010 changed this to limit users to responses linkable to Facebook sites. For example, if one's religious group or favorite band is not "linkable," the response written in it will not show up on the profile page.

Match.com has interspersed "quizzes" into their profile construction pages with questions such as, "If you could go on any vacation you wished, which of the following would you choose," followed by 5 or 6 possible choices. Eharmony offers a relationship questionnaire and "personality profile" for members. All of these multiple-choice opportunities are an effort to match compatible members. On SNS, even when not focusing on dating, the sites aim to make profiles searchable based on similar interests/likes/dislikes, and so forth.

Due to their very architecture of drop-down menus and carefully guided means of "helping" users express themselves, profiles are obviously restrictive in terms of how users can present themselves through the site. Users do not have to answer all the questions and can leave blank those which they feel unwilling or unable to answer, but as Lampe, Ellison, and Steinfold have proven with their 2006 study of SNS, the number of contacts one collects on a site is proportional to the amount of profile elements completed (435). The more information one offers through profile-based sites, the more willing/able others are to interact through that profile. Profiles with less information get less "traffic." And, as discussed above, users of dating websites in particular have a vested interest in revealing more information about themselves in order to attract a potential intimate partner.

Some might argue that, indeed, profiles are somewhat limiting of self-expression, but (a) users are still able to control the information given; (b) information given off is still quite limited; and (c) because these profiles are designed to be unisex, they do not seem to be patriarchal or heteronormative. While it is true that users are able to control their answers to some extent (by choosing which prompts to answer or which drop-down response to pick), they are only able to negotiate between the choices offered and all of these choices are, essentially, cultural signs rooted in mainstream Western culture. Cultural signs, the hieroglyphics of our dominant ideologies, permeate popular culture, relying on the political, social, and ideological unconscious of Western societies to decipher their weighty meaning. Age, for example, is a cultural sign. Assumption and beliefs about particular age groups are deeply imbedded in societal ideologies. That one can limit his/her search for other users by age group exemplifies this—one may not wish to interact with someone they deem "too old" or "too young." Religious affiliation, political beliefs, smoking, drinking, tattoos, education levels, and so on do not, essentially, have the ability to tell us about a whole human being. Yet, serving as cultural signs they connect the user with the ideological systems with which the signs are associated. Though none of these indicators truly offers insight into an individual, the *sign* of these indicators—the collective cultural understanding of the significance of these pieces of information—can, society thinks, tell us if someone is hard-working, motivated, intellectual, lazy, morally conservative, open-minded, and so on. On networking sites like Facebook, indicators are typically more cultural than ideological, such as prompts which ask "what kinds of music do you like?" The signs of musical genres indicate personality types and group affiliation, particularly for teenagers and young adults. The fact that one can peruse potential connections through search limiters like body type or political affiliations without any other form of communication means that the power of signs, like non-verbal indicators, is magnified in profile culture. Any connection and chance for actual discourse is initially limited by assumption and cultural context.

Though users may feel they have control over which prompts they choose, the nature of the affiliations of those answers becomes a part of their online identity. For example, though one may identify oneself as a Catholic and have a particular set of personal beliefs about that faith, the term "Catholic" on online profiles becomes a generic term at the mercy of popular ideas associated with it, good and bad, true and false.

But how, one might ask, is any of this heteronormative or patriarchal? On SNS and dating sites, the initial emphasis of profile construction is on establishing the gender of the user, his/her relationship status, and their intentions in terms of what type of relationship(s) he/she is seeking with other users. Though most sites allow for identification as homosexual or bi-sexual, the architecture of the profile still requires that users identify themselves as a particular gender and with a particular sexual preference. Regardless of sexual preference, profiles still insist on creating a clear gender role for each user, placing the users in a specific position with regard to their relationship status. This is, in essence, a heteronormative system.

A heteronormative ideological system is inextricably linked with the system of patriarchy. Studied extensively by scholars in women's and gender studies for decades, recent popular media has drawn serious criticism for its perpetuation and adulation of a strong, patriarchal system. Stephanie Meyer's *Twilight* series is a notable example. In their essay "Undead Patriarchy and the Possibility of Love," Leah McClimans and J. Jeremy Wisnewski explore the issue of patriarchy in the series. They offer a very clear explanation of patriarchal society, which is useful in exploring the control dynamic between the two characters.

> Patriarchal societies support inequality between men and women: Men are strong and rational; women are weak and silly. For many feminist theorists, controlling behavior is a consequence of patriarchy: Men will try to control those situations in which their dominance is threatened. Controlling behavior, however, also reinforces systems of domination and subordination, in that women whom men attempt to control are taken to be in *need* of control—in need of guidance, protection, and oversight [McClimans and Wisnewski 169].

In contemporary Western cultures, many citizens often feel at liberty to take equality between the sexes (and races and religions, etc.) for granted. Yet recent feminist criticism of popular culture is effective in articulating the prevalence and continuation of the problem today. Internet profile culture is very much a part of the system of new media and technologies perpetuating patriarchy and integrating it into the lives of a new generation of young adults.

Though profiles are designed theoretically as unisex technology, their reliance on cultural signs for the creation of an online identity inextricably links the drop-down menus and prompts with a system dominated by patriarchal belief. Collective, societal ideologies that favor youth, Western standards of beauty (thin, white, tall, able-bodied, etc.), and conformity are dominated by a patriarchal system that genders traits as either "masculine" or "feminine," empowering the masculine while devaluing the feminine.

The panopticonic nature of the Internet, in which one enters the online world very aware that he/she is being observed, monitored, and judged, means that users are entering a "world" dominated by patriarchal, heteronormative belief, fueled by heterosexual masculine fantasy, which is dominated by a heterosexual, male gaze. The assumed male gaze is ubiquitous in the online world. One only need be aware of the amount of online pornography and the pseudo-pornography of the visual culture of the World Wide Web to understand the power of this fantasy in the online world. Rather than a utopian forum for a new, equal system untouched by gendered, racialized, or ageist belief, the Internet has proven to be largely an extension of the same media that scholars have criticized as being harmful to women and other oppressed peoples for decades.

Photographs and Women for Sale

Because profiles on SNS, dating, and business networking sites are immersed in the culture of the Internet dominated by masculine fantasy, women[9] trying to "sell" themselves[10] through their profiles (for networking, dating, or simply friendly connections) are therefore, to a large extent, forced to engage with this fantasy to attract others to their profiles. This may not be a conscious decision, and I would argue that for many it is not, but simply the product of a life-long immersion in a heteronormative, patriarchal culture in which the media fetishizes (and creates) such underlying ideologies. For adolescents, in particular, rather than create their online presence uniquely, "by looking at others' profiles, teens get a sense of what types of presentations are appropriate; others' profiles provide critical cues about what to present on their own profile" (Boyd 76). According to Goffman's theory of impression management, in the online world, just as in our offline world, "social norms emerge out of situational definitions as people learn to read cues from the environment and the people present to understand what is appropriate behavior" (Boyd 75). Much of this conformity and social normalization comes from popular media.

As Goffman and Jhally suggest, advertising hyper-ritualizes the patriarchal system and the submission of women. Profile photographs are excellent examples of how the visual culture of media hyper-ritualizes this system as well. The main photograph of a profile is the picture associated with one's user name on profile-based sites. It accompanies the name of the user to be found during searches as well as comments one makes on the site or when contacting other users. It is the initial and primary symbol associated with users on such sites. Although the self-description aspects of profiles form a large portion of the self-presentation of users online, the photograph dominates the profile screen (it typically takes up a large portion of the upper-left-hand corner of the profile screen) and is seen more frequently than any other user information.

In their study of online impression management on dating sites, Ellison et al. found that the textual descriptions of appearance formulated through drop-down menu responses produce semantic problems for users: if someone suggests they posses an "average" body type, for example, this means different things to different people and, therefore, users tend to adopt "a strategy of relying on photographs as visual, objective evidence" of their potential mate's appearance. Beyond appearance, photos allow users to rely on artifacts as cultural signs to help formulate their online identity. The types of clothes and accessories worn are cultural indicators of the type of personality, class, and lifestyle the user wishes to project. Locations included in photographs also work as artifacts for non-verbal communication of self-presentation. These, of course, are impressions given, but more than anywhere else on profiles, photographs are responsible for information given off. My particular concern is how the photographs young women include on the profile "give off" signals of submission, vulnerability, and a lack of empowerment.

In Goffman's original work on advertisement and gender codes, he offers over 80 pages of examples of ads that portray women in what he calls a "parent-child" relationship with men. From body poses to camera and character proxemics, Goffman analyzes the ways in which women are continuously physically subverted in visual culture. Jhally's 2009 video expands upon this and examines the same issues (now exaggerated further) in contemporary ads 30 years later. Though they both examine over a dozen different ways in which women are undermined by their physical placement in ads, I will look at only a few examples of how these same positions are seen in the profile photos of young women: body positioning, placement in photos with male partners, infantilization, and interactions with offspring.

Goffman defines what he calls the "ritualization of subordination" in advertising in which women are perpetually placed, physically, in positions of deference to either the men in the photographs with them or the viewer (*Gender* 40). These positions include women being prostrate on floors or beds, lowering their heads and/or eyes, exposing their necks and/or bellies, or simply positioning themselves in a way that suggests instability and vulnerability. Such poses are ubiquitous in profile photos. One such gesture that implies instability and vulnerability is what Goffman calls the "bashful knee bend," a position "that seems to presuppose the goodwill of anyone in the surround who could offer harm" as it can "be read as a foregoing of full effort to be prepared and on the ready in the current social situation, for the position adds a moment to any effort to fight or flee" (45). The knee-bend and corresponding postures in which the body's weight is shifted so that the subject is off-centered and unbalanced are popular in profile pictures as they are seen as "feminine" and "pretty" poses learned from a lifetime of fashion imagery and advertising. The latent messages, however, as Goffman suggests, are indicative of vulnerability, weakness, and dependability. Weakness, vulnerability, and dependability are also seen in "canting positions" in which either the head or upper-body are lowered or tilted. "The resulting configuration can be read as an acceptance of subordination, an expression of ingratiation, submissiveness, and appeasement" (Goffman, *Gender* 46). Again, these popular profile photo positions of deference are either in response to males within the photographs themselves or to the world at large.

Images of vulnerability are further emphasized when women are infantilized.[11] One such expression is the exaggerated grin, a popular expression dominating profile photos of young women. Such a hyperexpressive symbol can be seen, as Goffman argues, as a ritualistic mollifier, or an offering of an inferior to a superior (*Gender* 48). Other images of childlike behavior, or "clowning," such as poses of wild abandonment, expressions of confusion or general goofiness, and playful jumps or kicks, suggest a lack of seriousness, formality, and self-assuredness (Goffman, *Gende*r 68–69).

A lack of self-assuredness is further emphasized by clinging and grabbing gestures, typically seen between women and male partners. Women are often featured leaning on men for support, clinging to male partners in glee or as a mark of possessiveness. This is a much more dominant image than that of men leaning on or clinging to women (Goffman, *Gender* 54–55) suggesting a sense of neediness and dependence or of passivity, with men taking the lead. This clinging form is very common in women's profile photos that feature them with their male partner. In profile photos that include a heterosexual couple, the man is nearly always the dominant image, even when the profile photo represents the woman's profile, clearly indicating a dominant/subservient relationship.

Such gestures and poses in photos indicate submission, vulnerability, and dependence, but proxemics in photos with men and women furthers such suggestions. In photos with men and women, men most frequently are seen in dominant positions, such as elevated or above women (Goffman, *Gender* 43), leaning over women, or shielding women by serving as body to be "peeked" around (Goffman, *Gender* 72). Men often typically take up more space in the photos than women and often serve as the dominant image while women constitute the subsidiary.

Women being pushed out of their own profile photos is a common theme on SNS (less so on dating sites). It can either be that their male partner dominates their profile photo or their children do so. In the profile photos of young mothers, children often either serve as the dominant image or replace the mother completely, standing in as her visual identifier. The woman is no longer the focus of her own profile; she has shifted the emphasis entirely onto her child/children.

A generalized reading of a large sample (approximately 3700 profiles) of female profile photos across both dating and SNS shows a majority of young women (roughly 85 percent) presenting themselves as either sexualized objects, submissive figures, or mothers (either by replacing their own photos with those of their children or by presenting photos in which the child is the dominant image). All three roles are representative of the idealized roles women play in a heteronormative, patriarchal system.

As stressed above, submissive, vulnerable presentations of self may not be conscious acts, but rather the result of a lifetime's immersion in popular media dominated by images of patriarchy. Yet many women are conscious of their gendered negotiation through CMC. For example, in Clancy Ratliff's "Blogging Feminism: (Web)Sites of Resistance," the author explores the relationship between sexuality online and the popularity of women's blogs. Ratliff suggests that "it should be noted that some women participate in this seeming objectification, or, rather, they consciously and purposefully use their sexuality and beauty as a way to attract readers" (5). If, as many of the article's commentators suggest, this is true and effective, Ratliff argues that "as a rhetorical strategy, even a feminist rhetorical strategy, women might take advantage of their femininity and appropriate it in order to reach a wide audience. Doing so on the Web is nothing new" (5). This discussion of sex and audience suggests that marketing oneself with the goal of appealing to heterosexual, masculine ideals of women is an appropriate and effective way of making one's voice and opinions "heard" through the clamor of noise online. Whether consciously or unconsciously, such a practice is clearly mainstream in profile culture.

In Ellison, Heino, and Gibbs's study of impression management and online dating, they found some female participants to be very aware of their own gendered negotiations of their profiles. In a specific case, "the participant 'really analyzed' her self-presentation cues and avoided any mention of sexuality, which she felt might indicate promiscuity in the exaggerated context of the profile" (Ellison, Heino, and Gibb's 424). The participant's fear of seeming promiscuous suggests that any mention of a female's sexuality in a profile is an invitation for predation or is indicative of sexual deviance. That women fear they cannot express a normal, healthy part of their humanity in the "exaggerated context" of a profile clearly expresses the power of profiles and social cues.

The above research suggests that women who are aware of their online communication as affected by their gender are maneuvering around pre-established, pre-determined ideologies related to patriarchal views of womanhood, thus maintaining the established status quo of gender relationships. Communication for women online is clearly colored by the dominance of heteronormative patriarchy.

Communication and Power

In her article "Grooming, Gossip, Facebook and Myspace," Zeynep Tufecki draws on the work of Robin Dunbar (on gossip and social grooming) to argue that social networking online, much like gossip, works as a kind of social grooming in contemporary culture. And social grooming, she articulates, "should be seen as both a bonding activity and a *competitive* activity: it is a means to improve one's reputation and status as well as access to resources and social and practical solidarity" (Tufecki 546). On social networking and dating websites, profiles facilitate the bonding and competitive nature of this grooming activity. One gains access to a number of others, forming a network for support and engagement, but it is also competitive in that one is gaining social capital, and any activity in which one seeks to gain capital is, by its very nature, competitive. Thus, one must "sell" oneself through a personal profile to gain this capital and, as seen from the research above, for women to sell themselves in today's online market, they generally must present themselves in ways that subscribe to heteronormative, patriarchal ideals to gain friends, dates, or networking contacts. This is achieved through submissive presentations of the self, created predominantly through non-verbal communication cues and connections to cultural signs.

If the accumulation of social capital occurs through means which present women as submissive and less powerful than men, what is this teaching young women about their own empowerment in general? Popular culture is riddled with contradictory messages about what it means to be a powerful woman, an issue that is by no means new, but particularly important at present as witnessed during the U.S. 2008 Presidential election, when influential female leaders centered in the debate. Every day successful, strong women are reduced to objects in advertisements, in films, and on television. Famous athletes, for example, regularly pose naked or nearly naked, in order, as Jhally suggests in *Codes of Gender*, to reassociate themselves with traditional gender signs, to assert their heterosexuality, and appeal to men's need for a sense of dominance. For example, Danica Patrick, the first successful female driver in NASCAR history, has appeared in a series of "Go Daddy" commercials that overtly sexualize her and place her at the mercy of the men in the ads. Popular female super-heroes, as "kick ass" as they may be, are restricted to sex-symbol status and lycra outerwear regardless of how tough they may initially appear. If it is not sexual objectivity that undermines influential women's power, then they are presented time and time again as bitches, power hungry, and manipulative. From the *Devil Wears Prada* to *Damages,* women in power, if they cannot be sexualized, are demonized. The extremes of this issue were clearly present in the controversy surrounding both Sarah Palin and Hillary Clinton during the 2008 election. Throughout popular culture young women are taught that they cannot be successful and powerful without subscribing to patriarchal ideals of womanhood. Internet profile culture, I argue, reinforces these messages, robbing young women of the freedom to articulate their own ideals of power and forcing them to package themselves into pre-established, heteronormative, patriarchal images of what women should be. Rather than a new forum for communication unaffected by traditional ideologies, the advancements in computer-mediated communication and online identity creation have been saturated with antiquated ideals of womanhood.

NOTES

1. See Kevin Robins and Frank Webster, *Times of the Technoculture* (London: Routledge, 1999) and Frank Webster, *Theories of the Information Society* (London, Routledge, 1995).

2. This article explores the issues of women, most of them heterosexual, functioning in a heteronormative system. Work focusing on the study of LGBT peoples within this framework is called for.

3. "Power" is a complicated term with endless connotations. For the purpose of this project, I refer to power as that which implies the possession of ability to wield force, authority, or substantial influence. "Empowerment" is the term I use to identify a woman's sense of her own power, her own ability to wield force, authority, or substantial influence.

4. I identify trends and generalized problems, discussing them from a cultural studies perspective rather than from a social science perspective.

5. The subjects studied for this article are those with an established online presence. All are based in the U.S. and between the ages of 16 and 25. Most are students, though several are recent graduates. These parameters mean that all of the women I will be discussing are privileged by both an education and regular internet access. This unfortunately excludes those disenfranchised by issues such as poverty or geographical constraints. Though I have tried to include women of all races, the majority of profiles easily accessible to me through public contacts were of Caucasians. Few were visually physically disabled. Further study exploring issues of empowerment online should include a discussion of difference among, for example, races, classes, and those with disabilities.

6. http://www.web-strategist.com/blog/2008/01/09/social-network-stats-facebook-myspace-reunion-jan-2008/

7. For more information see Walther, J.B. "Computer-mediated Communication: Impersonal, interpersonal, and hyperpersonal interaction." *Communication Research* 23.1 (1996): 3–44.

8. The drop down forms for gender on mainstream sites offer only "male" or "female" as choices.

9. This article is dealing primarily in the heterosexual realm of contact. Further work needs to be done specifically focusing on LGBT conscious navigation of this system. My work, again, is a generalized, theoretical exploration of profile culture and those who are excluded by my hypotheses are excluded because they deserve a great deal more attention than I can offer in the scope of this article.

10. By the term "sell themselves" I am not necessarily insinuating that this is a conscious act. On dating sites women are, of course, trying to market themselves for a mate, but profiles in general are designed to attract attention, so my use of the term "sell" can beread as simply a means of gaining contacts.

11. Jean Kilbourne uses the term "infantilized" in her series of films "Still Killing Us Softly" 1–4 to describe women in childlike dress or postures or with expressions reminiscent of children.

Works Cited

Boyd, Danah. "Why Youth (Heart) Social Network Sites: The Role of Networked Publics in Teenage Social Life." *Youth, Identity, and Digital Media.* Ed. David Buckingham. Cambridge: MIT P, 2007. Print.

Buckingham, David. *Youth, Identity, and Digital Media.* Cambridge: MIT P, 2007. Print.

"Codes of Gender." *Media Education Foundation.* Media Educ. Foundation, 2010. Web. 21 October 2009.

Codes of Gender: Identity and Performance in Popular Culture. Dir. Sut Jhally. Media Educ. Foundation, 2009. DVD.

Ellison, Nicole B., Rebecca Heino, and Jennifer Gibbs. "Managing Impressions Online: Self-Presentation Processes in the Online Dating Environment." *Journal of Computer-Mediated Communication* 11 (2006): 415–41. Print.

Ellison, Nicole B., Charles Steinfield, and Cliff Lampe. "The Benefits of Facebook 'Friends': Social Capital and College Students' Use of Online Social Network Sites." *Journal of Computer-Mediated Communication* 12 (2007): 1143–68. Print.

Goffman, Erving. *Gender Advertisements.* Cambridge: Harvard UP, 1979. Print.

_____. *The Presentation of Self in Everyday Life.* Garden City: Doubleday Anchor, 1959. Print.

Jansen, Sue Curry. *Critical Communication Theory: Power, Media, Gender and Technology.* Lanham: Rowman, 2002. Print.

Jhally, Sut. *The Codes of Advertising: Fetishism and the Political Economy of Meaning in the Consumer Society.* New York: St. Martin's, 1987. Print.

Lampe, Cliff, Nicole Ellison, and Charles Steinfeld. "A Familiar Face(book): Profile Elements as Signals in an Online Social Network." *Proceedings of ACM CHI 2007 Conference on Human Factors in Computing Systems.* San Jose: CA, 1 May 2007. Print.

McClimans, Leah, and J. Jeremy Wisnewski. "Undead Patriarchy and the Possibility of Love." *Twilight and Philosophy: Vampires, Vegetarians, and the Pursuit of Immortality.* Ed. Rebecca Housel and J. Jeremy Wisnewski. Hoboken: Wiley, 2009. 163–76. Print.

Ratliff, Clancy. "Blogging Feminism: (Web)Sites of Resistance." *The Scholar and Feminist Online. Barnard Center for Research on Women.* Barnard Center for Research on Women, 15.2 2007. Web. 4 January 2010.

Robins, Kevin, and Frank Webster. *Times of the Technoculture.* London: Routledge, 1999. Print.

Sautter, Jessica M., Rebecca M. Tippett, and S. Philip Morgan. "The Social Demography of Internet Dating in the United States." *Social Science Quarterly* 91.2 (2010): 554–75. Print.

Schau, Hope Jensen, and Mary C. Gilly. "We are What We Post? Self-Presentation in Personal Web Space." *The Journal of Consumer Research* 30.3 (2003): 385–404. Print.

Still Killing Us Softly 3. Dir. Sut Jhally. Creator Jean Kilbourne. Media Educ. Foundation, 2000. DVD.

Subrahmanyam, Kaveri, and Patricia Greenfield. "Online Communication and Adolescent Relationships." *Children and Electronic Media.* Spec. Issue of *The Future of Children* 18.1 (2008): 119–46. Print.

Tufekci, Zeynep. "Grooming, Gossip, Facebook, and MySpace: What Can We Learn from These Sites from Those Who Won't Assimilate?" *Information, Communication, and Society* 11.4 (2008): 544–64. Print.

Walther, J.B. "Computer-Mediated Communication: Impersonal, Interpersonal, and Hyperpersonal Interaction." *Communication Research* 23.1 (1996): 3–44. Print.

Webster, Frank. *Theories of the Information Society.* London: Routledge, 1995. Print.

Part IV

Technological Spaces: Transforming "Talk" in the 21st Century

12

Women, Kin-Keeping, and the Inscription of Gender in Mediated Communication Environments

Julie Dare

The notion of the Internet as a transformative communications platform, through which concepts such as embodiment, gender, and identity can be transcended, deconstructed, or subverted, represents an enduring theme in communications literature over the last two decades.[1] Underpinning early analyses was the premise that new opportunities presented by the Internet were driving innovative communication and behavioral practices. For example, the ability to interact anonymously opened the door for identity play and gender swapping, the implications of which, as Nancy Baym suggests, were "theoretically intoxicating" (41).

Such discourses offer a fairly narrow, technologically deterministic framework for examining the relationship between gender and new media spaces. Not only does this approach overlook a range of other factors shaping communication, but such analyses tend to underestimate the ways in which gender is inscribed in even the most mundane of conversations and behaviors. Indeed, a focus on the signs of gender in computer-mediated communication (CMC), rather than a more holistic examination of the purposes and motivations *for* communicating, arguably misses the "forest for the trees."

Of course, challenges to the notion of truly "gender-free" communication emerging in online environments are not new. For example, in the mid 1990s, Nancy Kaplan, in her analysis of the early interactive spaces of MUDs and

MOOs,[2] contended that "the practices suggest that even when personae try to construct genderless avatars, there is no social, communicative space without gendered speakers" (qtd. in Spender 244). And yet the idea that technological spaces offer a platform which is essentially disconnected from everyday life and normative patterns of behavior continues to resonate in contemporary scholarly discourse:

> Digital technologies of the self can contribute to self-disclosure (revealing secrets, confessing...), transvestism (trying on new identities to test the self and the other), fantasising, etc. The fact that most of the others that we encounter online are anonymous, unknown or invented characters creates a "strangers on the train" effect (McKenna et al. 2002) that facilitates all these phenomena [Abbas and Dervin 5].

Abbas and Dervin's claims draw attention away from the range of online channels which have been adopted as additional and supplementary pathways for connecting within *existing* networks. In this context, issues of anonymity and masking of gender are likely to be completely irrelevant, while other opportunities afforded by different media, such as convenience and affordability, may assume a more important role.

This chapter aims to tease out some of these issues relating to gender and media spaces by drawing on previous research on women's use of a range of communications media, as well as the findings from a recent ethnographic research project exploring women's communication practices,[3] to consider the degree to which gender is enacted through women's talk in mediated communications environments. A focus on communication technologies used most often in everyday life — the landline telephone, the mobile phone,[4] and email — is likely to reveal more nuanced insights into the ways in which technology is implicated in the gendering of communication in even the most banal of activities. Such an approach requires us to examine women's language, and their uses of these technologies, in the context of their everyday lives. Reflecting on the importance of social context to communication practices, this chapter begins with a brief overview of the social environment framing women's behavior and communication practices.

Kin-Keeping and Women's Talk: The Social Context

There is ample evidence that relationships play a pivotal role in women's lives. Women's communion in the private sphere — the realm constituted through family, domestic, and intimate relationships — reflects widely held social attitudes and beliefs concerning women's "natural" abilities and appropriate roles (Rakow 33). As Vicki Helgeson contends, women are socialized to be "kin-keepers" (412), with studies consistently confirming that women have traditionally been assigned, and in turn assumed responsibility for, sustaining familial and social networks (Millward 18; Young and Willmott 81; Wajcman 62; Lacohee and Anderson 7; Rosenthal 972; di Leonardo 443). Indeed, so central are women's activities to the notion of kin-keeping that Micaela di Leonardo went so far as to suggest that communication among kin members is actually dependent upon "the presence of an adult woman in the household" (443). Women's kin-keeping activities can be likened to a service role; part of the gendered job description assigned to women (Rakow 55). As di Leonardo notes, "the creation and maintenance of kin and quasi-kin networks in advanced industrial societies is *work*; and, moreover, it is largely women's work" (443).

Perhaps the most significant mechanism through which this relationship "work" is enacted is through women's talk. As Lana Rakow's research revealed, "women's talk holds together the fabric of the community, building and maintaining relationships and accomplishing important community functions" (34). This construction of women's talk — as something which is critical to the wellbeing of individuals and the community — contrasts sharply with common constructions of women's talk as insignificant, "gossip," or trivial chit-chat (Coates 135; Conforti 160). A more sympathetic definition by Deborah Jones positions gossip as "a way of talking between women in their roles as women, intimate in style, personal and domestic in topic and setting" (qtd. in Coates 135). Such a description, reflecting as it does women's social position, fits well with Nicholas Emler's construction of gossip as a mechanism through which women access "information essential to their capacity to cope with their social worlds, to solve the various problems they face, and to deal with the people around them" (qtd. in Coates 136).

While historically women's kin-keeping activities were most often conducted through face-to-face contact with family and friends who lived in close physical proximity (Young and Willmott 41), contemporary women are more likely to perform this socially designated role through mediated communication channels such as the telephone, text messages, and email (Uy-Tioco 259; Wilding 131). Such technologies enable women to manage family and social networks that may be geographically dispersed (Holloway and Green par. 9; Boneva, Kraut and Frohlich 541). It follows therefore that an examination of women's use of communication technologies is likely to reveal the degree to which gender is embedded in women's everyday practices. The following part takes up this challenge by examining how gender is enacted through women's appropriation of three particular communication technologies: the landline telephone, the mobile phone, and email.

Gender on the Line[5]: Women, Kin-Keeping, and the Telephone

Arguably no other communication technology has become so closely associated with women's gendered kin-keeping responsibilities as the telephone. A number of cross-cultural studies have identified the telephone as a critical conduit through which women perform gendered emotional work.[6] As Rakow noted, as well as sustaining family relationships through their telephone calls, women also "make calls to friends and other community members to make sure they are well and safe, to cheer them, to remember their birthdays and other special occasions, to draw them into the life of the community" (57).

Research indicates that women have also been tacitly assigned the task of answering the household telephone (Frissen 85). In this context, the telephone is constructed as a "domestic appliance, much like an oven or washing machine, operated by women as an extension of their other familial responsibilities" (Rakow 50). In this scenario, the telephone fits neatly within a social construct of women as "social secretaries," performing the gendered work of "domestic relations specialists" (Fischer 235). The classification of domestic technologies within a woman's "job description" has been previously examined in Ruth Schwartz Cowan's study of the impact of new household appliances on women's labor in the late 19th and early 20th centuries. As Cowan's analysis revealed, far from releasing women from menial work, the introduction into the home of "labor-saving" appliances such as washing machines and coal-burning stoves, along with a shift to mass-produced consumer goods, actually increased women's duties, in many cases requiring them to singlehandedly undertake household tasks which had, before industrialization, been shared with husbands and children (101).[7] Similarly, as Lana Rakow (50) and Valerie Frissen's (85) research indicates, the domestication of technologies such as the telephone has resulted in the corresponding expansion of women's service role within the home.

Gender on the Move: Women and the Mobile Phone

Just as the landline telephone has become an important channel through which women carry out their kin-keeping responsibilities, so too has the mobile phone. A study in the early 1990s found that perceptions of women as vulnerable and needing protection, particularly when travelling alone in a car, were a key factor which prompted many men to initially purchase a mobile phone for their partner (Rakow and Navarro 151). However, it did not take women long to exploit this new communication tool for their own purposes, and in ways which validated Frissen's prophetic comment that "the potential uses of new telephone services will be heavily influenced by the uses of the 'plain old telephone'" (80). Rakow and Navarro's study drew attention to the emerging dynamic of "remote mothering," whereby women were able to extend care to their children when they were separated from them (144). In this context, the mobile phone served to reinforce the construction of a "good" mother as someone who is literally "on call" at all times. An Australian study conducted at the same time revealed that far from challenging gender roles, the functionality of mobile phones fitted neatly into the status quo. As Karen Wale and Patricia Gillard observed, "mobile phones did not make fathers into caregivers during the day. In the hands of mothers, mobiles extended what was already a clearly defined responsibility" (para. 4).

Recent research suggests that almost two decades after Rakow and Navarro's and Wale and Gillard's studies, gendered patterns of use continue to define women's mobile phone practices (Palen and Hughes 345; Kennedy and Wellman 654). A range of cross-cultural studies highlight the ways in which mobile phones have been co-opted into women's "relationship work." For example, Sadie Plant's study of the social impact of the mobile phone indicated that, despite cultural differences, women from a range of different backgrounds have adopted the mobile phone for kin-keeping activities: "A Thai girl working in Bangkok uses her mobile to keep in touch with her family in a remote village upcountry. A Filipina cook in Hong Kong users hers to contact her children in Manilla" (58). In the Philippines, the mobile phone allows poor urban Filipina women to monitor their children's whereabouts and activities (Portus 109), while Dobashi's research on mobile phone use in Japan highlighted "Japanese expectations of gender roles, particularly those of housewife and mother" (qtd. in Donner et al. 326). Similarly, Julie Dare's research with Western Australian women found that the mobile phone has become a valuable tool enabling women to extend care and support to their aging parents (186). As one participant, Robyn, explained:

> I use my mobile phone when I'm in the car. Like I'll phone Mum, if I'm going up north on the freeway, I'll phone her then, because I know ... I've got the time to sit still and talk to her, which I know you shouldn't do ... but that's when I like to ring Mum as well, because I'm driving there, and I know I'm having to sit for half an hour [Dare 186].

As Robyn's comments imply, the value of the mobile phone lies not only in its convenience as a mobile form of communication technology, but perhaps more importantly because it allows her to perform several roles and duties at once. As such, it fits well with many women's multitasked lifestyles and responsibilities.

Gender in Cyberspace: Women and Online Communication Technologies

Arguably, both the landline and mobile telephones can be positioned as technologies through which women's socially designated roles as kin-keepers and primary caregivers have in many ways become even more reified. A logical extension of this claim concerns the degree to which women's uses of online communication technologies continue to reflect similar gendered patterns, or, as was presaged in early cyberculture literature,[8] whether women are exploiting the novel opportunities offered by this new media in order to challenge or subvert restrictive roles and obligations. Perhaps an early indication that many women use online communication channels for purposes and in ways that are remarkably similar to their uses of traditional communication tools such as the telephone, is revealed by considering which online communication technologies are used most often. Despite an ongoing fascination with the "politically empowering" (Slack and Wise 151) opportunities anonymous online environments might present to create and re-invent identities (Abbas and Dervin 5; Turkle 125), it is important to note that the overwhelming majority of online interaction takes place between people who are already known to each other through existing offline connections (Baym 43). Evidence of this can be found in research which consistently indicates that email is the most popular online activity for both males and females; indeed, email use significantly outranks other online activities such as blogging, online gaming and social networking.[9] A critical analysis of new media and gendered communication practices therefore requires a focus on particular communication channels, such as email, which have become most deeply embedded in women's everyday lives.

Empirical research conducted over the last 10 years indicates that one of the most striking differences between men's and women's use of the Internet relates to their use of email; while both men and women are heavy users of email, the motivations for using email appear to be quite different, with women valuing email as a tool to enhance relational and social communication significantly more so than men (Boneva, Kraut, and Frohlich 546; Pew Internet and American Life Project 19; Fallows 12). Such findings underscore the increasing importance of email as a communication tool through which women are actively sustaining existing familial and social relationships, at both the local and geographically dispersed level.

Research indicates that women use email to communicate with siblings and parents (Boneva, Kraut and Frohlich 539; Pew Internet and American Life Project 23; Dare 192); to maintain contact with children who have left home (Holloway and Green par. 13); and to connect with friends (Boase et al. 11; Matzko 50). As Dare's study found, emails exchanged between women and their elderly parents can facilitate deeper and more enjoyable connections, particularly in situations where family members are separated by thousands of kilometers. Such was the case for 55 year old Janette, who moved permanently to Australia as a young woman in the 1970s. As Janette explained, emails she exchanged with her widowed mother in the United Kingdom enabled both women to bridge the kilometers separating them (Dare 191). While Janette's experiences were not representative of the majority of the women interviewed in this research project,[10] they nevertheless illustrate that text-based channels such as email can in some situations be a key conduit through which cross-generational connections can be maintained, particularly when family members are separated by distance.

Significantly, the introduction of email to family networks appears to be subtly shifting gendered communication patterns, as revealed in a Western Australian study of communication among "transnational" migrant families (Baldassar, Baldock, and Wilding 120). Baldassar, Baldock, and Wilding's study found that the use of email in geographically dispersed family networks not only increased the overall quantity and quality of communication, but also resulted in an increase in the number of family members participating in that communication. While in the past, transnational family communication—manifested predominantly through letters or long-distance telephone calls—was distributed through the family matriarch, once email was introduced into these family communication networks, an "all-channel or distributed network" emerged (Baldassar, Baldock, and Wilding 119). As Raelene Wilding's research revealed, "rather than mothers and daughters forming the dominant nodes of communication, emails were sent between siblings and cousins and across other extended kin relationships, such as nephews and aunts" (135). In such a scenario, "otherwise silent members of the family—especially brothers, sons, grandchildren and cousins—use email to communicate across distance when they would not normally have participated in the routine exchange of telephone calls or letters" (Baldassar, Baldock, and Wilding 129).

A similar reshaping of family communication practices was found in Dare's study. As one participant, Beth, explained, "they're [Beth's brothers] more likely to whack back a quick response than they would be ... you would never get a letter from them, or a phone call, or rarely anyway" (Dare 195). Likewise, another participant, Janette, reported that email was more likely to be used by the male members of her family than traditional communication tools:

> Men don't write, but it's amazing that they do email. I can barely remember when my husband last wrote [a letter] except to his Mum [in the UK]. In our case, because my husband is one of four boys, it's all the sisters-in-law that keep

in contact all the time. All the wives. So there may not have been any communication there for seven or eight years except for the wives writing to each other.
But now you find that your husband and the other men...?
He communicates with his brothers a lot more now than he ever did [Dare 200].

Despite this optimistic view of more egalitarian patterns of family communication emerging, evidence suggests that there remain gender disparities in who performs the bulk of "relationship work" (Baldassar, Baldock, and Wilding 121). As Baldassar, Baldock, and Wilding noted, "some parents are grateful that their daughters-in-law maintain contact, as their sons are inexpert or disinterested in this aspect of kin-work, whereas we did not encounter any examples of the reverse, when sons-in-law undertake this responsibility for their wives" (121). Such dynamics suggest that socially constructed notions of whose job it is to maintain family relationships using ICTs — originally highlighted in the late 1980s in Moyal's research on women's telephone practices (65) — continue to frame communication practices within families, albeit in the context of online communication.

New Media, Women's Talk, and Gender

Gendered communication practices are also evident in discourse analysis of men's and women's text messages. For example, Yates and Lockley's study noted statistically significant differences in both the length and the content of messages. The study revealed that the longest text messages were between women, while conversely the shortest were between men. According to the authors, these differences in message length are significant because they are indicative of underlying gendered patterns of communication:

> For a woman to send curt and factual messages to a female friend would inherently threaten the ongoing relationship either during the interaction or at the next point of face-to-face interaction. Conversely, for a man to send another man a long message including the opening and closing comments, elements and socioemotional content of a typically woman-woman interaction would again raise issues for the relationship [Yates and Lockley 86].

Yates and Lockley's study raises several issues pertinent to an analysis of gender and communication technologies. Firstly, despite the opportunities text messaging offers to streamline communication to short messages, it is apparent that gendered communication practices continue to shape at least some women's use of this relatively new technology. Secondly, the degree to which women's text messages include socio-emotional content is not only an indication of gendered communication practices, but also reflects women's socially sanctioned roles as care-giver and nurturer, both to each other as well as to others.

Despite the evidence that gender influences texting patterns, it seems counterintuitive that the ability to send succinct messages would appear to be a good match for contemporary women's "multitasked" lives. Such a notion finds support from a number of qualitative studies, which indicate that women view email and text messages as convenient and efficient forms of communication (Matzko 50; Pew Internet and American Life Project 18; Boneva, Kraut, and Frohlich 541; Dare 167). This perspective is reflected in the following comments by Ellie, a participant in Dare's study:

> That's the other thing about communicating via phone, when you phone up a friend, you've got to go through all the niceties, and all the "How're you going [doing]?," and you can't make it too quick often, whereas email, or ... MSN [Instant Messenger], you're just straight to the point, no fluffy bits. And [those are] really a time-waster. It goes on forever [saying hello/goodbye] and you haven't got time for that....Even somebody that I only see once a year, I've just been thinking lately, I'll just give her a text saying "I'm available, how about we get together?," rather than ring her up. 'Cause when I ring her up I'll be on the phone to her for an hour.... It's the succinct message that you can get across that I really like [Dare 167].

Ellie's comments not only reflect her appreciation of the convenience of new communication channels, but also suggest an understanding of common conventions of telephone communication between women which require that they preface their conversations with stylised "chit-chat." Thus, in contrast to Yates and Lockley's findings, which suggested that even with text-based communication channels, females still find it necessary to conform to gendered styles of interaction, Ellie uses such channels specifically *because* they allow her to avoid such gendered obligations, and literally "cut to the chase." However, while Ellie has no problem sending factual messages through email or text messages, she finds text messaging an equally convenient channel through which to extend brief messages of care and support. In explaining how she communicated with a young adult son who had been struggling with depression, Ellie commented: "I'll text him 'Thinking of you, catch up with you soon'" (Dare 107). Ellie also used text messages to support a friend whose marriage had broken down, using short messages letting her friend know she cared: "How's it going, still thinking of you, I can come over now... I know it's a bad time" (Dare 167). Ellie was not alone in exploiting new media channels in this way, with other participants in Dare's study also describing using email and text messages in ways that enabled them to continue to carry out important "relationship work" in a way that fitted best with their hectic lives. In this way, women's use of text messaging can be positioned as conforming to social expectations of women's role as kin-keeper, while simultaneously enabling women to step outside gendered discursive patterns.

Email can also facilitate a more liberated and honest form of expression — one which can challenge gendered communication conventions. Indeed, one of the key themes emerging from Rosemarie Conforti's research on women's self-development through CMC is the degree to which online communication enables women to depart from culturally constructed definitions of appropriate female behavior. As Conforti found in her research, CMC allows women to "speak in voices that are self-focused and self-oriented" (194), in contrast to cultural expectations which, as Mary Belenky suggested, "hold that women should be listeners, subordinate, and unassertive"(qtd. in Conforti 193).

However, while it is tempting to interpret Conforti's observations as an endorsement of the power of anonymous environments to challenge gendered communication styles, it should be noted that most of Conforti's respondents were communicating with family and friends, and thus were far from anonymous. In this situation, factors such as the asynchronous and text-based nature of much CMC — in particular email — are more likely to influence communication patterns. While normative constructions of femininity promote qualities such as concern for others and selflessness as desirable, it seems CMC provides a platform through which women "enjoy not feeling selfish about talking about themselves, their opinions, and their ideas" (Conforti 192). The knowledge that they can speak without fear of being interrupted, challenged, or the conversation being derailed, means that women can explore issues of personal relevance in ways that are meaningful to them. Such a dynamic was revealed in Dare's research, as evidenced in Ellie's discussion on how the nature of her communication with her cousin in the United States subtly changed depending on the medium:

> Actually with my cousin ... I can actually write [email] a lot more. Yeah, because when I'm with her, and perhaps over the phone, she tends to be a little bit more domineering.... Sometimes I prefer to email her and I get more out, because I can express myself more to her, whereas when we're communicating either on the phone or... [face-to-face], she may not let me finish my sentence or something, and she will be more dictatorial to me. She'll say, "No, this is how you should feel," or "this is how this or that" ... there's an ease there with email....But that's the key, *that's the difference* ... I don't get that in emails. I don't feel that authority [Dare 169].

Moreover, both Conforti's and Dare's participants valued CMC as an environment in which they could discuss issues that were important to them, but which are often perceived by others as trivial women's issues. Significantly, the ability for CMC to offer a platform for women to talk about things that matter to them (Conforti 253) not only highlights the degree to which women's talk continues to be marginalized, but also hints at how new communication channels may be the vehicles through which women might achieve a greater sense of self-awareness and empowerment.

Conclusion

Just as Lana Rakow noted over 20 years ago that women's use of the telephone reflected their social position and "uses of talk" (9), an examination of women's uses of newer mediated channels similarly reveals that gender continues to be a pivotal factor shaping women's communication practices, choices of communication tool, and the nature of their talk. As this chapter has outlined, an analysis of the literature on three of the most commonly used communication tools — the telephone, the mobile phone, and email — reveals how women are using both traditional and new communication technologies to perform gendered kin-keeping responsibilities in ways that are at once very familiar, and at the same time represent new and innovative ways of interacting and managing relationships. For the most part, these women are not using new media to escape from their "real world" lives into a virtual reality, or consciously challenging gendered identities and subjectivities. Instead, women are strategically integrating a range of communication technologies *into* their existing "real world" networks, and in doing so, they are articulating even more clearly the gendered roles and responsibilities which continue to provide the framework to women's lives.

Notes

1. For critiques of the Internet as a potentially transformative medium, see Baym 35–54; Woolgar 1–22; Lupton 477–488.

2. MUDs (multiple-user domains) and MOOs (multiple object-oriented) are virtual environments. MUDs are text-based, and as users enter the MUD, the features of the space are described to them. In MOOs users have more creative freedom to build and alter the virtual environment (Green xxi).

3. See Dare, Julie. "The Role of Information and Communication Technologies in Managing Transition and Sustaining Women's Health During Their Midlife Years." Diss. Edith Cowan University, 2010. Print.

4. Throughout this chapter the term mobile phone is used inclusively to describe mobile, cellular, and wireless.

5. I have borrowed this term from Lana Rakow's study of women and the telephone in a small rural community in the United States: Rakow, Lana F. *Gender on the Line: Women, the Telephone, and Community Life.* Chicago: University of Illinois Press, 1992. Print.

6. See, for example, Moyal 51–72; Rakow 61–80; Frissen 79–94.

7. As Cowan notes, before industrialization in the 1800s, many tasks would have been shared between family members. For example, men and boys were largley responsible for the production, processing and grinding of grains such as corn and wheat, necessary for making bread, and women were responsible for baking (48–49). Since meal and flour

deteriorate quickly, grinding of grain was a task that was both tedious and never-ending. The introduction of commercial mills, which led to the production of mass-produced white flour at reasonable prices, meant that men and boys were now relieved "of one of the most time-consuming chores for which they had been responsible" (Cowan 49). However, the switch to white flour signalled a shift to more labor and time-intensive methods of cooking, since the finer white flours "required hard labor (in the kneading) and considerable attention to details (particularly in maintaining yeast cultures)" (Cowan 51). As a result, females found their workload in the home expanded, at the same time as the kitchen now became a place of comparative leisure for males. As Cowan noted, "as the nineteenth century wore on, in almost every aspect of household work, industrialization served to eliminate the work that men (and children) had once been assigned to do, while at the same time leaving the work of women either untouched or even augmented" (63–64).

8. For an overview of theories concerning the liberatory potential of online technologies, see Wajcman chapter 3.

9. For a statistical representation of the most popular online activities by American Internet users over the last decade, see Pew Internet and American Life Project Online Activities, 2000–2009.

10. 25 percent (10) of the 40 participants in Dare's study had used email to communicate with their parents.

WORKS CITED

Abbas, Yasmine, and Fred Dervin. "Digital Technologies of the Self: Introduction." Ed. Yasmine Abbas and Fred Dervin. 2009. *Digital Technologies of the Self.* Web. 29 Nov. 2009.

Baldassar, Loretta, Cora Vellekoop Baldock, and Raelene Wilding. *Families Caring across Borders: Migration, Ageing and Transnational Caregiving.* New York: Palgrave Macmillan, 2007. Print.

Baym, Nancy K. "Interpersonal Life Online." *The Handbook of New Media: Social Shaping and Social Consequences of Icts.* Eds. L.A. Lievrouw and S. Livingstone. London: Sage, 2006. 35–54. Print.

Boase, Jeffrey, et al. "The Strength of the Internet Ties: The Internet and Email Aid Users in Maintaining their Social Networks and Provide Pathways to Help when People Face Big Decisions." *Pew Internet and American Life Project,* 2006, 2006. Web. 20 May 2010.

Boneva, Bonka, Robert Kraut, and David Frohlich. "Using Email for Personal Relationships: The Difference Gender Makes." *The American Behavioral Scientist* 45.3 (2001): 530–50. *Sage Premier.* Web. 28 May 2009.

Brooks, John. "The First and Only Century of Telephone Literature." *The Social Impact of the Telephone.* Ed. Ithiel de Sola Pool. Cambridge, Mass: MIT Press, 1977. 208–24. Print.

Coates, Jennifer. *Women, Men and Language: A Sociolinguistic Account of Gender Differences in Language.* 2nd ed. London: Longman, 1993. Print.

Conforti, Rosemarie J. *An Interview Study of the Role of Computer-Mediated Relationships in the Experiences and Self Development of a Small Group of Women Users of Computer Mediated Communication.* Diss. New York University, 2001. Ann Arbor: UMI, Print.

Cowan, Ruth Schwartz. *More Work for Mothers: The Ironies of Household Technology from the Open Hearth to the Microwave.* New York: Basic Books, 1983. Print.

Dare, Julie. "The Role of Information and Communication Technologies in Managing Transition and Sustaining Women's Health During Their Midlife Years." Diss. Edith Cowan University, Western Australia , 2010. Print.

di Leonardo, Micaela. "The Female World of Cards and Holidays: Women, Families and the Work of Kinship." *Signs* 12.3 (1987): 440–53. *JSTOR Arts and Sciences III.* Web. 14 Jan. 2010.

Donner, Jonathan, et al. ""Express Yourself" and "Stay Together": The Middle-Class Indian Family." *Handbook of Mobile Communication Studies.* Ed. Katz, James E. London: MIT Press, 2008. 325–37. Print.

Fallows, Deborah. "How Women and Men Use the Internet: Women are Catching up to Men in Most Measures of Online Life. Men Like the Internet for the Experiences it Offers, While Women Like it for the Human Connections it Promotes. " *Pew Internet and American Life Project,* 2005. Web. 22 May 2010.

Fischer, Claude S. *America Calling: A Social History of the Telephone to 1940.* Berkeley, CA: University of California Press, 1992. Print.

Frissen, Valerie. "Gender Is Calling: Some Reflections on Past, Present and Future Uses of the Telephone." *The Gender-Technology Relation: Contemporary Theory and Research.* Eds. Grint, Keith and Rosalind Gill. London: Taylor & Francis, 1995. 79–94. Print.

Green, Lelia. *Technoculture: From Alphabet to Cybersex.* Crows Nest, Western Australia: Allen and Unwin, 2002. Print.

Helgeson, Vicki S. "Relation of Agency and Communion to Well-Being: Evidence and Potential Explanations." *Psychological Bulletin* 116.3 (1994): 412–28. *PsycARTICLES.* Web. 28 Mar. 2009.

Holloway, Donell , and Lelia Green. *Home is Where You Hang Your @: Australian Women on the Net.* Canberra, Australia: Department of Communications, Information Technology and the Arts, 2004. Web. 1 Oct. 2007.

Kennedy, Tracy, and Barry Wellman. "The Networked Household." *Information, Communication & Society* 10.5 (2007): 645–70. *Taylor and Francis Online Journals CAUL.* Web. 12 Jan. 2010.

Lacohee, Hazel, and Ben Anderson. "Interacting with the Telephone." *Special Issue of the International Journal of Human-Computer Studies* 554.5 (2001): 665–99. Print.

Lupton, Deborah. "The Embodied Computer/User." *The Cyber Cultures Reader.* Eds. Bell, David and Kennedy, Barbara M. London: Routledge, 2000. 477–488. Print.

Matzko, Marilyn. *Putting Herself on the Line: Women's Relational Use of E-mail.* Diss. Harvard University,2002. Ann Arbor: UMI, 2002. Print.

Millward, Christine. "Keeping in Touch: Extended Family Networks." *Family Matters* 32 August (1992): 14–19. Print.

Moyal, Ann. "The Gendered Use of the Telephone: An Australian Case Study." *Media, Culture and Society* 14 (1992): 51–72. Print.

Palen, Leysia, and Amanda Hughes. "When Home Base Is Not a Place: Parents' Use of Mobile Telephones." *Personal and Ubiquitous Computing* 11.5 (2007): 339–348. *ProQuest 5000 International.* Web. 12 Jan. 2010.

Pew Internet and American Life Project. "Daily Internet Activities, 2000–2009." *Pew Internet and American Life Project,* 2010. Web. 18 May 2010.

_____. "Tracking Online Life: How Women Use the Internet to Cultivate Relationships with Family and Friends. " *Pew Internet and American Life Project,* 2000. Web. 22 May 2010.

Plant, Sadie. "*On the Mobile: The Effects of Mobile Telephones on Social and Individual Life.* " Motorola, 2001. Web. 18 Feb. 2008.

Portus, Lourdes M. "How the Urban Poor Acquire and Give Meaning to the Mobile Phone." *Handbook of Mobile Communication Studies.* Ed. Katz, James E. London: MIT Press, 2008. 105–18. Print.

Rakow, Lana F. *Gender on the Line: Women, the Telephone, and Community Life.* Chicago: University of Illinois Press, 1992. Print.

_____, and Vija Navarro. "Remote Mothering and the Parallel Shift: Women Meet the cellular Telephone." *Critical Studies in Mass Communication* 10.2 (1993): 144–57. Print.

Rosenthal, Carolyn J. "Kinkeeping in the Familial Division of Labor." *Journal of Marriage and the Family* 47.4 (1985): 965–74. Print.

Slack, Jennifer Daryl, and J. Macgregor Wise. "Cultural Studies and Communication Technology." *Handbook of New Media: Social Shaping and Social Consequences of Icts*. Eds. Lievrouw, L.A. and S. Livingstone. Student ed. London: SAGE, 2006. 141–62. Print.

Spender, Dale. *Nattering on the Net: Women, Power and Cyberspace*. North Melbourne: Spinifex, 1995. Print.

Turkle, Sherry. "Always-on/Always-on-You: The Tethered Self." *Handbook of Mobile Communication Studies*. Ed. Katz, J.E. Cambridge, Mass.: MIT Press, 2008. 121–37. Print.

Uy-Tioco, Cecilia. "Overseas Filipino Workers and Text Messaging: Reinventing Transnational Mothering." *Continuum: Journal of Media and Cultural Studies* 21.2 (2007): 253–65. *Taylor and Francis Online Journals*. Web. 12 Jan. 2010.

Wajcman, Judy. *Technofeminism*. Malden, MA.: Polity Press, 2004. Print.

Wale, Karen, and Patricia Gillard. *Adventures in Cybersound: The Impact of New Telecommunications Services on Family and Social Relations* . Melbourne, Vic.: Telecommunications Needs Research Group, RMIT, 1994. Print.

Wilding, Raelene. "'Virtual' Intimacies: Families Communicating across Transnational Contexts." *Global Networks* 6.2 (2006): 125–42. *Wiley-Blackwell Full Collection*. Web. 12 Jan. 2010.

Woolgar, Steve. "Five Rules of Virtuality." *Virtual Society? Technology, Cyberbole, Reality* Eds. Woolgar, S. Oxford: Oxford University Press, 2002. 1–22. 2002. Print.

Yates, Simeon, J., and Eleanor Lockley. "Moments of Separation: Gender, (Not So Remote) Relationships, and the Cell Phone." *Remote Relationships in a Small World*. Ed. Holland, Samantha. New York: Peter Lang, 2008. 74–97. Print.

Young, Michael, and Peter Willmott. *Family and Kinship in East London*. Rev. ed. Harmondsworth: Penguin, 1962. Print.

13

Gendering the Construction of Instant Messaging

Koen Leurs and Sandra Ponzanesi

FIREKISS23: tomm's national kissing day! Lol [laughing out loud]
FIREKISS23: so that means u and me gotta kiss
SLIMMXX44: lol suuuuuuuuure ;-)
SLIMMXX44: ok fine
SLIMMXX44: what about jenni?
FIREKISS23: i thought u liked ariel
SLIMMXX44: wtf [what the fuck]
FIREKISS 23: do u think she's cute?
SLIMMXX44: do u
FIREKISS23: how would I kno? im a gurl
SLIMMXX44: i wana kiss u
FIREKISS23: lol stop playin
SLIMMXX44: Sunny i do
FIREKISS23: lol im gonna make out w/ so many ppl tomrw~ [people tomorrow]
SLIMMXX44: k me and u ok
FIREKISS23: OK lol [Thiel-Stern 69–70].

In the fragment above, Sunny (Firekiss23), an adolescent girl, engages in a flirtatious conversation using Instant Messaging with a male friend she knows from school. National Kissing Day is coming up and the two teenagers draw on this topic to flirt with one another. This exchange is illustrative of how Instant Messaging (IM) culture provides a window into gendered day-to-day routines, social life, and teenage intimacy. As interactively written diaries, IM "may be emerging as a primary source for how some adolescents conceive of themselves and take on an identity" (Thiel-Stern 59). In recent years, IM has gained a reputation as a gendered technological space where gossip, "girl talk," and "best-friend culture" prevail (Thiel-Stern 44; Tufte 72). This remark somewhat essentializes the gendered positioning of girls as sociable communicators. However as the opening quote suggests, and as we will also elaborate on below, in everyday use of IM the cultural stereotypes of girls as friendly gossips also get resisted and transgressed. Before turning to the specifics of IM, the broader landscape on gender and computer mediated communication (CMC) will be sketched.

Moving Gender and CMC into the Fabrics of Everyday Life

Empirical and theoretical literature on IM is scarce; therefore this argument is grounded first in the wider context of text-based computer mediated communication. IM, similar to email, discussion groups, newsgroups, and chat, involves the exchange of typed words that are read from computer screens. Email and the Bulletin Board System (BBS) have been around ever since the beginning of the 1970s. Instant Relay Chat (IRC), Multi-User Dimensions (MUD's), and object oriented MUDS (MOOs) were introduced in the 1980s, while instant messaging applications such as I Seek You (ICQ), AOL Instant Messenger, Yahoo!, Tencent's QQ, and the Microsoft Network (MSN) date to the mid–1990s. The practice of Instant Messaging has come of age in the 2000s.[1] Parallel to this, literature on embodiment and computer-mediated communication has flourished over the last two decades. From a variety of perspectives, feminists have been reflecting on the usages and implications of these applications as they grew in popularity.

Three key conceptual contours can be mapped in the feminist research landscape on the gendered features and contexts of these various forms of computer mediated communication, technologies, and the Internet. The three strands are the utopian perspective of online gender as a malleable signifier; the dystopian strand of gender and technology as fixating structures; and the third strand of mutual constitution of gender and technology in everyday, situated contexts (Van Doorn and Van Zoonen 260; Wajcman 150).[2] In this chapter, the aim is to look beyond the exaggerated hype and panic surrounding CMC, by considering instant messaging as an everyday practice. However, in order to puncture utopian and dystopian myths, a number of the most important contextualizing reference points will be discussed first. We will first address the utopian view and then engage the dystopian perspective

From the mid 1990s until only a couple of years ago, the Internet was often hailed as offering a place where people could deliberate freely while leaving categories of difference such as age, ability, gender, sexual preference, race, class, and ethnic-cultural positioning behind in the "offline," real world.

Illustratively, new media advocate John Perry Barlow wrote *A Declaration of the Independence of Cyberspace* in which he argues that the Internet is a space apart from the real world:

> Ours is a world that is both everywhere and nowhere, but it is not where bodies live [...] We are creating a world that all may enter without privilege or prejudice accorded by race, economic power, military force, or station of birth [Barlow par. 6–7]

Barlow insists on the disembodied nature of cyberspace; he believes "Nothing could be more disembodied than cyberspace. It's like having your everything [*sic*] amputated" (qtd. in Nunes 8). Feminist activists and scholars alike have argued that gender as a personal marker can be experimented with online.

Elizabeth Reid wrote that users of Internet Relay Chat can self-select their gender, opening up a great variety of possibilities to experiment with social roles and deconstruct the "fixed" and "sacred" institution of gender. "This fixity, and the common equation of gender with sex, becomes problematic when gender reassignment can be effected by a few touches at a keyboard" (Reid 63). In these writings, computer culture was analyzed through the lens of postmodernism. Sherry Turkle wrote about online interactions, "gender bending," and identity experiments. She concluded, "We have moved in the direction of accepting the postmodern values of opacity, playful experimentation, and navigation of surface as privileged ways of knowing" (Turkle 267).

In describing the "digital revolution" more broadly, Sadie Plant developed a celebratory woman-centered cyberfeminism. Bringing together biological essentialist and technological determinist views, she suggests women have "natural" affinity with technology. The non-hierarchical character of the internet resembles feminine weaving more than masculine technology mastery, as the network reflects constructed, fluid, and multiple gender identities (Plant 60–73). Also, socialist feminists saw opportunities in technologies. Most famously, Donna Haraway, in her 1991 manifesto, uses the figuration of the cyborg as a post-human solution to social injustices.

Kevin Robins stressed that metaphors on technologies seduced people to believe in a dream world. He argues that in early writings "the mythology of cyberspace [was] preferred over its sociology" (Robins 153). The perspective reconciling postmodernism and neo-liberal progress has also been dubbed the Californian ideology.[3] Marketing experts put techno-utopianism forward; it became vented in popular writings such as the magazine *Wired;* and it was taken up in feminist scholarly work. Digital communication was often seen as taking place in a space standing apart from the mundane, everyday, geographical and political spheres of influence.

On the other more dystopian side of the spectrum, authors have underscored the gendered structuring principles of technoscience. Radical and socialist feminists have recognized respectively how technologies have been based on male instead of female values and how masculinity got embedded in machineries since the Industrial revolution. Radical feminists were concerned over the Western masculine project of exploitation of women and nature. Fierce debates arose over new reproductive technologies such as in-vitro fertilization and connected worries about patriarchal exploitation.[4] Besides recognizing opportunities to fight against social injustices, socialist feminists also exposed the gendered hierarchical division of labor and male domination and monopoly of technology. [5]

Two studies, on the darker sides of gender experimentation, became touchstones for techno-pessimistic understanding of text-based interaction. These cases are "Julie Graham," the cross-dressing feminist psychiatric therapist chatter and "Mr. Bungle," a character inflicting rape and violent sexual abuse in a text-based virtual world. Mr. Bungle's practices left users in great distress behind their computers. He was a participant in *LamdaMoo* and spread a subprogram called "voodoo doll." This program overtook the control of other characters, and Mr. Bungle had them carry out sexually humiliating acts on the screen. After this event, borrowing from offline conventions, users developed a sophisticated set of rules and sanctions to govern the shared communicative space (Dibbell 11–32).

The other case, Julie Graham, refers to an extrovert online persona created by Sanford Lewin, a New York psychiatrist. Julie was a self-declared bisexual female counselor. Suffering from paraplegia and a disfigured face after a car crash, she was left homebound. She turned to chat to offer and gain support. The role Julie played allowed Sanford to enact a different gender with different physical capacities. After two years, Sanford, who had created Julie as an enjoyable experiment, wanted the weight of the online "deception" off his shoulders. He had formed numerous therapeutic relationships using the Julie persona. When Julie's clients found out she was not who they thought she was, they felt violated and heavily betrayed (Stone 65–82).

From these landmark cases, we turn our attention to studies examining more mundane interactions. Examining the content of online chat, Herring shows how patterns of linguistic inequalities between women and men get established and perpetuated on the Internet in message content, third person pronouns, and nicknames. Males are more likely to open and close discussions, voice opinions as facts, use harsh language, and take up an adversarial stance towards their interlocutors. Females are more likely to post shorter messages, provide qualifications and justifications for assertions, express support, and voice an "aligned" orientation towards their interlocutors. Writing about synchronous chat, Herring states that gender bending takes place infrequently.

She explains that chat users "give off" gender cues, on average, once every three to four typed lines. This makes it difficult to sustain a bended gender, as the longer people participate in chat, the more likely their "actual gender" gets disclosed. Women and men use different discourse styles, she concludes (Herring 207–212).

The content of communication is bound to constraints and affordances of Internet applications. Nakamura seeks to de-naturalize web interfaces, arguing that interface design and algorithm decisions are always political. Focusing on race and ethnicity, her argument is that interfaces structure self-presentations online. In self-presentations, axes of difference such as race, ethnicity, but also gender are often restricted to a limited set of clickable boxes; they are "menu-driven" (104). Nakamura discusses the bounded menu-choices from which users have to chose and argues that this process "limits the ways that race can happen in cyberspace" (102). The imposed order of interfaces is necessarily reductive, as users have to comply with pre-given, often fixed categories that are provided to them. Thus, interface restrictions may deny the possibility to perform hybrid or multiple (racial) identifications.

Over time, awareness grew of how the online and offline interplay. Rather than being in opposition to it, online life gets woven into the fabrics of offline life. Early technological determinist accounts focused mostly on post-modern opportunities, and in this dominant discourse the internet was analyzed as a "dazzling light," where "everything was possible" that was "shining above everyday concerns" (Haythornthwaite and Wellman 4). Others were panicky or employed gender essentialist outlooks in describing how technologies are masculine power mechanisms. Gendered power relations and hierarchies also perpetuate the content of communication. Furthermore, the restricting medium specificity of interfaces was also recognized as leaving its trace on the contents users circulate online.

The question remains how to take the most informative elements from these insights to grasp the normalcy of how adolescent girls do everyday things in Instant Messaging spaces. To do so we turn to contemporary feminist technoscience; this perspective accepts gender as the result of a process of active articulation among various actors. By showing that gender is something people *do* rather than something people *are*, Judith Butler deconstructed the category of gender and argued it gets performed in a matrix of power relations. Butler asks how gender performativity as a process of stylized repetitions, through which one acquires subjectivity, sets norms, and remains open to subversion:

> How precisely are we to understand the ritualized repetition by which such norms produce and stabilize not only the effects of gender but the materiality of sex? And can this repetition, this rearticulation, also constitute the occasion for a critical reworking of apparently constitutive gender norms? [x].

In IM, the gendered self gets constituted through the performative repetition and re-signification of gendered norms and routines. These rituals are, however, influenced by both the interface structure and the user's actions. Using the lens of feminist technoscience the ongoing articulation of the gendered self through IM can be seen as mutually constituted. Haraway deconstructs our experiences as situated in a universe that is both material and semiotic (*Modest_Witness* 11–16). As a space where different axes of differentiation also play their part, instant messaging will be understood here as an experiential practice that is at once material and semiotic. Thus, the performance of self in IM can be seen as inscribed by the material and semiotic affordances and constraints of the medium and shaped by the users' material and semiotic actions.

Adolescent IM Connectivity

Online social networking sites (e.g. MySpace, Facebook), micro-blogging (e.g. Twitter) and video sharing sites (e.g. YouTube) have received increasing attention in the popular press and in academia. It is highly fashionable to publish about these publicly accessible, multimodal communication platforms. However, with the focus on these new applications, the more straightforward communicative space of Instant Messaging (IM) gets ignored. This omission is, however, unwarranted, as instant messaging remains an important part of being in the world for a large number of teenage youth: "the majority of teenagers have embraced instant messaging in a way that adults have not ... instant messaging has become an essential feature of their social lives" (Lenhart 10, 16).

Even though instant messaging is ancient in the ever-changing digital culture — having been around for almost two decades — it remains immensely popular among youth throughout the world. There is a growing presence of teenage girls and young women on the Internet. As the gender dimension of the digital divide — in terms of access — is decreasing, research shows that there are differences in how boys and girls make use of the internet. Girls use technologies such as text messaging, talking on mobile phones, communicating via email, using social networking sites, and instant messaging more than boys, while boys are more likely to download music and play computer games (Mazzarella 2; Tufte 72–73; Livingstone 56). In the context of the U.S., three quarters of all adolescents use IM frequently. Girls especially turn to IM as a place to socialize (Lenhart 38).

Online spaces become central gathering spots for teens, where conversation partners most often know each other quite well. As boyd argues, "while the sites teens go to gather at has changed over time, many of the core practices have stayed the same" in online gathering spots (boyd 80). Earlier, youth hung out in shopping malls, streets, schoolyards, and sport fields. And they passed paper notes in class. Now they also engage in forms of online adolescent connectedness, such as everyday peer negotiations using IM applications. Youth turn to instant messaging to fulfill needs to socialize while being confined to the house (Boneva 201). These socialization and peer negotiation practices include "making friends, performing friendship, articulating friendship hierarchies, and navigating issues of status, attention, and drama" (boyd 81). In the process of articulating identities, updating display names and display pictures, gossiping, flirting, joking, and fighting, gendered conventions get established in the communicative space of IM. This is, however, not to say that youth only engage in informal, personal, and private practices; IM is also used among youth to share information and collaborate in cultural productions (Leander 2006).

In this chapter we focus on the ways in which this space is made a significant representation arena for adolescent youth. Journalists, teachers, policy makers, and parents have expressed concern over the popularity of technologies such as IM. Often dressed up in moral panic rhetoric, IM has been dismissed as an avenue in which written versions of informal speech circulate. The practice is feared to ultimately corrupt formal writing skills and cause harm to print culture institutions (Jacobs 116; Baron "Always On" 46). However, in the lives of young people especially, its private character is highly appreciated. IM is a socializing space that can be kept away from the eyes of public and parental scrutiny. The allure of the medium is that users in relative autonomy can engage in private conversations, while using their own screen name, publishing their own display picture, and maintaining a personal list of contacts (so-called "buddy lists"). IM is used to stay in contact with different people. In the context of IM, sets of two people have one-to-one conversations, while individual users most often conduct multiple conversations simultaneously.

> I'll talk to my best friends, and me and my friends, it's like, "Oh it's 9 o'clock, I gotta get on the computer!" And it's like, if we can't, it's like, what am I going to do?! ... I don't know. It's just part of my night.—Abby, 14 years old [Lewis and Fabos 486].

Abby's description of her peer group's nightly engagement with IM illustrates how it has become a key spot for identity work. There, new linguistic codes get constructed and new, shared systems of meaning are being created. Display names, subject matter, voice, tone, and emoticons can be manipulated to emphasize, hide, and add nuance to their identities and monitor responses and interactions of others. This way, IM fulfills two important "modes of adolescent connectivity": one-to-one and one-to-many communication (Boneva et al. 202). In the transition from childhood to adulthood, youth find themselves in a process of negotiating definitions of selves (Erikson 87). At this juncture in life, individual and private reflection through person-to-person contact over IM help youth to make sense of themselves in their process of self-identity formation. Girls can verify their own positionality and can ask for support and attention. While IM facilitates one-to-one conversations, the expression of nicknames in buddy lists is one of the examples of how IM also fosters one-to-many communication. This mode of communication enables adolescent girls to publish expressions of shared affiliations with particular groups of their peers. Boneva et al. describe the significance of these two modes persisting in IM as follows: "through maintaining individual friendships (that help them "decipher" the self) and through belonging to peer groups (that help them map the self onto the social categories of the larger world)," girls may find their place in their worlds (202).

However, in the everyday life of girls, IM has become an invisible technology. IM gets taken for granted, and one "expects to be connected to friends at the stroke of a key, and expects to read and write in particular ways that lead to fulfilling connections with those friends" (Lewis and Fabos 470). By reviewing earlier work on IM, this study demonstrates how IM — as a practice that has become unremarkable and invisible to its users — reveals much about how social subjects shape and are shaped in everyday routines of technology use. Using gender as a red thread, the focus is on how girls construct spaces of their own in the day-to-day rituals that they perform using Instant Messaging. We aim to remain aware of the affordances and restraints of the medium, the ideological and commercial interests of the cultural industry, and gendered norms and discursive frameworks.

Rituals of Gender in IM

> The Internet then can be seen as an "unformed place," which depends to some degree on its use to find its structure. It is at the interface of user and technology that socialization instills order to the disorder of the Internet [Durham 37].

Everyday exchanges on MSN are bound but not fully determined by interfaces, algorithms, and discursive norms. The establishment of a new system of meaning within IM is illustrative. IM conversations have a specific composition that may be seen as a new genre of writing. The transmission style of messages includes the breaking up of single utterances into several lines of chat. Baron gives three reasons why users employ this particular style. Her first reason is technological. To maintain the attention of the interlocutor, utterances are often broken up into smaller pieces. By pressing "enter" while continuing to write an utterance, the conversation partner can begin reading the message, while the sender types the remainder. Her second reason refers to the readability of the message. Conversations are easier to follow when messages consist of short lines instead of larger chunks of text appearing on the screen. Finally, users reported to her that in their division of utterances over multiple turns "they are consciously attempting to make the results visually resemble a poem" ("See You" 417).

More specifically, users in their interaction with the application construct IM as a gendered space. Screen-names or display-names, used to self-identify and express affiliations, illustrate this process. In the context of the U.S., teenagers in IM for instance go by names such as "starchicachic," "Nikeguy1," "sportswoman," or "SlimmXx44" (Thiel-Stern 48–76), while in the Netherlands, "Adolescent youth sign in with email addresses and use display names that include 'chick,' 'girl,' 'lady,' 'miss,' 'boy' both in Dutch, English and other languages" (Leurs and Ponzanesi, "The Performance" n. pag.). Screen-names appear on the screen over and over, every time a new line is typed and the "enter" button is pressed. By naming themselves in these specific ways, they come into being as gendered beings in the context of IM. Through repeating these names, IM installs the user's gender.

Display names get updated to express one's personal status to a wider public of befriended contacts. For instance, 13-year old girl Leanne changed her name into "Leanne is SEXY!!!" (Thiel-Stern 38), while Soad, a 13 year old girl, updated her display to announce her love feelings: "I am Crazzy in love with you ... my feelings for you cannot go away " (Leurs and Ponzanesi, "Communicating Spaces" n. pag.). Kevin Hillis reads such transmissions as ritual acts: "the act of transmission itself becomes an ersatz place and constitutes a ritual act or performance" ("Digital Sensations" 63). He foregrounds how, as people are increasingly online, "networked rituals give order" and can accommodate different ways of being in the world: "ritual allows participants to performatively enact or rehearse strategies to cope with the crucial changes they may undergo" ("Online a Lot" 56). In performing IM rituals, youth's attention is divided among screens, but also among other activities and tasks such as listening to music, playing games, talking on a mobile phone, watching television, and doing homework.

The crafting of an appealing display name is an example of identity work that is communicated from one-to-many. It not only appears in person-to-person conversations, but it also appears in the buddy list of IM contacts. By double-clicking on someone's display name in one's list of friends, youth can start conversations. Elsewhere, we have argued that to attract attention from potential conversation partners, youth reveal in their display names masculine and feminine qualities: "Buddy lists are virtual real estates; in an ongoing verification of complimentary feminine and masculine conventions youth sell their gendered selves in a masculine and feminine peer economy" (Leurs and Ponzanesi, "The Performance" n. pag.). This attention economy is mutually shaped by teenagers' use of IM and the set up of IM applications.

Gender rituals are also apparent in the content of IM exchanges. The content of conversations uncovers how specific gender scripts can become apparent. Earlier research established that boys use more slang in everyday speech than girls[6]; however, we found elsewhere that in IM, slang is not restricted to the male domain. Girls were avid slang producers and consumers in the IM conversations we analyzed ("Communicative spaces" n. pag.). When analyzing IM rituals beyond the exchange of slang, other gendered dimensions become apparent. Fox et al. found in their study on IM that "women sent messages that were more expressive than those sent by men" (389). Studying IM exchanges among college students, they noticed female students differed from male students in, for instance, the use of emphasis, occurrence of laughing, use of emoticons, and reference to emotions (Fox et al. 394). Baron also compared IM conversations between female and male conversation partners and argues that women are more "talkative" which may reflect a "female writing style" ("See You" 418).

Baron found that "female-female conversations were roughly a third longer (in turns and time) than were male-male conversations." While males used more contractions, females were prime users of emoticons. "When it came to closing IM conversations ... females clearly used a greater number of turns, and lengthier time spans, than did males" ("See You" 415). The meaning of IM ritual practices in the lives of teenage girls, however, goes beyond these findings, but it can be better understood by exploring how they make IM spaces their own.

"Jammer Girls" on IM: Gatekeeping Spaces of Their Own

> "I get kind of shy when I meet new people face-to-face," explained Cherry (age 14). "But over MSN, it's just kind of, like, I can be myself without having to, like, be embarrassed because I'm not, like, standing there" [Kelly et al. 27].

The cultural industry is actively seeking ways to intrude in the private space of IM. For instance, this is done with pop-up screens. Discussing BP Nordstrom advertisements appearing in the Yahoo! IM environment, Thiel-Stern argues, "adolescent girls are asked to identify themselves with these flirty, sexy teen models, discuss shopping and fashion with their friends over IM and then click on the BP Nordstrom Web site" (97). In the context of MSN

Messenger, an "MSN today" pop-up screen tries to lure users to advertisements. Thirteen-year-old Midia reports, "sometimes there are nice scoops," but adds "what I find irritating is for instance when you go on your hotmail or so I sign in on msn there, and then I would like to press on someone to talk to, then I press on the advertisement on the side, which is irritating... or ads that pop up!" Often, girls say they disregard these advertisements, as Fatiha, a 17-year-old simply states, "I ignore those commercials" (Leurs and Ponzanesi, "Communicative Space" n. pag.).

The girls' navigation of advertisements is an example of a tactic used to gatekeep IM as a private communicative space. Gatekeeping, or "jamming," is done both physically — in the offline — as well as digitally — online. Coalescing with sociological and technological changes and informed by third wave feminism, Merskin specifies how "jammer girls" negotiate their subjectivities by making the best of the Internet to "enjoy a sense of freedom and a sense of control" (56). IM-girl-culture illustrates how girls can express a sense of active "girlhood" or "new femininities." By articulating such "new femininities," girls update the understanding of feminism in contemporary contexts. Technologies are used to highlight moments of celebration, freedom, and fun (Nayak and Kehily 59).

Physical examples of jamming include making sure no one can eavesdrop on the conversations taking place. Such gatekeeping is also done by crafting new linguistic codes. For instance, girls in Thiel Stern's study "all knew the various IM 'codes' to alert one another that a parent was present, such as *brb* for 'be right back' or *mh* for 'mom's here'" (52). Girls can also set digital boundaries. One way of doing so is by deciding who gets to be included on one's buddy list, and who gets blocked from it (Jacobs 125). Midia explains: "you can have people stalking you, such as people adding you and telling you they know you orsoo [sic], then you just have to block & delete" (Leurs and Ponzanesi, "The Performance" n. pag.). When asked how she would respond after getting sworn at, Cherry, aged 14, replies, "First, I tell them off, and then, I block them" (Kelly et al. 21). Linguistic conventions are also used as boundary markers; not knowing how to abide by the rules and conventions of IM culture works as an exclusionary mechanism.

But why is it so important that girls get to claim and defend the virtual turf of IM? Livingstone has emphasized the significance of online expressive girl-cultures. "Because their lives are often represented more powerfully by others than themselves, the exuberance and diversity of a girls' subculture online seems especially compelling" (Livingstone 116). Merskin describes the importance of the Internet and how it can offer jammer girls a place in which they share "common joys as well as trials and tribulations" (57). In their performance of self in IM, girls can encode personalized and contradictory messages.

Being able to author the self and represent the self to others in ways in which girls decide by themselves is significant, because personal voices of young people often get washed away in the wider flows of mainstream public culture.

In this space of relative autonomy, away from adult supervision, IM is a place to hang out; it is a representational arena with a peer public in which "young people learn about the opinions and values of their peers through testing of social norms and expectations in everyday negotiations over friendship, popularity, and romantic relationships" (Ito et al. 340). Lewis and Fabos argue that "this technology affords to redesign new social relationships," which includes for instance "new ways of talking to boys" (248).

More specifically, IM allows girls to exert a different voice. Fourteen-year-old Marcia explains: "I can talk more freely to boys, and I know more boys [online]. If it wasn't for MSN, I would know no boys [laughter]. That's a guarantee" (Kelly et al. 15). "With MSN," Marcia elaborates, "you can kind of think about, like a good comeback or something" (Kelly et al. 17). MSN is sometimes preferred over face-to-face conversations as, in the former, awkward silences can be avoided, says Cheryl, age 15. "Say the guy you like is on [MSN], you can always plan what you're going to say, and like, make it perfect ... And then, you can send to your friends and be like, "Can I say this? Is this okay?" (Kelly et al. 18). This statement resonates with the exchange quoted at the beginning of the chapter, that is, when girls turn to each other for help in dealing with relationships and intimacy. IM allows youth to build relationships, says Vera: "you talk to people online, it's like you know them in reality" and get closer (Kelly et al. 18). "So the next time you see each other, like, in real life, right, it's sometimes easier to talk to them" (Kelly et al. 18). As Alana, also 13, attests with regard to MSN: "I've definitely gotten to be more comfortable around guys" (Kelly et al. 18).

When Amy, age 13, was asked about her most powerful online experience, she discussed how she battled sexual harassment. Her narrative is worth quoting at length:

> Oh, some jerk was like, "Hey, let's have sex." And I was like, "No, screw you! What's wrong with you? Why do you do this?" ... I felt really good afterwards because I totally, like, yelled at him. It was like, "It's stupid like asking young girls to do things like that. So do the police know you're doing this? Should I tell them?" [Kelly et al. 19].

Exploiting the affordances of the medium, Amy actively safeguards herself in her communicative space. Jammer girls may become powerful members of "the constant contact generation" in the space of IM; "it holds for young women the promise of being able to manage relationships through their written communication skills, which are generally better than those of their male counterparts" (Clark 216). As Thiel Stern sums up:

> The point that adolescent girls feel comfortable and positive about expressing sexuality is very important; girls in decades past tended to feel embarrassed about expressing sexuality outside the pages of their private diaries (and even within them) [69].

In the process of boundary making, girls find themselves more at ease in (dis)engaging with lovers, in building relationships, and exploring intimacy. Being able to maintain IM as a connected, but personal, space is very significant in their lives as they start to explore their subjectivity and place in the world.

Conclusions

Youth are increasingly online for much of their free time. Instant messaging (IM) is one representational arena that often gets overlooked, particularly due to the recent increase of attention paid to public communicative spaces such as social networking sites and blogs. However, as we have set out, IM remains an important space to "hang out" in the lives of adolescents (Ito et al. 38). IM is a mainstay for synchronous one-to-one and particular forms of one-to-many computer mediated communication. IM practices exemplify how computer mediated communication gets interwoven into the fabrics of everyday teenage life. The discursive energy invested in this space of relative autonomy, away from unwanted onlookers such as parents, reveals how "teenagers play out their entrenched understandings of social relations in their uses of the technologies" (Durham 37). Studying IM practices may help to uncover and highlight gendered constructions of agency, structure, power, and resistance.

Abstract hype and panic over CMC remains largely cut-off from present day-to-day online rituals. Fearful and utopian perspectives on technologies miss out on the everyday complexities of IM use among teenagers. A binary distinction between the embodied experience of a person before a screen and the symbolic interaction on the screen is untenable. Instead, being aware of the experiential material, and semiotic dimensions of IM, we demonstrated how ideas about age, ability, gender, sex, race, ethnicity, and identity continue to be constituted and re-constituted every time we log on. Focusing on the fluid and situated mutual constitution of gender and technology, IM can thus be seen as a source as well as a consequence of gender relations (Wajcman 149).

In this communicative space, crucial adolescent "modes of adolescent connectivity" (Boneva et al. 202) are played out, as youth decipher themselves and explore peer-group belongings. In ritualized performances of selves, boys and girls distribute themselves in specific gendered roles. Girls are said to be more "talkative" and employ a "female writing style" (Baron, "See You" 418).

Through these gendered performances, distinct cultures arise with a particular aesthetic. Most importantly, in seizing control of the medium through physical and digital boundary work, girls using IM become "jammer girls" (Merskin 57) by reconfiguring their experience of instant-messaging spaces materially, and semiotically to meet their personal demands, interests, and goals.

NOTES

1. Currently, the most used IM applications are Yahoo!, MSN Messenger (the application has recently been renamed Windows Live, but youth still refer to it as MSN) and Tencent's QQ (QQ was first called Open ICQ, which was later changed into QQ). The first application is most popular in the United States, the second in Europe, South-America, Africa and the Middle East and the third in China. At the time of writing, Yahoo! ranks as the 4th most popular page globally and 3rd in the U.S.; MSN, globally ranks as the 9th most popular website online; while QQ globally ranks as the 10th most popular website online, and the 2nd most popular in China ("Search Analytics"). QQ instant messaging service registered 990 million user identities in the summer of 2009 ("QQ: China's Monster 'Facebook'" par. 5). In the month of February 2010, 300 million people logged in to MSN (Kunins par. 9) and Yahoo had 250 million registered users in January 2008 (Arrington par 1).

2. Van Doorn and Van Zoonen survey literature on the topic of gender and the internet and Wajcman synthesizes work on feminist theories of technologies. Both studies examine what lies between technological determinism and gender essentialism and point towards a mutual shaping perspective. This perspective argues that "gender relations can be thought of as materialised in technology, and masculinity and femininity in turn acquire their meaning and character through their enrolment and embeddedness in working machines" (Wajcman 149).

3. "The Californian ideology" is a world-view described by Richard Barbrook and Andy Cameron which "promiscuously combines the free-wheeling spirit of the hippies and the entrepreneurial zeal of the yuppies" (qtd. in Meikle 190). Barbrook and Cameron criticize its free market, techno-determinism, individualism and libertarianism ideology.

4. E.g. Spallone and Steinberg.

5. E.g. Cockburn.

6. E.g. Gordon.

WORKS CITED

Arrington, Michael. "Yahoo Implements OpenID." *Tech Chrunch*. Tech Chrunch, 17 Jan. 2008. Web. 24 August 2010.

Barlow, John P. "A Declaration of the Independence of Cyberspace." *EFF.org*. Electronic Frontier Foundation, 9 Feb 1996. Web. 20 July 2010.

Baron, Naomi S. *Always On: Language in an Online and Mobile World.* Oxford: Oxford University Press, 2008. Print.

_____. "See You Online. Gender Issues in College Student Use of Instant Messaging." *Journal of Language and Social Psychology* 23.4 (2004): 397–423. Print.

Boneva, Bonka S, et al. "Teenage Communication in the Instant Messaging Era." *Computers, Phones, and the Internet: Domesticating Information Technology.* Ed. Robert Kraut, Malcolm Brynin and Sara Kiesler. Oxford: Oxford University Press, 2006. 201–17. Print.

boyd, danah. "Friendship." *Hanging Out, Messing Around and Geeking Out.* Ed. Mizoko Ito. Cambridge: MIT Publishers, 2010. Print.

Butler, Judith. *Bodies That Matter.* New York: Routledge, 1993. Print.

Clark, Lynn Schofield. "The Constant Contact Generation." *Girl Wide Web.* Ed. Sharon R. Mazzarella. New York: Peter Lang, 2005. 203–22. Print.

Cockburn, Cynthia. "On the Machinery of Dominance." *Women's Studies Quarterly* 37.1–2 (2009): 269–73. Print.

Dibbell, Julian. *My Tiny Life: Crime and Passion in a Virtual World.* New York: Henry Holt and Company, 1998. Print.

Durham, Meenakshi Gigi. "Adolescents, the Internet and the Politics of Gender." *Race, Gender & Class* 8.4 (2001): 20–41. Print.

Erikson, Erik H. *Identity: Youth and Crisis.* New York: Norton, 1968. Print.

Fox, Annie B., et al. "The Medium Makes a Difference: Gender Similarities and Differences in Instant Messaging." *Journal of Language and Social Psychology* 26.4 (2007): 389–97. Print.

Gordon, Michael. "Sexual Slang and Gender." *Women and Language* 16.2 (1993): 16–21. Print.

Haraway, Donna. "A Cyborg Manifesto." *Simians, Cyborgs, and Women.* Ed. Donna Haraway. New York: Routledge, 1991. 149–181. Print.

_____. *Modest_Witness@Secondmillennium.* New York: Routledge, 1997. Print.

Haythornthwaite, Caroline, and Barry Wellman. "Part 1. Moving the Internet out of Cyberspace." *The Internet in Everyday Life.* Ed. Barry Wellman and Caroline Haythornthwaite. Malden: Blackwell, 2002. 1–41. Print.

Herring, Susan C. "Gender and Power in On-Line Communication." *Handbook of Language and Gender.* Ed. Janet Holmes and Miriam Meyerhoff. Oxford: Blackwell, 2003. 202–28. Print.

Hillis, Ken. *Online a Lot of the Time.* Durham: Duke UP, 2009. Print.

_____. *Digital Sensations.* Minneapolis: U of Minnesota, 1999. Print.

Ito, Mizoko, et al. *Hanging Out, Messing Around and Geeking Out.* Cambridge: MIT P, 2010. Print.

Kelly, Deirdre M., Shauna Pomerantz, and Dawn H. Curre. "'No Boundaries'? Girls' Interactive, Online Learning About Femininities." *Youth Society* 38.3 (2006): 3–28. Print.

Kunins, Jeff. "Windows Live Messenger — a Short History." *The Windows Blog.* Windows, 9 Feb. 2010. Web. 24 August 2010.

Leander, Kevin. "The Aesthetic Production and Distribution of Image/Subjects among Online Youth." *E-Learning* 3.2 (2006): 185–206. Print.

Lenhart, Amanda, Lee Rainie, and Oliver Lewis. "Teenage Life Online." *Pew Research Centre.* Pew, 21 June 2001. Web. 20 July 2010.

Leurs, Koen, and Sandra Ponzanesi. "Communicative Spaces of Their Own: Migrant Girls Performing Selves Using Instant Messaging Software." Forthcoming.

_____. The Performance of Gender by Migrant Girls in Instant Messaging Spaces." *Handbook on Gender, Sexualities and Media.* Ed. Karen Ross. London: Routledge, forthcoming. N. pag. Print.

Lewis, Cynthia, and Bettina Fabos. "Instant Messaging, Literacies and Social Identities." *Reading* Research Quarterly 40.4 (2005): 470–501. Print.

Livingstone, Sonia. *Children and the Internet.* Cambridge: Polity, 2009. Print.

Mazzarella, Sharon R. *Girl Wide Web.* New York: Peter Lang, 2005. Print.

Meikle, Graham. *Future Active: Media Activism and the Internet.* New York: Routledge, 2002. Print.

Merskin, Debra. "Making an About-Face. Jammer Girls and the World Wide Web." *Girl Wide Web.* Ed. Sharon R. Mazzarella. New York: Peter Lang, 2005. 51–67. Print.

Nakamura, Lisa. *Cybertypes.* New York: Routledge, 2002. Print.

Nayak, Anoop, and Mary Jane Kehily. *Gender, Youth and Culture.* Hampshire: Palgrave MacMillan, 2008. Print.

Plant, Sadie. *Zeroes + Ones: Digital Women and the New Technoculture.* NY: Doubleday, 1997. Print.

"QQ: China's Monster 'Facebook.'" *Telco2research.* Telco, 2009. Web. 24 August 2010.

Reid, Elizabeth. "Electronic Chat: Social Issues on Internet Relay Chat." *Media International Australia* 67 (1993): 62–70. Print.

Robins, Kevin. "Cyberspace and the World We Live In." *Cyberspace/Cyberbodies /Cyberpunk: Cultures* of Technological Embodiment. Ed. Mike Featherstone and Roger Burrows. London: Sage. 135–156. Print.

"Search Analytics." *Alexa.* The Web Information Company, 2010. Web. 20 July 2010.

Spallone, Patricia, and Deborah Lynn Steinberg. *Made to Order.* London: Pergamon Publishers, 1985. Print.

Steiner, Peter. "On the Internet, Nobody Knows You're a Dog." Cartoon. *New Yorker* 5 July 1993: 61. Print.

Stone, Allucquère Rosanne. *The War of Desire and Technology.* Cambridge: MIT Publishers, 1995. 65–82. Print.

Thiel-Stern, Shayla. *Instant Identity.* New York: Peter Lang, 2007. Print.

Tufte, Birgitte. "Girls in the New Media Landscape." *Nordicom Review* 24.1 (2003): 71–78. Print.

Van Doorn, Niels, and Liesbeth Van Zoonen. "Theorizing Gender and the Internet." *Routledge Handbook of Internet Politics.* Ed. Andrew Chadwick and Philip N. Howard. New York: Routledge, 2009. 261–274. Print.

Wajcman, Judy. "Feminist Theories of Technology." *Cambridge Journal of Economics* 34.1 (2010): 143–52. Print.

14

Gender Blogging: Femininity and Communication Practices on the Internet

Adriana Braga

Throughout history, the control and management of available technologies have been strategic factors on power relations and hierarchies. And, as in many other fields of discourse, like religion, warfare, or politics, access to available technology is remarkably defined by a gender bias. Since its inception, the Internet was a male-operated medium (Turkle 58). Nowadays, the growing number of women on the Internet is slowly changing the traditional male dominance of technologically-mediated activities. This chapter analyzes the social interactions among a group of women and their definitions of femininity, sexuality, and motherhood in a Brazilian blog environment. The social environments available on the Internet can be utilized in several ways. In this case, participants use the blog's guestbook to recover a social practice they were missing in their private lives, that is, "women's talk," a kind of interaction often regarded in a male-centered perspective as useless and futile gossip.

This blog's use as a forum for issues of femininity and motherhood resulted in numerous comments, vast information exchange, and engaged discussion on topics relating to feminism from hundreds of women from different locations and life experiences. The constant flow of opinions, comments, interpretations, definitions, and information on the blog reveals an important panel of positions regarding conflicts and dilemmas of contemporary femininity expressed in an Internet environment. Some of the topics in this debate that will be analyzed in this chapter include: (1) the voluntary interruption of pregnancy; (2) attributes and definitions of contemporary motherhood; (3) the blog's place in participants' lives; (4) the social, domestic, and affective implications of women's labor after motherhood; and (5) women's everyday life experiences.

The positions presented on that forum represent an idealized version of "modern mothers," expressed in the title of the blog, the neologism "Mothern" (Mother + modern). This phrase, as defined by these women, denotes a modern attitude towards femininity, sexuality, and motherhood, as well as a tolerance for social differences, such as a regard for alternative methods for the education of children and respect for one's individuality. However, such positions coexist with traces of ethnic, class, and gender prejudices, evidencing some ambiguities and dilemmas of contemporary femininity.

The Research

This nethnographic study on the topic of contemporary femininity in blogs has been ongoing since 2004, and investigates the communicative interactions among a group of women who participate in a specific environment. The technologically-mediated interaction produced on this blog allows for an interesting study on the relation between motherhood, communication technology, and contemporary feminine interaction in Brazil.

Assuming the existence of a gendered culture in contemporary society, that is, a complex set of definitions and social practices regarding femininity, masculinity, and their articulations of meanings, this chapter argues that the terms of this dimension of culture are updated in everyday life through the ordinary interactions and practices of men and women. Thus, the phenomenon that this chapter investigates refers to a specific and contemporary revision of gendered culture, related to the social uses of technology by a group of women in interaction with one another.

Within the blog environment, social definitions of motherhood and femininity are proposed by participants, in what can be taken as an informal theorization on contemporary femininity. Such definitions express the ways in which a group of women ponders the challenges and contradictions between traditional features of femininity and contemporary practices regarding gender relations, work, family, and motherhood. It is interesting to note that blog environments — in this one and in many others — seem to offer a renewed place for recovering a traditional feminine practice, "women's talk," which is seen as outdated in face-to-face environments. Although women's conversations about children, marriage, and domestic life have been framed in public spaces as futile and useless gossip, in blog environments the same topics are expressed without such pejorative connotations; on the contrary, these conversations are framed by participants as important practices of modern women.

Feminism has promoted changes in the forms of social control, hierarchy, and authority in family relations, changing behaviors and moral values through the last four decades. Much of this social change derived from industrialization, urbanization, accumulation, and distribution of knowledge. The impact of the feminist movement in Western societies has challenged patriarchal power, fostered gender equity (to a certain extent), and influenced social practices. One such stimulated change can be seen in that of traditional family organization. The last several decades have shown an alternative perspective toward motherhood and femininity. In this tense dialectic between permanence and change, women still choose to have children although their childrearing practices may not mirror that of previous generations.

Another important topic in the contemporary configuration of femininity relates to the position of women in labor activities. This is a very complex issue which goes far beyond the actual disadvantage of women in terms of salaries and prestige in comparison to men. If, on the one hand, feminine work has been deemed as a necessary economic activity, on the other, it has been connected to ancient expectancies that associate women with the home, creating what is sometimes called double duty: the burden felt when professional work is added to the work of housekeeping and caring of children. It is necessary to consider that in emergent countries, like Brazil, women's ability to engage in professional activities is often dependent on the delegation of the second part of their "double duty," such as housekeeping responsibilities, to domestic workers. This dependency is complicated further when class tensions are taken into consideration. For example, in Brazil, these domestic workers are most often comprised of women from the lower economic classes, whereas the women entering into the professional work force are of middle class status or higher (Braga, *Personas* 216). In underdeveloped countries, feminine emancipation is a matter of social class — an emancipation that involves affective, ethnic, and labor conflicts, as will be discussed later.

On the Presentation of Self in Blog Life

Online activities are inscribed in practical conditions of use, applying resources from other contexts according to specific situational demands. Such online activities (commenting, replying, blogging, etc.) do not substitute for traditional ones (chatting, visiting, meeting, etc.), but seem to be their complements or transformations. Many aspects of oral-auditive conversation can be identified on computer mediated communication (CMC). However, many other models of interaction are used in online activities, such as letter writing, phone calling, face-to-face conversation, and so on.

According to Erving Goffman, social interaction takes place in widely two different regions or settings called backstage and front (29). When people are in the front region, they are generally polite and concerned with presenting themselves to the best of their roles, while people in the backstage region are relatively free to perform less polished presentations of self: criticizing, mocking, or complaining about others. In blog environments, topics are generally addressed in a backstage language, closer to spoken than written language, even if their comments are all written. In other words, blog communication is a written form of spoken language (Barnes 3). Although blog interaction has sometimes been described as an indistinct region between public and private, participants of the blog environment know very clearly where the distinction lies (Sibilia 1–12).

The structure of the blog allows it to exist as both a public and a private space wherein participants can engage in conversation that might transcend those constructed spheres. On the very structure of the blog, the homepage is different from the guestbook. The contents of both are public, although the homepage is edited only by the hosts. As spaces for private access, there are several links in the blog and in the guestbook for hosts' and participants' email addresses. These are important since an email address is sometimes seen as a proof of "authenticity" for a comment, as in signing a document. Within the borders of this communicational dynamics, it can be noted that intimate topics are not brought up for discussion on the blog given that this space is considered public. The blog is seen as a place for meeting people, among other things. Participants very often refer to interaction with fellows beyond the blog, using cell phones, instant messaging, private discussion lists — all private forms of media — for practical purposes.

Given that newcomers to the blog must adapt to this type of presentation of self, it is possible to identify patterns of attitude, or coping strategies which range from praising to criticizing the views of others. In a sort of interaction ritual, newcomers' first words on the guestbook usually praise the blog environment, with posts like "awesome," "brilliant," or "fantastic." At other times, however, such first words openly criticize the blog environment, sparing no one. Evidently, the reactions on the guestbook are completely different in each case, be it a warm welcome or a counterattack. Despite the fact that conflicts happen from time to time, by far the most regular pattern of attitude in the guestbook is kindness.

The study of social behavior on Internet environments presents a great methodological challenge. A first remark should be made on the historical period in which this research takes place. These forms of interaction are recent phenomena which fail to provide users with established forms of individual and group strategies for operation. In order to overcome this, users borrow and adapt already-existing rules taken from other relational contexts such as face-to-face interaction, phone calls, or letter exchanging. Such strategies are applied on a case-by-case basis, according to situational demands, prior to the eventual formation of explicit formal rules. These rules-in-the-making will probably consolidate later as online cultural activities go on.

Although it is claimed that the Internet offers a limitless freedom of expression, there is also the need for still-evolving rules that allow for collective co-existence. This being the case, the patterns of verbal expression held in these settings are in some way subordinated to the social control of participants. The freedom created by anonymity — the absence of physical presence that would expose ethnic, gender or class attributes — can serve either to foster friendship and intimacy or to spark aggression and disrespect towards others. In many discussion lists open to new members, newcomers are often ignored for not presenting the desired profile for a member, an often unspoken prerequisite for belonging. In situations in which a newcomer deviates greatly with the regular participants' norms, reactions vary from ostracism to open aggression.

Femininity and Communication on the Internet

The Internet is a multimedia environment which allows for the production and exchange of audiovisual data between users. However, it is still essentially a text-based medium. This essential feature of CMC defines the sort of interaction that takes place in blog environments. In a blog, one exists and occupies a position by writing. Being in a blog environment is to write. To not write means invisibility. To register a comment means to be there, and interaction only occurs as participants "are there" in written words. Thus, writing competence is a powerful tool in blog environments, and the messages posted convey a lot of information — sometimes involuntary — about their authors. Sometimes, authors express themselves in short, abbreviated, and voluntarily incorrect terms, as in chat or instant messenger situations. Many things can be inferred — such as age, school level, or social class — by the words and phrasal constructions utilized.

In the blog *Mothern*, the mastering of grammatical Portuguese is worth a great deal: during regular polite interactions, mistakes in construction or spelling are usually accounted for in advance with a joking comment by the author (when in doubt before writing a difficult word), or corrected in a further comment, or simply tolerated by the other participants. However, during conflict situations (as explained above), blaming terms such as "illiterate" or "ignorant" can be openly charged upon any opponent who commits a grammatical mistake of any kind. Additionally, a sort of symbolic hierarchy regarding the linguistic competence of a participant can be perceived, by connecting her to professions or activities that demand a sophisticated language use, such as advertising, translating, or teaching. Therefore, the way one writes imparts a sort of tacit hierarchy on the communication, as it is demanded from participants not only that they possess the technical competence of the medium but also an educational competence.

Thus, within this blog environment, power and hierarchy are inscribed in words. The explicit connection of the blog *Mothern* with femininity and motherhood brings out arguments, comments, representations, and interpretations on gender issues, presenting an interesting panel of positions regarding dilemmas on contemporary femininity, as presented below.

The Argument on Abortion

Abortion is a key issue in public policies regarding female rights (even more so in underdeveloped countries), and in the blog *Mothern* this topic raised a long and intense argument that evidenced contradictions and ambiguities among participants. The voluntary interruption of pregnancy challenges traditional views of conception which fixate on feminine "virtue" and the valoration of "life."

The examples below showcase some of the comments left on the guestbook on this topic. The argument in this case began when a participant asked for advice regarding an unintentional pregnancy.

> TATI: Hi... I am writing because I need help... as you know, I am one month pregnant and living all the doubts and fears of the "newly pregnant." I'm a 28 y.o., advertiser, still struggling to earn my independence and my space. I live with my mother, my boyfriend also lives with his parents, and he is currently unemployed. My pregnancy was completely unexpected... I always wanted (and still want) to have children, but under other circumstances... living in my own place, with my boyfriend employed... He does not want to, says it is not the right time. My family knows it and fully supports me, but I still think about many things: I can't earn my own living, I share a room with my brother, my baby's father is unemployed... Sincerely, all I think is about having an abortion, but I am very frightened of the consequences. I am completely confused and in anguish, I need advice, something to help me to decide what to do... Thanks.....
>
> LU: Look, Tati, no one can help you to decide this matter. What you have to do is to look at yourself and figure out if you can handle it or not. Having a child is really difficult, it will take a lot of time and money, at least for some years. But the truth is that almost everyone finds a way of dealing with it and in the end falls in love with the baby, so if you choose to have the baby, you can be sure that it will be hard, but in the end you will find your way. Now, the decision to not have the baby depends a lot on your own moral values. If you are ok

about that, it may be an option, but if you are in doubt, you must be sure whether you can handle it or if you will spend the rest of your life regretting and blaming yourself. In this case, the solution may be worse than the problem. I would say that, in the case you decide to have an abortion, don't tell this to anyone. Don't forget that we live in the largest Catholic country in the world, and people can be very aggressive when discussing this topic. Take care, and good luck.

ANDREA: Listen, ladies: I don't want to rule on this matter, nor to teach you morality. It is simple common sense. Abortion is a simple euphemism for killing the child. The same thing, right? Please correct me if I am wrong. Whoever aborts kills the child, right? Is life difficult? Yes it is! Raising a baby costs a lot of money. And love doesn't buy diapers. But frankly, didn't they know that having sex is the way babies come into the world? At that moment no one remembered, uh? No one remembered that the boyfriend was unemployed, that it was not the right time, and so on. Now that the PROBLEM is here, it is easy: use a knife and get rid of it. Oh, of course, the condom has burst, the pill didn't work, of course. I will tell you something, I feel very disappointed to hear this sort of advice (follow your heart, make your choice, kill) from people that participate in a blog like Mothern. It is a place for mothers, to talk about motherhood. I agree that women have the right to decide when they want to have a child. To do this, any drugstore is filled with condoms, pills, IUDs and 200 other things. But I think that once the child is in there, it is done. You must pull yourself together and face it! By the way, where are the people that are against killing children?

SORAIA: Sex, my friends, should be practiced only by people responsible for the consequences—pregnancy, for instance. Be they 15 or 35 years old. At the "don't stop, don't stop" moment, this possibility is not considered. Then, if something happens, is it just as easy as choosing a basic abortion? Easy, useful and modern, isn't it? A finger in the eye of such bloody bastards.

LU: Cool it, people! Let's keep the debate on the high level it once was. First of all, something must be clear: no one is "pro-abortion." An abortion is always an emergency choice, a trauma, a situation of suffering and despair. (...) Each person should know what he/she is capable of, and techniques for interruption of pregnancy have been known since the beginning of humanity. There is nothing modern about that. The argument about abortion being a form of "murder" or not is much more recent. And even today, no one is really sure about when life begins, about when an embryo becomes a child. I think no one here is square enough to condemn the IUD, and it is a method that works AFTER fecundation. (...) Let's not make life harder for someone who is already having a hard time, pressing her with positions that only have meaning for those who share the same beliefs. I want to state clearly that, as I am doing here, everyone has the right to express herself in this place. So let's cool it down, and start speaking like grown-ups again. Kisses.

Among participants, the specific topic lost its relevance, and metaphysics took place on the debate, splitting the group into "pro-life" versus "pro-choice." The episode left sequels: two of the most enthusiastic defenders of the "pro-life" position left the group forever. In two days, there were more than 150 comments on the guestbook, evidencing the explosive potential of this topic as well as the demand for adequate places for debating it. This conflict expresses some of the contradictions between tradition and modernity that compose a "mothern" theory of contemporary femininity.

Being *Mothern*: Between Tradition and Modernity

In an interview published in a Brazilian news magazine, one of the bloggers argued that she had created the blog *Mothern* because all the parenting magazines she knew were dedicated to "square mothers" ("Caleidoscópio" 58). She complained that although they had become mothers, it did not mean they had stopped being interested in issues like fashion, lifestyle, or music.

What would a "mothern" be? For participants, being mothern means to be a mother who has a career, a certain control of technological devices, who questions established knowledge, and is guided by an individualistic perspective because she believes the rights of every person should be taken into account, as in the quotes below:

> JACQUELINE: I guess I am a mothern because:
> - I have Orkut, msn, email and some virtual friends.
> - I work all day long and this year I will finish college.
> - I am a mothern because I have red underwear hidden in the drawer...surprise!!!
> - I read everything about child education, sleep, food, teeth, toys...
> - I believe there is time to play, time to sleep and nooooooo coke, nor pizza!

> FLAVIA: I am a mothern because I am not a "super-protective mother" that keeps her children under her wing all day long. I am a mothern because I let my boy play with all the toys, including dolls, and I don't worry if he will have his sexuality affected by this. After all, I am a mothern because every day I try to break rules and taboos, and I still am a dedicated and exemplary mother (yes, I am an exemplary mother!).

These beliefs allow them to break with traditional representations of motherhood, and rethink the "perfect mother" stereotype. The success of the blog is made apparent by the number of visitors and the intense activity of the guestbook. These women have identified with the new representations of motherhood, which they themselves have forged and found there a place to meet like minded people and exchange experiences and thoughts.

Public Utility: A Safe Dock in the Info-Sea

Mothern is usually defined by participants as a place of public utility. Their intense engagement in interactions regarding feminine issues evidences a demand for a place, a public arena, where meanings regarding the complex symbolic field of femininity can be exchanged. The blog offered such a place in which these issues could be debated, as in the examples below:

> SIMONI: Congratulations on the blog. Besides being so funny, it is a Public Utility Service!
> RENATA: Surgeon General Warning: Mothern is ESSENTIAL to health!!!
> MARILENE: Everything I always think about, doubt, imagine, complain and cry for is in here. There is nothing like knowing that you are not the only one who works, has children, a husband and house, goes out to parties, loves all of it and doesn't give up any part of it.

In interactional terms, online behavior is regulated by tacit rules. The absence of formal regulation — like laws for broadcasting — makes the production of contents and cultural representations in blogs to be self-regulated via interactional constraints. Usually, these constraints can be expressed in form of criticisms, interpellation, or even strategic indifference. However, the production of cultural representations, both by bloggers and by readers — who, in CMC are also co-producers of contents — demand social responsibility. As the blog is part of the public sphere, agents or representatives of social groups can overtly demand political commitment from the bloggers, generating criticisms, interpellations, adherences, and conflicts. Even if the bloggers declare they never had the intention to appear as "models" or "examples" to anyone, such roles are inherent to the fame they have earned. Such situations demonstrate the many complexities involved in the production of cultural representations in the blogosphere: becoming a blog celebrity or "microcelebrity" (Braga, *Microcelebridades*, 1–15) arises new obligations.

The emergence of a transformed feminine role challenges traditional conceptions of femininity. It implies dealing with the many contradictions and ambiguities between the two conceptions. For instance, on the guestbook and in interviews participants affirm to adhere to a set of modern values (religious tolerance, respect for minorities) but admit race and class prejudice, and regard the word "feminist" as problematic. One good example concerns domestic labor, which is the next topic of discussion.

Working Girls: Feminism and a Domestic Class Struggle

A central matter in the ordinary life of these mothers is the management of motherhood with professional life. Today, in Brazilian society, even though there is a consensus concerning the legitimacy of women's work outside the home, there are still fewer — if any — childcare laws which aid the working mother. Usually, this forces mothers to find their own private solutions for dealing with childcare, as will be shown below.

The most direct consequence of the lack of childcare laws is the accumulation of duties, in which the stereotypically feminine duties — housekeeping, child care, etc. — are added to professional demands of meeting deadlines, schedules, and business meetings. To meet these demands, middle-class mothers in Brazil usually hire maids (lower-class women who are expected to do domestic work that is often devalued) or rely on their mothers or mothers-in-law (usually women who do not work outside the home) to keep their houses clean and care for their children. A topic for discussion related to this was proposed on the *Mothern* community at the social network Orkut. *Ana:* "Day care, maid or Grandma's house? What do you do with your little ones while you work like dogs?" This topic generated 49 comments, when the average number of comments for a discussion topic on that community is under 10 comments. On the *Mothern* Guestbook, the complaint of a participant about her maid had generated an immense thread of more than 200 comments in less than 24 hours. The diversity of opinions evidenced some of the contradictions and paradoxes of domestic labor in Brazilian society: a silent class struggle. Some of the comments illustrate this:

> GINA*:* Is there anything more disgusting than getting home desperate to use the toilet and finding your "helper" sitting on it???
>
> CHRIS: Sorry, but that one was funny! The nerve of her!!!
>
> JU: Sorry, Gina, but I feel really bad for her. I think it is horrible those minimal "maid's dormitories" in which a person has to sleep with her feet on the wall and have a shower above the toilet. I don't like uniforms for nannies, it seems to me that the boss thinks that she is not "clean" enough to carry the baby. What I have seen around is that when a maid does something wrong, bosses tell the story in details to all their friends, but these bosses never mention when they don't pay health insurance, don't respect weekends, pay peanuts and still want the maid to live at her job and work 24 hours a day.
>
> GINA: Sorry, Ju, I didn't mean to hurt your feelings, I just needed to get it off my chest. I think you are right about being a nice socially fair boss, but it pisses me off to be taken advantage all the time.
>
> MONIX: I want to say that Victor's nanny sleeps in my house from Monday to Friday so that I can work (she lives 2½ hours away) and she wears a white uniform. I don't feel comfortable in seeing her walking around the living room in short-shorts in front of my husband, or wearing inappropriate clothes while walking with my baby — in my elitist opinion...
>
> CHRIS: Never mind, but I find it such poor taste when I see nannies with miniskirts or shorts at the playground. And I find some uniforms so fashionable... When I worked in a uniform store I was crazy about wearing some of them.
>
> DUDA: Racial democracy is wonderful, democracy at home is wonderful. But it doesn't work. You have a person that lives in your house. She may not sleep there, but she cooks your food and does your laundry. If one day she is late and you complain, she scorches your favorite blouse with the iron, she showers with your soap and combs her hair with your brush. It's class struggle. Brazilian society

was built upon slavery. A whole race has been oppressed, tortured and raped. What would one expect as outcome? Black women—and we all descend from them—learned to seduce, to bow her head and open her legs to the boss. And then, pretend being a fool for the boss' wife, who took revenge on her for masculine humiliation. I have seen a maid tell that she had given rat poison to her husband that used to beat her. I was frightened: my god, what will she do when she gets angry with her boss?

The uneasiness with this ordinary class contradiction makes this theme embarrassing for an environment occupied by modern women who define themselves by their accomplishments in the public sphere. The need to delegate child care to another person — usually a lower-class woman — demonstrates a breaking point for the position of women in Brazil.

Rethinking Femininity as Ethnomethod

Considering the topics discussed on the blog *Mothern*, one notes a sort of "practical sociological reasoning," or "ethnomethod" defined as ordinary methods for facing concrete situations (Garfinkel 11). This includes questioning the contemporary woman's situation and its contradictions with the traditional feminine role. Discussions on this subject present a sort of consensus about the coexistence of feminism — responsible for many direct benefits and rights for women—with a persistent, male-centered logic that balks at every feminine social advance. Participants of the blog reflect on their own situation, and seem to be conscious about the reproduction of gender relations inherent to the education of their children, as in the comments below:

LIU: It is harder to raise a boy than a girl these days, because feminism has come, but male chauvinism is still around, filling kids' heads with prejudice. How to raise a boy in such an ignorant society?

GABI: The other day we were at a birthday party with Sofia, and a friend from nursery gave her a "bear hug," and did not left her for a long time. My mother was around and commented: "Hey, it seems she got a boyfriend, uh?" Come on, we are talking about a "couple" under 2 years old! Ok, it was not the most horrifying thing in the world, but I thought about how fast people are to protest against early sexualizing of children, against media discourse, etc, but they don't think about how they contribute to the whole thing. Everybody thinks this is absurd, etc, but in everyday life there are lots of double messages and nobody seems to be aware.

JU: I was watching the Cinderella movie with Isabella, and I realized how we were prepared for being princesses. The message is clear: never complain of what others do against you, be kind and sweet even if they screw you up (the scene in which Cinderella's sisters destroy her dress is one of the most sadistic thing I have ever seen in the movies), always be a soft, good and silly girl. And hope some day someone will appear to solve your problems, like magic. To become a prince charming is much easier: you can yawn in boredom, while hundreds of beautiful princesses pass shamelessly flirting in front of you. Then, you choose the prettiest, and hopefully she will come with a bonus of having worked as maid in hell, and have learned all about housekeeping. Then, you can leave daddy's palace straight to the arms of your maid, oops, Cinderella.

CHRIS: what story should I tell so that my boy does not turn into a chauvinist pig?

An important point to be considered in these comments is that their proposals for social action are essentially individualistic. Participants have a critical view of reality, and identify many contradictions in contemporary gender culture. However, their proposals for facing these contradictions are private: each woman should care for the education of her own children, and hope that if every other woman does the same, in a few generations the world will be a better place.

Feminist rhetoric appears within their posts when they discuss the implications of their jobs and careers for growing their children:

LULU: I have read an interview of a feminist lawyer who defends "time reengineering" for women. She says that "eight hours workday is a complete anachronism in a virtual era. Women must denounce their exploitation." Wow! Finally somebody decided to say something. I think we could create a movement like "new feminism" re-discussing the role of women in society.

LUCIANA: I am pissed off about this "super-woman" stuff. It was just a way the job market found to exploit us to death. One day, I will rip my veil, have five children and jump off to be with my family. Life is much more than work. We have been fooled, but there is still time to change this.

ELEN: On the contrary to what feminists defend—and maybe they will tear their hair out with what I will say—I always have dreamed of the house+husband+children trilogy, and this is the main goal in my life. Throw the first stone you who never dreamed of it? The dedication of a woman is vital for the survival of a home-sweet-home and there is no salary in the world that pays for this!!

The comments above seem to engage in an effort to understand the situation of women that give priority to children's education before professional achievements. This desire to reconceptualize contemporary femininity appears as a way of dealing with concrete ordinary situations. By elaborating on this informal feminist theory, they seek to orient their actions for practical, individual purposes, feminism as a private, not political matter.

Conclusion

The ethnographic study of the interactions among a group of young mothers in a blog environment has revealed many important features of gender culture and contemporary femininity in Brazilian society. There seems to be a will among participants to challenge social expectancies regarding women's behavior when they become mothers. In their comments, they look for "modern" patterns of behavior. With tolerance for differences among them, they seek out alternative ways of child caring, and respect their own individuality. However, when these issues are addressed through online communication, they are not taken as political issues, but as private ones.

Technological change introduces some new social practices and leads others to disappear; it demands specific competences and makes other competences useless; it creates environments and transforms modes of interaction. The introduction of the Internet into a culture promotes great changes in social life, as has been proven in this discussion of a subset of Brazilian society.

Acknowledgments

The author gratefully acknowledges Dr. Édison Gastaldo of Universidade Federal Rural do Rio de Janeiro, Brazil, for his assistance in the translation, and Dr. Sarah Burcon and Dr. Melissa Ames for the careful review that greatly improved the manuscript. This research was supported by Conselho Nacional de Desenvolvimento Científico e Tecnológico/Brazil (CNPq) and Pontifícia Universidade Católica do Rio de Janeiro.

Notes

1. The blog analyzed in this research (*www.mothern.blogspot.com*) was published in Brazil, and written in Portuguese. There is a certain cultural specificity in this, as Internet was available in Brazil only in 1995, and participants of the blog belong to the first generation of Brazilian women who learned how to use computers for their everyday activities, as they witnessed the rise and spread of computer-mediated technology. The group is composed mostly of middle-class mothers, around thirty years old (average age at the time of fieldwork was 31 years old), who had attended college, and who used computers in their everyday activities. When personal computers became a device regularly used by lay persons in Brazil, in the mid–1990s, these women were around 15 years old.

2. Nethnography is a research method that uses ethnographic techniques applied to online interactions. See Braga, Nethnography, 488.

3. On technology and gender, see Paglia, 13.

4. See Braga, *Personas*, 116–140; Greiffenhagen and Watson, 92–94; Sternberg, 262–288.

5. In the first two years of activity, the blog *Mothern* had over one million visitors and registered more than 40,000 comments on the guestbook. The texts of the blog resulted in a best-selling book and a TV show with the same name.

6. Garfinkel defines ethnomethods as the "rational properties of indexical expressions and other practical actions as contingent ongoing accomplishments of organized artful practices of everyday life" (11).

WORKS CITED

Barnes, Susan. *Goffman and the Internet: Applying Goffman's Concepts to Online Communication*. IAMCR Conference. Porto Alegre, PUCRS. 24 Jul. 2004. Reading.

Braga, Adriana A. *Microcelebridades: Entre Meios Digitais e Massivos*. COMPÓS Conference. Rio de Janeiro, PUC/RJ, 11 Jun. 2010. Reading.

_____. "Nethnography: A Naturalistic Approach Towards Online Interaction." *Handbook of Research on Web Log Analysis*. 1st. ed. Eds. Bernard J. Jansen, Amanda Spink, and Isak Taksa. 2009 Hershey, NY: IGI Global, 486–503. Print.

_____. *Personas Materno-Eletrônicas: feminilidade e interação no blog Mothern*. Porto Alegre: Sulina, 2008. Print.

"Caleidoscópio Virtual." *IstoÉ 1755*, 21 May 2003: 58–62. Print.

Garkinkel, Harold. *Studies in Ethnomethodology*. New Jersey: Prentice Hall, 1984. Print.

Goffman, Erving. *The Presentation of Self in Everyday Life*. New York: Doubleday Anchor Books, 1959. Print.

Greiffenhagen, Christian and Rod Watson. "'Teoria' e 'Método' na CMC: identidade,género, e tomada-de-turno — uma abordagem etnometodológica e analítico-conversacional." *CMC, Identidades e Género: teoria e método*. Colecção Estudos em Comunicação. Ed. Adriana Braga. Covilhã, Universidade da Beira Interior, Portugal, 2005: 89–114. Print.

Paglia, Camille. *Personas Sexuais: arte e decadência de Nefertite a Emily Dickinson*São Paulo: Cia das Letras, 1992. Print.

Sibilia, Paula. "Os Diários Íntimos na Internet." *Antroposmoderno*. 27 Aug. 2008. Web. 20 Aug. 2010.

Sternberg, Janet L. "Misbehavior in Cyber Places: the Regulation of Online Conduct in Virtual Communities on the Internet." Diss. New York University. New York: 2001. Print.

Turkle, Sherry. *A Vida no Ecrã: a identidade na era da internet*. Lisboa: Relógio D'Água, 1995. Print.

About the Contributors

Melissa Ames is an assistant professor of English at Eastern Illinois University specializing in media studies, television scholarship, popular culture, and feminist theory. Her work has been published in a variety of anthologies and journals, ranging in topic from television, new media, and fandom to American literature and feminist art. Recent publications include two books, *Feminism, Postmodernism, and Affect* (2008) and *Television and Temporality* (2011), and chapters in *Grace Under Pressure: Grey's Anatomy Uncovered* (2008), *Writing the Digital Generation* (2010), and *Bitten by Twilight* (2010).

Giselle Bastin is head of English and Creative Writing at Flinders University in South Australia. Her research interests include gossip as a gendered discourse, biographies and biopics of the British Royal Family, narratives of fame and celebrity, and constructions and representations of "English-ness" in popular fiction and film.

Diana York Blaine is an associate professor teaching in the Writing Program at the University of Southern California. Her research focuses on gender and death in media, and her publications include analyses of William Faulkner, Thomas Pynchon, Michael Jackson, and JonBenet Ramsey. She has also lectured widely on death in advertising and is featured in "Birth of an Independent Woman," the *Mad Men* season 2 DVD documentary on the history of feminism in the United States. She is writing a book on representations of death in American popular culture.

Adriana Braga is a Brazilian researcher with a degree in psychology and a doctorate in communication science. She is a researcher and a professor in the Social Communication Department at the Pontifícia Universidade Católica do Rio de Janeiro. Her Ph.D. dissertation on "Computer-Mediated Femininity" received the 2007 Media Ecology Association's Harold Innis Award and 2007 CAPES [Coordination of Improvement of Higher Education Personnel] dissertation award. Among other publications, she is the editor of the book *CMC, Identidades e Género: Teoria e Método* (2005) and author of *Personas Materno-Eletrônicas: Feminilidade e Interação no Blog Mothern* (2008).

Sarah Himsel Burcon teaches composition and literature courses at Lawrence Technological University in Southfield, Michigan. She received her Ph.D. at Wayne State University in 20th century American literature, with a specialization in feminist theory. Other research interests are popular culture and linguistics. Among her publications are chapters in *Revisiting the Past through Rhetorics of Memory and Amnesia* (2011) and *Television and Temporality* (2011), and she has written articles for *Women and Popular Culture Encyclopedia* (2011).

Julie Dare received a Ph.D. from the School of Communications and Arts at Edith Cowan University in Perth, Western Australia. Her dissertation explored the nature of Western Australian women's use of the Internet as a tool to manage family and social relationships and support health. She is a lecturer in the School of Exercise, Biomedical, and Health Sciences at Edith Cowan University. Her research has been published in Australian and international journals covering the fields of communications, women's health, and ethical practice.

Ashley M. Donnelly is an assistant professor of telecommunications at Ball State University in Muncie, Indiana. She received a Ph.D. from the University of South Florida in English with a concentration in film in 2008 and an M.A. from Birkbeck College at the University of London in cultural and critical studies in 2003.

Koen Leurs is a Ph.D. candidate in gender studies at Utrecht University. His dissertation examines the gendered and ethnic interfacing of digital technologies, migration and global/local youth cultures. He conducted earlier studies at the National University of Singapore and Intergender and has participated in NOISE (Network of Interdisciplinary Women's Studies in Europe) and Oxford Internet Institute summer schools. Among his publications are "Communicative Spaces of Their Own: Migrant Girls..." in *Feminist Review* (2011), and "Performing Gender and Ethnicity in Techno-Social Networks" in *Where Have All the Cyberfeminists Gone?*

R. C. Lutz teaches English and works as a consultant for Madison Advisors in Bucharest, after graduating with a Ph.D. in English and film studies from the University of California, Santa Barbara, and teaching English and film studies at University of the Pacific. He is an active contributor to reference works on Pacific Rim literature, history and culture with a special interest in the relationship of Southeast Asia and the United States of America, and is writing a book on French-Vietnamese director Tran Anh Hung.

Miriam Muth is completing her Ph.D. at the University of Cambridge on women as ethical symbols in late Arthurian romance. Her areas of interest include gender within Arthurian literature, Old and Middle English representations of female voices, and the boundaries of genre as tools of authority in the reception of medieval literature.

Hanh N. Nguyen is a Ph.D. candidate writing a dissertation on Vietnamese national cinema in the English Department of the University of Florida, Gainesville. She has an M.A. degree in film studies from the University of California, Riverside. She has published two articles on the Vietnamese American experience, "A Bridge Between

Two Worlds," in *The Emergence of Buddhist American Literature* (2010), and "The Case of Nguyen Nguyet Cam's *Two Cakes Fit for a King,"* in *From Word to Canvas* (2009), both in collaboration with R.C. Lutz.

Sandra Ponzanesi is an associate professor involved in gender and postcolonial critique at Utrecht University in the department of Media and Culture Studies/Graduate Gender Program. She has been a visiting professor at the University of California, Los Angeles, and a visiting scholar at the University of California, Riverside, and has published articles on transnational feminist theories, Italian colonial history, visual culture and postcolonial cinema. Among her publications are *Paradoxes of Post-Colonial Culture* (2004), *Migrant Cartographies* (2005) with Daniela Merolla, and *Postcolonial Cinema Studies* (2011) with Marguerite Waller. She guest-edited a special issue on postcolonial Europe with Bolette Blaagaard for *Social Identities: Journal for the Study of Race, Nation and Culture* (2010).

Emily Ross received a Ph.D. from the University of Otago in 2009; her dissertation was "The Current of Events: Gossip about the Controversial Marriages of Lady Arbella Stuart and Frances Coke in Jacobean England, 1610–1620." She lectures in the English program in the Faculty of Policy Studies at Chuo University in Tokyo, Japan.

Aleysia Whitmore is a Ph.D. candidate in ethnomusicology at Brown University, researching the transnational movements and practices of salsa music and dance and the ways in which various conceptions of race and gender come together on dance floors. Her dissertation is on the influences of Cuban music in African popular music. She is looking specifically at African musicians who play Cuban music and who collaborate with Cuban musicians, and their engagement with the "World Music" industry.

Earla Wilputte is a professor of English, specializing in 18th-century fiction, at Saint Francis Xavier University in Antigonish, Nova Scotia. She has two published editions of Eliza Haywood: *Three Novellas by Eliza Haywood: The Distress'd Orphan, The Double Marriage, and The City Jilt* (University of Michigan Press) and *Adventures of Eovaai* (Broadview Press). A recent publication, "Eliza Haywood's *Poems on Several Occasions*," appears in *Eighteenth-Century Women* (2010). She is writing a book about passion and language in the Hillarian Circle of the 1720s.

Lindsay Yakimyshyn holds an M.A. in English from Queen's University, Kingston, Ontario, and is currently engaged in Social Sciences and Humanities Research Council–supported doctoral work at the University of Alberta. Her research interests lie in early modern English women's drama, especially translations or adaptations and the echoes of early modern texts in contemporary literature. As well, she studies colonial American women's legacy texts.

Index